Six Modern British Novelists

Six Modern
British Novelists

EDITED WITH AN INTRODUCTION BY

George Stade

COLUMBIA UNIVERSITY PRESS

NEW YORK AND LONDON 1974

823.03
S776S

Copyright © 1965, 1966, 1967, 1970, 1971, 1972, 1974
Columbia University Press
Printed in the United States of America
Library of Congress Cataloging in Publication Data
Stade, George, comp.
    Six modern British novelists.
    Includes bibliographies.
    CONTENTS: Wain, J. Arnold Bennett.—Lodge, D.
Evelyn Waugh.—Smith, G. Ford Madox Ford. [etc.]
    1. English fiction—20th century—Addresses,
essays, lectures. I. Title.
PR883.S8   823'.03   74-6141
ISBN 0-231-03846-1

10 9 8 7 6 5 4 3 2

Six Modern British Novelists

The six essays in this volume first appeared separately in the Columbia Essays on Modern Writers series published by Columbia University Press. This series of critical studies includes English, Continental, and other writers whose works are of contemporary artistic and intellectual significance. The editor of the series when these essays were written was William York Tindall. The current editor is George Stade. Advisory editors are Jacques Barzun, W. T. H. Jackson, and Joseph A. Mazzeo. The late Justin O'Brien was also an advisory editor. For this edition, the essays, where necessary, and the bibliographies have been updated.

Acknowledgments

Grateful acknowledgment is made to the following individuals and publishers: to A. P. Watt and Son for permission to quote from works by Arnold Bennett; to Doubleday & Company, Inc., for permission to quote from *The Old Wives' Tale, Clayhanger* (copyright 1910 by Doubleday & Company, Inc.), and *The Pretty Lady* (copyright 1918 by George H. Doran Company); to the Viking Press for permission to quote from *The Journal of Arnold Bennett*, 1896–1928 (copyright 1932, 1933, 1960, 1961 by The Viking Press, Inc.); to Mr. Frank Swinnerton for permission to use an extract from his *The Georgian Literary Scene;* to Chapman and Hall for permission to quote from the works of Evelyn Waugh and to Little, Brown and Company for permission to quote from *Decline and Fall* (copyright 1928, 1929 by Evelyn Waugh); and to the Trustees of the Joseph Conrad Estate, Doubleday & Company, Inc., New York, and J. M. Dent & Sons Ltd., London, for permission to quote passages from Conrad's works and letters.

GEORGE STADE

Introduction

The great English literature of the modernist era, from about the nineties until World War II, was written by Irishmen, Americans, a Welshman, and a Pole. It is hard to think of an important English contemporary of Stevens and Williams, Faulkner, Fitzgerald, and Hemingway, for example, who was as representative, as exemplary even, of the prevailing English type as these Americans were of the era's prevailing American type. It is hard, that is, to think of an important English writer of the modernist era who openly qualified for membership in the caste that set the styles, determined the values, and wielded the power that showed the world just what it meant to be English: it is hard to think of a modernist who was at once English, Protestant, male, middle–class, and heterosexual.

If the writers were not American or Polish or from one of John Bull's other islands, they were Catholics (usually by choice rather than by birth), like Ford, Waugh, and Greene, or from the working class, like D. H. Lawrence, or women, like Virginia Woolf, or homosexual, like Forster and Auden (and, perhaps, Lawrence and Woolf). Successful writers who were

indeed examples of the prevailing type, like Galsworthy and
Bennett, showed the others what they had at all costs to avoid,
and what they had above all to subvert. Self-consciously, deliberately, with programmatic zeal and polemical emphasis, the
others, those who were not of the prevailing type, made clear in
their writing just how little they were Galsworthy or Bennett or
their equivalents among poets. And those writers of the younger
generation who by birth and sexual preference qualified for
membership in the dominant caste declined the honor; they exiled themselves in one way or another: by identifying themselves
with the working class, like George Orwell, by leaving the
country, like Robert Graves (who in any case thought of himself
as spiritually an Irishman), or by pursuing strange gods, like Aldous Huxley—to single out one in a crowd.

The prevailing type, although in fact he still prevailed,
seemed somehow to have outlived his historical moment. The
complex of ideas, values, and relations to his culture, the set of
practices and attitudes that constituted his typicality and
guaranteed his prevalence, no longer seemed the ones from
within which anything of moment could be written. When the
prevailing type appeared in modernist fiction it was as a figure of
fun or as an occasion for justifiable parricide. To write anything
of moment seemed to require at least the adversary edge of
Irishmen or Americans trying to cut themselves free from the
cultural imperialism of a mother country whose language was
the one they had perforce to use. Or it required the implacable
antagonisms of class conflict, and with it that freedom from official pieties which sometimes comes to people who have been
deprived of the advantages that make the pieties plausible. Or it
required the cool refusals of feminist resentment, the withering
glance of someone who has discovered that what the emperor's
clothes no longer hide had never been worth looking at. Or it

required the satirical disenchantments of homosexuality, the oblique and disabused perspective of an abused outsider on that massive system of erotic, domestic, social, and artistic conventions built upon an alleged attraction between the sexes. Or it required a hatred of the present and a nostalgia for the past desperate enough to drive one into the arms of the Church.

Analogous things might be said about French and German writers, about writers from portions of what used to be the Hapsburg Empire, and about those Americans who worked at becoming English or European, in the style of Henry James and T. S. Eliot. Writers became modernist wherever advanced Western civilization had taken firm enough hold for advanced people to wish it were in decline. South American writers, for example, seem now to be in a modernist phase. Their felt relations to Spanish and Portuguese must be something like the Irishman's or American's felt relation to English during the days of Joyce and Pound. But the resentful love and reciprocated hate that modernist writers feel toward their own countries seem to have been especially pervasive among English moderns, perhaps because in the period just prior to the onset of modernism England was by most standards the greatest nation in the world. Its decline, or appearance of decline if you will, was that much more dramatic.

The decline of nations is like the decline of fathers, at least to boys and girls growing up. The children of discredited fathers and fatherlands seem both more free and more driven to do unheard-of things and to imagine compensatory worlds more attractive—more free and more driven, that is—than solid citizens assured of their succession. An astonishing number of writers— among them Shakespeare, Dickens, and Joyce, to name three of the greatest to write in English—had fathers whose fortunes declined as the sons were growing up. And Western modernists,

especially those born near the end of the last century, clearly felt
that their fatherlands were coming down in the world, that their
cultural patrimonies had become debased coin, that the very
principle of authority had compromised itself, that their release
from filial piety had only delivered them into the anxious com-
pulsions of a world whose center no longer held, that the aesthetic order of their work would have to compensate for the actual chaos of the world their fictions represented. During the
modernist period, fathers, fatherlands, principles of authority,
conventions and traditions were still there, sometimes insistently
there, but discredited. The insistent presence of these, and with
it the itch to subvert them and the longing for substitutes, is one
thing that distinguishes modernist literature from what followed
it.

The most general common characteristic of the modernist
writers, then, was an adversary or alienated relationship to their
own cultures. The most general common characteristic of their
work was the inverse relation between the rendered aesthetic
order and the represented chaos. The more disordered the world
represented, the more ordered the rendering of the work. In this
respect *The Wasteland* and *Ulysses* are exemplary, but so are the
novels of Ford, Conrad, Woolf, Forster, and Waugh. The very
techniques used to represent a world of dissolving appearances
and discontinuous selves, of crumbling institutions and discredited authorities, of the ruin of all space and time, shattered
glass and toppling masonry, are also the techniques that bind
part to part and part to whole with an unprecedented adhesive
force. For esemplasticity the modernist classics are unequaled.

This very esemplasticity, unlike Coleridge's organic variety,
has something un-English about it, as do the techniques used to
produce it. The techniques of the English modernists are not
simply those of their nineteenth-century predecessors brought

up to date. The English modernists did not look toward their immediate past for hints as to how to make it new. They wanted nothing to do with "the eunuch century, the century of the mealy-mouthed lie, the century that has tried to destroy humanity, the nineteenth century," in the words of D. H. Lawrence. They looked around them at new occasions calling for new practices. Or they looked toward the fiction of France, America, and Russia. They looked at Post-Impressionist painting, Russian ballet, Chinese ideograms, African masks, and American movies. They looked toward psychology, anthropology, and physics. They looked everywhere but at Meredith, Thackeray, and Dickens. "We are sharply cut off from our predecessors," said Virginia Woolf. "Every day we find ourselves doing, or thinking things that would have been impossible to our fathers." As a result, she continues, "no age can have been more rich in writers determined to give expression to the differences which separate them from the past and not to the resemblances which connect them with it." That determination required not only techniques different from those of the past, but techniques that called attention to themselves for their ostentatious and subverting differences.

The prevailing type of Englishman, who did not look at his past as across a chasm but as the ground under his feet, has still not forgiven the modernists for their ostentation and foreignness. If he reads twentieth-century literature at all, he prefers Georgian poets and realistic novelists, John Betjeman and the small portion of D. H. Lawrence that looks like Thomas Hardy, or, among more recent writers, those antimodernists who used to be called Angry Young Men. It is no accident that John Wain, whose practice as a novelist may be described as antimodernist and who used to be called an Angry Young Man, chose Arnold Bennett to write about. Mr. Wain can look at Bennett, "this most prosaic of novelists," as the ground under his feet, as a predecessor in the great tradition of English realism stretching without break all the way back to Defoe, if not to Chaucer. Great as that tradition has been, impressive as its achievements continue to be, the modernists rejected it, and at the same time rejected the assumptions about nature, human nature, and human society upon which that tradition is based. "Can it be," asks Virginia Woolf, "that owing to one of those little deviations which the human spirit seems to make from time to time Mr. Bennett has come down with his magnificent apparatus for catching life just an inch or two on the wrong side? Life escapes; and perhaps without life nothing else is worth while." D. H. Lawrence's disparagement of Bennett, who had been characteristically generous in trying to help Lawrence out, is on the same ground of technical obsolescence as Virginia Woolf's: "Tell Arnold Bennett that all rules of construction hold good only for novels which are copies of other novels. A book which is not a copy of other books has its own construction, and what he calls faults, he being an old imitator, I call characteristics." The prevailing type of Englishman has never forgiven the modernists for their rejection of the assumption about nature, human nature, and human society upon which realism has rested. Modernism, like psychoanalysis, was and is more congenial to Americans.

The reasons for that congeniality can be explained without reference to invidious myths of national character. In his discussion of "the negative side of the spectacle on which Hawthorne looked out," Henry James remarks that "one might enumerate the items of high civilization, as it exists in other countries, which are absent from the texture of American life, until it should become a wonder to know what was left." James's enumeration of thirty-five or so absent institutions moves from "No

state" to "no Epsom nor Ascot!" The natural remark in the face
of such an indictment, says James, "would be that if these things
are left out, everything is left out." Such was the natural remark
of the prevailing type of Englishman, which James strove to
become, in the face of all that the modernists left out. But what
the modernists left out was all that had been removed from the
texture of national life by recent history. And recent history had
Americanized the Western nations, so to speak, by cutting them
off from their own institutions, those which America had never
had. Americans are the oldest people in the world, said Gertrude Stein; they have been in the twentieth century for over
one hundred years. Looking through America to the future,
Tocqueville fearfully predicted "that the productions of demo-
cratic poets may be surcharged with immense and incoherent
imagery, with exaggerated descriptions and strange creations;
and that the fantastic beings of their brains may sometimes make
us regret the world of reality." As D. H. Lawrence put it, "the
European moderns are all *trying* to be extreme. The great Americans I mention just were it." European and English modernism
soon enough achieved American extremism, and in the same
way: by adapting a parricidal relation to whatever had spawned
them, by developing techniques for expressing an adversary relation to those items of high civilization in the texture of their
national lives that recent history had discredited.

In spite of its international or alien or American quality, or
perhaps just because of it, there is in English modernist fiction a
slow return of the native. He wakes up like old Rip to discover
that he is no longer at home in his home, and his unease is
precisely what makes him a subject of interest. The prevailing
type became a subject of interest at precisely that moment when
his prevalence could no longer be taken for granted. The great
nineteenth-century English novelists revealed national char-

acter—they represented it through their characters and expressed it by being themselves—without having to look for it. They did so by the way, usually while setting out to do other things. But writers like Ford, Conrad, Woolf, Forster, and Waugh, like indeed Gide in France and Mann in Germany, and like American writers from the beginning, found national character not only a problem but problematic as well, something to be discovered and defined. The English modernists again and again posed their national types against a background of others, Americans, Irishmen, Europeans, Indians, Africans, South Americans, and these home-grown New Men of relentless aspiration. The idea was to throw the native into sharp relief, to see what in fact was the design in his lineaments. Ford's Tietjens, Conrad's Jim, his Gould, his Lingard, Woolf's six characters in search of a Percival who died in India, Forster's Wilcoxes and Ango-Indian boors, Waugh's landed gentry and traveling rascals, however, are thrown by what surrounds them into an ambiguous light that makes vices of their virtues, and vice versa. The native type became most illuminating just as his light began to fade, when like Lord Jim he found himself "under a cloud."

Even Arnold Bennett was enough of a modern to measure the vices and virtues of his provincial English town of Bursley against the more flamboyant ones of Paris. But his conclusion showed that even Paris had no lasting effect on the Bursley principle in wise Sophia, who at the end of it all remained inwardly identical to the stay-at-home and constant Constance. Bennett did not have an adversary relation to his own culture; his liberalism is the thing itself. The aesthetic order of his novels is not extraordinary; the disorder they represent is ordinary. Conversely, the other writers discussed in this volume tended to be as conservative in their politics as they were radical in their aesthetics. Whether from the right or from the left or from some-

where beyond the pale, what the modernist writers hated most
in politics was liberalism, although the Bloomsberries sometimes
pretended otherwise; what they hated most in fiction was realism, which according to them left reality out.

These remarks of mine are only meant as a gesture toward a
few of the matters that the six critics whose essays form the
body of this volume reveal by the way, rather than as a summary of what they have set out to do. Each set out to write an
introductory essay that would at the same time make an original
contribution to our understanding of a recent English novelist.
All six essays were first published as separate pamphlets in the
Columbia Essays on Modern Writers series. Where necessary,
they have been brought up to date. Bound together, they not
only introduce six important novelists; they also provide a basis
for the beginnings of a much needed look into the English variety of modernist fiction considered as a discrete body of work.
Arnold Bennett was to the modernists, at least, a definitive example of what modern English fiction should not be; the others,
none of whom was at once English-born, Protestant, male,
middle–class, and heterosexual, are definitive examples of what
it was.

Contents

JOHN WAIN

Arnold Bennett

Arnold Bennett's conventional reputation, his niche in the textbooks of literary history, is that he was "the English Realist." That, growing up in the seventies and eighties of the nineteenth century, he broke with the tradition of English fiction that runs down from Fielding through Dickens and Thackeray and expresses itself in kindliness, sentimentality, profusion of incident, and love of oddities. That he was the first, and remains the only, English novelist to have made a determined effort to cultivate in English soil the Continental, and primarily French, realistic novel with its matter-of-factness, its gray and truthful atmosphere, its disenchanted look at the realities of modern life. That he is the only English writer to have captured anything of the spirit of Balzac, Flaubert, and Zola.

I agree with this view, and the essay that follows will consist mainly of footnotes to it. Bennett's work is sufficiently robust and various to yield interesting crops to any kind of critical husbandry, and in fact one critic, Mr. James G. Hepburn, has devoted an interesting book, *The Art of Arnold Bennett* (1963), to putting forward an interpretation that ignores the "realistic" side and looks instead for symbolism. Mr. Hepburn manages to make this most prosaic of novelists seem very much like a poet, and the result is valuable because it emphasizes that there is no one "correct" approach to literary art, that a body of work imagined with sufficient solidity will look solid from any angle. Neverthless, it is Bennett the realist who concerns me. Though his early interest in French realism and naturalism faded steadily, so that by 1910 his private touchstone for his own work was not Balzac or Flaubert but Dostoevsky, his mind took its permanent shape under the pressure of that universal drive toward realism which dominated the arts in every Western country. The causes of this pressure are easy enough, at this distance, to see.

Industrialism, in Europe and America, moved into high gear about 1850: or, to fix on a more precise date, the Great Exhibittion of 1851 in London provided the occasion for a collective hymn in praise of the new spirit of uncontrolled productivity. And year by year, as the sheer profusion of objects multiplied and multiplied again, humanity reacted by developing more and more complex forms of organization. The electric telegraph, which had been practicable since 1837, demanded that an incessant flood of data should be received and processed throughout the twenty-four hours; the steam locomotive made it possible to haul the thousands of tons of food and materials needed every day by a city the size of Victorian London. Within a few decades, "civilized" life became more complex than anyone had foreseen. Such enterprises as the running of a hotel, the command of a regiment, the editing of a newspaper, became specialized skills involving the coordination of many elements. Simultaneously, ordinary activities such as wage-earning work became opaque to the very people engaged in them. Instead of practicing recognizable skills within a mile or so of their homes, men disappeared into the fog of the city and toiled at fragmented, specialized tasks, with only the barest glimpse of the total end to which they were contributing.

It is no surprise that such an epoch as this witnessed the rise of that literary and artistic phenomenon known as realism. For the main struggle of the realist is to comprehend, to classify, to enumerate. The romantic artist, living in the comparatively simpler days of the late eighteenth and early nineteenth centuries, had sought to throw a veil of mystery over the world of his daily experience. The realist was in abrupt revolt against this. Necessarily so, for the problem had changed, and the enemy of human sensibility was no longer dailiness and familiarity, but complexity and material plethora. In the Great Exhibition which piled up and spread out before his eyes, man was in danger of becoming one more item, ticketed and priced. His only defense against this was to enumerate, describe, assess, and comprehend the other exhibits. Like Adam in a nightmare Eden, he had to assign names to the animals in order to establish his ascendancy over them.

It follows that the precise descriptions of the realist are incantatory. When Zola, in the opening pages of *Thérèse Raquin*, describes with obsessive care the exact contents of the two windows of the little haberdashery, having previously described the airless passage in which the shop lurked, his motive is not merely to show us a sheaf of photographs. These objects are important characters in the story. They are crowding and suffocating the human souls that live among them, producing a distortion that finds issue in frightful outbursts of lust and murder.

St. Luke's Square, Bursley, is not the Passage du Pont-Neuf. But it is equally under the domination of the artifact, the product of man's labor that has invaded every corner of man's life. Bennett's descriptions of the contents and business methods of

Baines's, or the Clayhanger steam printing works, have the same suppressed passion as similar descriptions in Balzac and Zola. Realistic fiction, which must describe everything, had always described the artifact. But in Bennett's work a new note has crept into these descriptions. Dickens had familiarized English readers with a world in which the inanimate had human characteristics, and human beings the characteristics of the inanimate, so that they met together on the level of that strange Dickensian dream from which the reader is never allowed to awake. But in Bennett's work, the artifact takes on the one human characteristic Dickens did not grant it. It is allowed its role in history. Like humanity, it lives in time, and time enriches, illuminates, and finally despoils it. Consider the description of "the old machine" at Clayhanger's (Chapter 12, Section IV):

Then there was what was called in the office the "old machine," a relic of Clayhanger's predecessor, and at least eighty years old. It was one of those machines whose worn physiognomies, full of character, show at once that they have a history. In construction it carried solidity to an absurd degree. Its pillars were like the piles of a pier. Once, in a historic rat-catching, a rat had got up one of them, and a piece of smouldering brown paper had done what a terrier could not do. The machine at one period in its career had been enlarged, and the neat seaming of the metal was an ecstasy to the eye of a good workman. Long ago, it was known, this machine had printed a Reform newspaper at Stockport. Now, after thus participating in the violent politics of an age heroic and unhappy, it had been put to printing small posters of auctions and tea-meetings. Its movement was double: first that of a handle to bring the bed under the platen, and second, a lever pulled over to make contact between the type and the paper. It still worked perfectly. It was so solid, and it had been so honestly made, that it could never get out of order nor wear away. And, indeed, the conscientiousness and skill of artificers in the eighteenth century are still, through that resistless machine, producing their effect in the twentieth. But it needed a strong hand to bestir its smooth, plum-coloured limbs of metal, and a speed of a hundred an hour meant gentle perspiration. The machine was loved like an animal.

This is not the Dickensian personification of an object. It is a recognition of the object's role in the long unfolding of time. And anything that plays a role acquires an identity. The identity of objects is a prime theme of Bennett's. One thinks of the display cards, Mr. Povey's inspiration, on which he and Sophia work so happily until stopped by the disapproval of Mrs. Baines. "Mr. Povey had recently been giving attention to the question of tickets. It is not too much to say that Mr. Povey, to whom heaven had granted a minimum share of imagination, had nevertheless discovered his little parcel of imagination in the recesses of his being, and had brought it effectively to bear on tickets." When Mr. Povey discovers that the insides of collar boxes make admirably shiny tickets, and Constance discovers that sugar, mixed with ink, will enable it to "take" on the glossy surfaces, their relationship takes a significant step forward. They are fellow-inventors, fellow-workers, and, when their scheme is quashed, fellow-martyrs. And all this is done through shiny pieces of cardboard, and ink mixed with sugar. These objects move Mr. Povey and Constance quite as much as Mr. Povey and Constance move them.

That is one pillar of Bennett's work. The other, of course, is his regionalism. And here again he is very much a man of his time. His mature years coincided exactly with the heyday of the railway system. And the chief result of the railway age was the growth of metropolitan cities. The stagecoach had dispersed the population, bringing information and business to country towns. The railway created large capital cities. As we noted above, the railway engine was the only force capable of hauling the mass of material needed by a big city. And it was natural that during the railway age the disparity between the capital city and the provinces should grow more and more conspicuous. The railway made access to the metropolis easy and cheap, while itself fostering the rapid growth from metropolis to megalopolis. The railhead became the center of power, of fashion, of information. So that energetic provincials yearned for the capital city with a new yearning. Arnold Bennett's first novel, *A Man from the North* (1898), opens with these words:

There grows in the North Country a certain kind of youth of whom it may be said that he is born to be a Londoner. The metropolis, and everything that appertains to it, that comes down from it, that goes up into it, has for him an imperious fascination. Long before schooldays are over he learns to take a doleful pleasure in watching the exit of the London train from the railway station. He stands by the hot engine and envies the very stoker.

Not unnaturally. Because the stoker is the attendant priest of the black, thunderous god who has made that same metropolis into a reality. Nowadays, when the petrol engine has dispersed population into vast anonymous suburbs with no centers, when every remote cottage with its radio and TV set is as close to the scene of action as the nearest bystander, the difference between metropolitan and provincial has been ironed out to an extent that makes it hard for us to recapture this "imperious fascination." But Bennett, though he saw this change well under way before he died in 1931, grew up in the railway age, when capital cities really were capital. Hence his lifelong absorption into the metropolitan world, beginning with his hurried exit from Burslem in 1889. It has sometimes been said of him that his work lacks interest when it deals with anything other than his provincial roots, that he ought to have stayed in the Five Towns and been content to be their chronicler. But this is to overlook the fact that London and Paris, in his day, were genuinely metropolitan. And Bennett, whose object was to comprehend the society in which he lived and to pass on that comprehension, simply could not afford to neglect the metropolis.

On the other hand, he knew that all great writers have understood a provincial life. His French and Russian masters had inculcated this with great firmness. Realistic fiction must always concern itself, to some extent, with mass—with crowds, with majorities, with averages. And obviously, even in a society that goes in for enormous capital cities, the majority of lives are lived away from the capital. Bennett understood from the start that to comprehend life in the Five Towns was not to turn his back on the essential task he had set himself, but on the contrary to approach it directly. Yet provincial life was only half the picture. The eye that he trained on it, if he was to reflect his age accurately, must be a metropolitan eye. Hence the slight but all-pervading irony which we find in his descriptions of Five Towns scenes and people. The crowd that gathers in St. Luke's Square, Bursley, to stare at the house in which Daniel Povey has murdered his wife, is described ironically. The not dissimilar French crowd which gathers to watch the guillotine at work, a few chapters later, is not seen with this irony. Bennett set out to interpret the provincial scene from without, not from within. Unlike his beloved Wordsworth, he had to establish a stance markedly different from that of his fellow-natives, before he could begin his observations.

Georges Lafourcade, Bennett's principal French critic, remarked, oddly, "He is that rare thing in English literature, a novelist without a purpose." This, in a Frenchman, is a strange lapse. Bennett's "purpose" is surely the purpose of all realist writing: to establish the truth. The eighteenth-century novelist had tended to exhort his readers, or to lash their follies and vices with satire; and this was still a living tradition in the pages of Dickens, Thackeray, and George Eliot. Realistic fiction, however, with its roots in a more complex and difficult world, proceeds on the assumption that moral honesty is not possible until we have sorted out appearance from reality. Its tone, therefore, is sober and unimpassioned, its surface unvarnished. The realist's ideal of prose style is well represented by Stendhal's remark that a novelist, before starting work for the day, ought to read through a few pages of the Civil Code. "Fine writing," lyrical or symphonic, is a falsification in itself. All that matters is the unflinching pursuit of truth.

We should now have a tolerably clear picture of how the realist approaches his work. He sees himself, in the best and most accurate sense of the term, as a historical novelist. So far from being "without a purpose," Bennett aimed to come to grips with the essential nature of his age, to work on it as a historian works: disentangling motives, tracing cause and effect, deciphering the intelligible pattern that lies beneath a heap of confused detail. As late as 1907, an important entry in his Journal (September 13) shows him deploring the lack of "objective" data about human life, the kind of thing it ought to be a writer's business to accumulate.

I bought Taine's *Voyage en Italie*, and was once again fired to make fuller notes of the impressions of the moment, of *choses vues*. Several good books by him consist of nothing else. I must surely by this time be a trained philosophic observer—fairly exact, and controlled by scientific principles. At the time one can scarcely judge what may be valuable later on. At the present moment I wish, for instance, that some schoolmistress had written down simply her impressions of her years of training: I want them for my novel. The whole of life ought to be covered thus by "impressionists," and a vast mass of new material of facts and sensations collected for use by historians, sociologists and novelists. I really must try to do my share of it more completely than I do.

The idea of a pool of "facts and sensations," like a blood bank for anaemic writers, sounds quaint. Yet when we remember how long and deeply Bennett researched among printed sources and verbal anecdotes in putting together his picture of the Siege of Paris, we can see that such a corpus might have helped, in the days before film and tape recording took over from the written word the whole business of "documentary." What is interesting, today, about that passage is the troika of historian, sociologist, and novelist. To Bennett, as to the realists in general, the three had one aim: to discover, by patience and insight, the truth about the human being as they knew him in their time; and to pass on that truth with the minimum of distortion.

Today, we have moved away from that ideal. Novelists, when they can be induced to be serious at all, either satirize, or exhort, or retreat into a purely private vision of the world. The ideal of the late nineteenth century, that "objectivity" which is the reward of a clear eye and a steady hand, is forgotten. Bennett's fiction, at its best, is a striking reminder of how much we are missing.

Arnold Bennett, like Denry Machin, "first saw the smoke on the 27th May 1867." This smoke, as everyone knows, came from the fat black kilns of "the Potteries," the chain of six industrial towns lying along the valley of the Trent in North Staffordshire, surrounded on either side by pretty dairy-farming countryside and dominated at its northern end by the strange conical hill of Mow Cop, from which the eye can take in the noble sweep of the Cheshire plain in one direction and the mysterious huddle of the Potteries in the other. The fact of having been born and bred in such a place gave him several undeniable advantages. The "Five Towns" (he reduced their number by one for the sake of euphony) provided a rich mine of local color; for various historical and geographical reasons, those towns have always been peculiarly isolated and their way of life idiosyncratic, so that any description of them is exotic and interesting, even to other people from the English midlands.

Understandably enough, what seems to have remained in Bennett's mind about the Five Towns is their narrowness, dirt, and provinciality. He had no real contact with the working class who make up the overwhelming majority of the inhabitants; his own background was the small trading and (occasionally) professional middle class, whose lives, governed by the harsh dictates of Victorian respectability, were much more joyless and arid than the lives of the miner and the potter. Drabness, in such a milieu, was everywhere. It must have been during Bennett's early childhood that George Moore was directed to Hanley in his search for "an ugly town without any amusements," "a town . . . which would not excite the imagination even of George Borrow," which was to serve as the background for *A Mummer's Wife*.

The source of most of our knowledge about Bennett's early youth is, of course, *Clayhanger*. The facts may have to come from elsewhere, but the *feeling* of being young in the Potteries at the end of the nineteenth century is best conveyed there. His father, like Clayhanger's, was a self-made man; he adopted several professions in turn, including that of a pawnbroker, before achieving supreme respectability as a solicitor. Like Darius, he set the seal on this respectability by sending his son to school in Newcastle-under-Lyme, then as now the local center of polite learning.

There, Bennett's education was probably as unsatisfying to the artist within him as Clayhanger's. Nor was his religious training any more palatable than his secular instruction. The six hours spent every Sunday either in church or at Sunday school

remained a bitter memory throughout life, and the association of
religion with harsh and arbitrary discipline gave Bennett a bias
toward materialism, which naturally appeared to his young
mind as a liberation. "In my opinion," he wrote in an article in
1909, "at this time of day it is absolutely impossible for a young
man with first-class intellectual apparatus to accept any form of
dogma." His attitude to religious belief, and the part it plays in
human life, became more interested and more tolerant as time
went on; but for many years he associated it only with those
dreadful Sundays in Burslem.

As his minority drew near its end, Bennett was evidently in
exactly the same position as Clayhanger, save that the father
who employed him was a solicitor and not a steam printer. As
the son who was to inherit the practice, he was expected to work
for a nominal wage, and to live in totally uncongenial surroundings. But the historical young man had more determination than
the fictional counterpart—*Clayhanger* is the story of what *almost*
happened—and before he was twenty-one Bennett had taught
himself to write newspaper articles that were good enough for
the local press. He was also writing fiction that was not good
enough; the possibility of its having been too good, and above
the heads of the editors, is remote in the extreme; his first short
story and his first serial, both submitted to local newspaper
competitions, were rejected. In any case life in Burslem was not
to be tolerated once he had been handed his latchkey. "I came to
London at the age of twenty-one, with no definite ambition, and
no immediate object save to escape from an intellectual and artistic environment which had long been excessively irksome to
me."

To piece together the story of the next few years is no easy
matter, because the two sources of information are both more or
less fictional. There is the quasi-autobiography, *The Truth about*

an Author, in which Bennett writes about himself in the first person, and the novel *A Man from the North*, in which (we may venture to say) he writes about himself in the third person. The fact that the true story (for true, as to fact, it evidently is) gives a less interesting and fundamental impression of Bennett's character than the fiction brings us sharply into contact with one of the most important facts about him. He was not, directly, analytical about himself; when Miss Cheston (to use her own words) "gave the subjective side of his mind an airing" he does not seem to have been reassured by what came out, and the need to pose to himself is evident not only in his numerous autobiographical fragments but in the famous Journal itself. *The Truth about an Author* is less an autobiography than a swaggering anonymous manifesto; it was serialized in *The Academy* in 1898, when he was still a long way from real success, and though it appeared in book form in 1903, Bennett did not formally admit authorship of it until the second edition of 1914. There is much more of the real Bennett—shy, hard-working, anxious to prove himself capable above the average, but by no means confident that he could do it—in Richard Larch, the hero of *A Man from the North:* a solicitor's clerk, desperately eager to become an author, dazzled by London, thirsty for polite knowledge, glad of advice from his elders. Those who require external evidence of the autobiographical nature of the book may note that Richard, forcing himself to write a story, produces "Tiddy-fol-lol," which is unquestionably Bennett's own story of that name. There is no evidence that the story was written at this time; it was included seven years later in the collection *Tales of the Five Towns*, and my own feeling is that it was an afterthought. If Bennett had already put himself to the trouble of devising a plot and a title for a story to be written by one of his characters, he would (being Bennett) naturally write that story sooner or later on the princi-

ple of letting nothing go to waste. Of course my interpretation
makes the facts less important as external evidence (if Bennett
wrote the story *afterwards* it tells us nothing of his state of mind
when writing the novel) but it strengthens their significance as
internal evidence: if Richard writes a story so Bennettian that
Bennett himself is subsequently impelled to write and publish
it, the identification becomes impossible to resist. This, in any
case, is the significant fact: that while the directly autobiographical book is aggressively confident, and its hero a Denry of
literature, both the novels which mirror the inward experiences
of their author during these years—*Clayhanger* and *A Man from
the North*—are in a sense novels of failure.

The fugitive from Hanley arrived in London in 1888, a year
of some importance. George Moore's *Confessions of a Young Man*,
Yeats's *Fairy and Folk Tales of the Irish Peasantry*, Wilde's *The
Happy Prince*, all published in that year, indicate the direction in
which literature was moving—*The Yellow Book* was started six
years later—while the general activity of the scene is indicated
by the fact that Archer, Gissing, William Morris, Stevenson,
Henley, Doughty, Quiller-Couch, and Bosanquet all published
books. Matthew Arnold and Edward Lear died; far away, T. S.
Eliot and Katherine Mansfield were born. It was a year in which
a young man might see the future as expanding, not shrinking.
The young solicitor's clerk (for Bennett had not entirely deserted his early training) showed no undue eagerness to hurl
himself into literature. To him London was first and foremost a
city of romance. Four years before Bennett's birth, Dostoevsky,
in his *Winter Notes on My Summer Impressions*, had left a shocked,
half-incredulous record of the teeming vice and squalor of the
city, and of its picturesque tawdriness.

In London may be seen multitudes in such numbers and in such surroundings as you will see nowhere else in the world. For instance, I

was told that on Saturday night half a million working men and women
with their children spread like a flood over the whole town, for the
most part gathering in certain districts. All night, it is said, up to five
o'clock in the morning, they celebrate their holiday, that is, they fill
themselves like cattle with food and drink and so make up for the whole
week past. These people bring here their weekly wages, all that has
been earned with hard work and curses. In the butchers' shops and in
the eating-houses gas begins to flare in great jets, brightly illuminating
the streets. It is just as if some ball had been arranged for these white
negroes. The people crowd together in the open tavern and in the
streets. There they eat and drink. The beer-houses are decorated like
palaces. Drunkenness is everywhere, but it is joyless, sad, and gloomy;
a strange silence seems always to prevail. Only now and then do abuse
and brutal fights disturb the silence which weighs upon you so heavily.
The whole crowd make haste to become intoxicated as quickly as possible, and to the point of unconsciousness. . . .

I saw in London, too, just such another crowd the like of which in
point of number you will not see anywhere else. There, too, the setting
is unique. Anyone who has been to London has no doubt gone, at
night, at least once to the Haymarket. This is the district where thousands of public women crowd at night. The streets are illuminated by
flares of gas such as we have no idea of in our own country. Magnificent coffee-houses, decorated with mirrors and gold, may be seen at
every step. There people gather, these are their haunts. It is painful to
walk among this crowd. And of what strange elements does it consist.
Here are old women, there—beautiful girls at the sight of whom you
are struck with amazement. In all the world there is no more beautiful
type of woman than the English. The crowd, densely packed, finds
room with difficulty in the streets. The pavements cannot accommodate
it; it sways over the whole street. All the women are eager for prey,
and with shameless cynicism throw themselves at the first comer.

The second of these two crowd pictures links up with the
purposely vague world into which Richard Larch disappears at
intervals during *A Man from the North*, with the difference that to
Richard the life of pleasure is offering itself as a contrast to the
deadness of puritanical Bursley. It was natural that the pleasure-

starved youth, whether we call him Richard Larch or Arnold Bennett, should look on such sights as "the immense façade of the Ottoman Theatre of varieties, with its rows of illuminated windows and crescent moons set against the sky." in a mood of callow eagerness.

In 1891 Bennett moved to the home of his friend Marriot in Chelsea, and found himself at once in another world. "I was compelled to set to work on the reconstruction of nearly all my ideals. I had lived in a world where beauty was not mentioned, seldom thought of. I believe I had scarcely heard the adjective 'beautiful' applied to anything whatever, save confections like Gounod's 'There is a green hill far away.' Modern oak sideboards were called handsome, and Christmas cards were called pretty; and that was about all. But now I found myself among souls that talked of beauty openly and unashamed." He had already, it seems, decided to become a man of liberal culture, and to provide those about him with evidence of the fact (" 'What's all this?' he inquired politely. 'This, sir? Bayle's *Dictionnaire Historique et Critique*,' I replied"), but now these vague aspirations were given a definite direction. He would become an author.

The first steps were slow. For two years after the removal to Chelsea, nothing happened. Then, in 1893, he won twenty guineas in a parody competition set by *Tit-Bits;* in the same year he became subeditor of *Woman.* Journalism was, at any rate, better than a solicitor's office.

In 1896 the Journal was begun, and henceforth we can put a precise date to almost every important action and decision. But it has another function besides that of a chronicle, as we see as soon as we open it. The first entry finds him hurrying, in the wake of a fire engine, toward the scene of the rumored outbreak. It has been extinguished without the help of the brigade, so that the scene, when he arrives, is one of inactivity and anticlimax.

Nonetheless he notes its main features and describes them. That evening he overhears "two soberly dressed young women— perhaps actresses" in conversation at the Comedy Restaurant. He cannot catch all that they say, but makes out a few sentences, and down they go, together with a careful description of the speakers and their voices. The Journal is, in fact, a product of Bennett's knack of seeing himself in the appropriate role. From 1890, when he had flogged himself through Daudet's *Fromont Jeune et Risler Aîné*, he had been a passionate student of the French novel. We must try to imagine him, as the nineteenth century ebbed away, not as a bouncing young journalist dreaming of the day when his books will sell like Hall Caine's, but as an intensely serious and industrious apprentice to the craft of authorship, anxious above all to write well, excitedly aware that the novel is entering a new phase, pouring the contempt of the neophyte on the traditional English concept of the novel, with its clumsiness and lack of rigid form.

I believe in the course of a few years I could write such a history as would cast a new light on English fiction considered strictly from the craftsman's standpoint. As regards fiction, it seems to me that only within the last few years have we absorbed from France that passion for the artistic shapely presentation of truth, and that feeling for words as words, which animated Flaubert, the de Goncourts, and de Maupassant, and which is so exactly described and defined in de Maupassant's introduction to the collected works of Flaubert. None of the (so-called) great masters of English nineteenth-century fiction had (if I am right) a deep artistic interest in form and treatment; they were absorbed in "subject" . . . just as the "anecdote" painters of the Royal Academy are absorbed in "subject". . . . Certainly they had not the feeling for words in any large degree, though one sees traces of it sometimes in the Brontës,—never in George Eliot, or Jane Austen, or Dickens, or even Thackeray or Scott. (Journal, January 11, 1898.)

The combination of crude materialism and repressive religiosity, which had disgusted his youth, had had the effect of orienting

Bennett toward the ideal of objective truth and close observation; this led him to the French realists, and they in turn strengthened and guided his tendency.

When Bennett announces, "An artist must be interested primarily in presentment, not in the thing presented," that is because the problem of what to present does not exist; it has been settled in advance. The subject of the new novel was to be everyday life, the kind of thing the French naturalists noted in their *carnets;* hence the Journal. Every moment is filled, either with the collecting of material or with its remolding by means of "technique." He laments, at the end of a fortnight during which he had had no time to spare for the Journal, that "several impressions have been lost": and his comment after spending a few days at home to attend the funeral of his sister's fiancé is characteristic. "The Goncourt brothers would in my place have noted every item of it, and particularly watched themselves. I had intended to do as much, but the various incidental distractions proved too strong for my resolution."

Despite "incidental distractions," he worked, as he was to work all his life, like a slave. He poured out articles; he became editor of *Woman;* he contributed a short story to *The Yellow Book;* by the end of the century he had written a number of plays, alone and in collaboration with Eden Phillpotts, finished *Anna of the Five Towns* (published in 1902), and published *A Man from the North, Journalism for Women,* and *Polite Farces.*

As his thirty-third birthday approached, Bennett decided finally to launch out as a self-supporting author. He left London and settled with his parents and his sister Tertia at Trinity Hall Farm, Hockliffe, Bedfordshire, on September 30, 1900. Two years later, the death of his father altered the family circumstances; Bennett settled his mother comfortably in Burslem, and found himself free to do what he had so long wanted to do: take up residence in Paris.

During Bennett's first few years in Paris, his chief source of income was the stream of newspaper and magazine articles soon to be collected in book form as *The Reasonable Life*, *How to Live on 24 Hours a Day* (both 1907), and *The Human Machine* (1908). Meanwhile he was pelting the as yet indifferent British public with a shower of novels. Their names are not important: they have a place in Bennett's story for the quantity alone. Did any novelist, did even Scott at the height of his self-imposed slavery, write so quickly and so much? Two novels by Bennett appeared in 1903, two in 1904, one in 1905, three in 1906, three in 1907. "I constantly gloat over the number of words I have written in a given period," he wrote on April 5, 1908.

This period of Bennett's life ended abruptly in 1907 with his marriage to Marguerite Soulié. Since 1905 he had been looking forward to marriage and a more regular routine of work; evidently he hoped, by living quietly, to induce the concentration necessary to write the book he had been carrying inside him since 1903. But more of that later. Bennett selected the woman he wished to marry—Miss Eleanora Green—in the spring of 1906, but their engagement lasted only six weeks. In his disappointment he wrote his most serious novel since *Anna: Whom God Hath Joined*. But the mental efficiency expert was at work. The following January he engaged a charming and accomplished young Frenchwoman as his part-time secretary; and on July 4, 1907, Mlle Marguerite Soulié became Mrs. Arnold Bennett.

The couple rented and furnished a small house at Les Sablons, near Fontainebleau, and, allowing himself adequate leisure for cycling and taking solitary walks in the forest, Bennett settled down to the composition of that masterpiece which he had felt moving in his mind since 1903. The stage was set; house, wife, and furniture were duly grouped around him. He even experimented on the effect of a sympathetic presence by asking

his wife to do her sewing in his study while he wrote, but she
was soon banished for failing to maintain absolute silence. His
desire for complete concentration was at last satisfied; as a further demonstration of cool craftsmanship he even undertook to
write the manuscript in a stately and careful script—he himself
called it his "fine writing"—suggested to him by the illuminated
manuscripts in the British Museum. Professor Lafourcade
claims, and very plausibly, that the lightness and humanity of
Part I, written that autumn before he took his wife for a few
months on a duty-visit to England, is evidence of Bennett's serenity during these early months of marriage. The right conditions were present, and he made the most of them. By August,
1908, *The Old Wives' Tale* was finished, and a few weeks later it
was published in England by Chapman and Hall. Characteristically, Bennett gave himself no rest; after a sketching tour
through France in September, 1908, he was back at his desk.
The following January found him deep in *The Card*, and in May
he had begun careful plans for the construction of *Clayhanger*.
With furious activity and an unwonted wealth of research, he
had completed his preparations by the end of the year and in
July, 1910, the book was finished. Still without pausing, he
finished *The Card* and added *Hilda Lessways*, both of which were
published in 1911. That autumn he set out on a triumphant
publicity visit to the United States. Photographed, interviewed,
feted, he realized all that fame can mean to a popular author in a
prosperous age and a materialistic society.

His name and his income were no longer appropriate to the
life of an expatriated and retiring literary man. In 1912, wealth
could show to its best advantage in the English countryside. He
left Fontainebleau in April, and installed his wife in a country
house, "Comarques," at Thorpe-le-Soken, Essex.

At this point the early, obscure, desperately serious young

craftsman disappears; not gone away, but hidden within the
widely familiar and enveloping *persona* of the later successful
Bennett, caricatured all over the world as the self-made man of
letters, with his huge income, his yacht, his immense power in
the world of literary journalism, and (inevitably) his dwindling
reputation as a serious artist. It is this later Bennett who is
mainly remembered, often derisively, sometimes affectionately.

Let me try to present him to you as he appeared to those who saw him
in the flesh. He was stoutly built, and about five feet nine inches in
height. He held himself very erect and his shoulders very rigid, so that
his body had no natural swing as he walked, but rather swayed stiffly
from side to side. He always walked slowly and with great seriousness.
His brow was square, and rose straight from eyes that looked tired,
because of rather heavy eyelids, to the small flourish of hair that lately
replaced the famous coif made fun of by caricaturists. His cheeks were
clear and shewed a faint colour, his mouth was irregular, and his upper
teeth were also irregular. The eyes, once the first impression of
tiredness was passed, were a warm brown, and smiled. . . . In repose
his expression . . . represented calm melancholy. But his smile was
very sweet, and the aura of kindness which surrounded him was such
that he was very popular with children. (Frank Swinnerton, *The
Georgian Literary Scene*, 1935.)

His stammer, significantly enough, continued to torment him.
"Few realised the exhaustion it cost him to speak," Somerset
Maugham noted. "It tore his nerves to pieces." As his world
fame was consolidated, and the money poured in, Bennett seems
never to have considered the idea of relaxing and taking life
more easily. He worked as hard as the poorest city clerk, pon-
dered his writing as anxiously as a young novice out to make his
first impression.

But that is to anticipate. We left Bennett in 1912, just settled
at Thorpe-le-Soken. The next major event in his life, as in everyone's, was the First World War. Many critics have blamed

the strain of these years for Bennett's decline as a novelist. Walter Allen, for instance, says flatly, "It is scarcely possible not to see him as a war casuality. In 1914 Bennett was a brilliant novelist; after 1914 he was generally no more than a brilliant journalist." The trouble is that the year 1914 cannot be made to bear this weight of significance in Bennett's story. It would be more precise to draw the dividing-line at 1911, by which date he had produced most of his really good novels with the notable exception of *Riceyman Steps* (1923). That would make success, and advancing years, the villains of the story rather than the war.

Nevertheless, the coming of the war meant that from now on there was to be no real rest in Bennett's life. He was forty-seven years old, and suffering from various physical and nervous ailments. But he plunged headlong into any activity which might be supposed to contribute to the war effort. He became president of the local branch of a society for the relief of the Belgian refugees, and sent, for a time at any rate, a weekly check of £50 to its funds, to which his wife added parcels of clothes and shoes, and a hamper of fruit and vegetables from the garden. "Comarques" became an unofficial rest-center for officers on leave. Possessed by an urge to show willing, he one day mounted a horse (for the first time since 1901) and rode at the head of a detachment of cavalry officers to Frinton-on-Sea. When Mrs. Bennett followed a few yards behind in the car, in case he should give up the struggle en route, Bennett was understandably piqued, but had to admit to an attack of lumbago on the following day. Needless to say, he did not spare his efforts in a field to which he was better accustomed, producing propaganda pamphlets and articles in mounting volume. His experience of the American temperament led to his *Liberty: A Statement of the British Case;* his lack of experience of the German temperament did nothing to prevent his equally assertive article

on *What the German Conscript Thinks*. In 1915 he visited the
trenches ("he was nearly killed," declares Mrs. Bennett roundly,
but gives no details) and from now until 1918 his pen was more
or less wholly at the service of Allied propaganda. As work of
this kind is not regarded by subsequent readers as creditable, it
is fair to add that I have read a considerable number of Bennett's
propaganda articles, and found them far less offensive than
might be expected.

All this meant a mental struggle and a physical strain. Noises,
real or imaginary, shattered his sleep, and he shattered his
wife's. As the tension grew worse, Bennett took to sleeping with
a loaded revolver at his bedside. Happily he never had occasion
to make the discovery that his wife had prevailed on a male
friend to unload the weapon. His doctor, summoned to an attack of influenza, prescribed less work in future, but Bennett ignored the warning and threw himself into propaganda work
more deeply than ever, this time in collaboration with Max
Aitken, later Lord Beaverbrook. For two months, in 1918, he
was Director of British Propaganda for France. The appoint-
ment was a result of Beaverbrook's admiration for Bennett's understanding of the French psyche, as evinced in *The Pretty Lady*,
published in that year. Since the central character of the novel is
a French prostitute, whose motives are an odd mixture of pru-
dential caution, bourgeois carefulness about money and appearances, sensuality, and a strange hallucinatory Catholicism, the
decision is not, at first sight, flattering to French vanity. Yet
Beaverbrook's estimate is borne out by the fact that no less a
critic than Georges Lafourcade wrote in 1939, "The central
character is well-nigh faultless, and bears evidence of having
been composed not merely with care and patience—with something like actual tenderness." Because the girl's Catholicism is
central to her nature, the book offended English Catholics. The

lay secretary of the Catholic Federation wrote a vaguely menacing letter: "Several remedies can be employed by my Committee. Before using any of them I am writing to you in the hope that you will take adequate action in the matter." "Adequate action" could only have meant withdrawing or mutilating the book. Bennett's answer, in a letter to his publisher, was courteously uncompromising. "I can only reply, with respect and regret, that such a course is absolutely out of the question. The book is a serious and considered work." We shall take up this matter of Christine's Catholicism again. Meanwhile it is enough to note that Bennett, who never took a penny for his war services and who paid ten thousand pounds in income tax during the war years, found himself squarely in what the rather pompous vogue phrase of the 1960s calls "the corridors of power."

Very little appears to be known about Bennett's effectiveness in the important post of Director of British Propaganda for France. From Mr. Reginald Pound's biography, the most nearly complete to appear so far, we can glean a few facts: that Bennett left England every Monday morning and spent the week, till Saturday, in Paris; that he had an assistant named W. S. Hawley, a native of the Five Towns and an accomplished polyglot; that, at a time when the French were belittling the English war effort, Bennett sent to Paris several thousand copies of a series of small booklets setting out the bare facts about England's achievements in the war, which were duly confiscated by the French government and never seen by the French public. Beyond that, there seems to be no information, even the conscientious Mr. Pound falling back on vague statements such as that Bennett "sat grandly at his desk initialling minutes, drafting directives, reading and writing reports." So one imagines! But it would be interesting to know more details. These pamphlets so warily handled by the French: did Bennett take any part in their

composition? If he did not, who did? Did his efforts make any
difference to the French image of England? In these days, when
miscellaneous "research" is undertaken in such vast quantities
by universities all over Europe and America, it is a pity that
some university does not put a research student on to the subject
of Bennett's two-month career as chief British mouthpiece in
France.

Serving on committees, pouring out propaganda articles, and
still finding time and energy for his fiction were a severe strain
on an aging man. In addition, his private life at this time appears
to have been very disturbed. He was separated from his wife on
November 23, 1921, some months before his meeting with Miss
Dorothy Cheston, under whose influence he regained a measure
of serenity which lasted till his death. Miss Cheston did not actually share his household until after the birth of their daughter
in the spring of 1926; about this time, Bennett's wife being
unwilling to grant him a divorce, she took the name of Bennett
by deed poll.

This was by far the most important experience of the novelist's last fifteen years. Obviously it was not an entirely smooth
one. There was a good deal of adjustment to be done, and Bennett had never had any talent for adjustment. "The relation between husband and wife is very different from that between
lover and mistress," he wrote to Miss Cheston, "and . . . ours
must inevitably be the latter—and it is much better that it
should be the latter. Each has its advantages and disadvantages,
but nobody can have everything. Our relation, while just as
close in one way, in several ways in fact, is decidedly freer in
others. It involves fewer duties and fewer rights, especially in
the smaller things of life. This is the price of liberty." This was
not the only price of liberty, for he complains in the same letter
that "it is decidedly disturbing to be told that one is a stranger,

that you don't know whether in coming to me you are being
guided by Satan or by heaven, that I forget you when you are
not there, and that I regard you only as an agreeable mistress."
There were other jars and jolts. If the relationship Bennett described and desired is freer, it is also the sworn enemy of regular
work. This of course he could not stand. "Now I do want you
imaginatively to understand that I shall be seriously undone if I
do not start on what lies before me on the first of this month.
This doesn't in the least mean that I shall not see you. I shall
want to see you, and shall work better, incidentally, for seeing
you, but my machinery, the mechanics of my work, must not
be deranged. The mere thought of upsetting it sets every nerve
in my body on edge. So that's that."

Still, though the new demands he was making upon himself
were heavy, they were also healing. The state of semineurosis
wore away. His money worries became more acute than they
had been for years, but that is an easier problem to fight. Bennett's way of fighting it was, as everyone knows, to turn himself
into a star reviewer. I do not know if there is any precise information as to the sums he was able to make, in the postwar years,
by his newspaper articles; Mr. Allen mentions the sum of a
hundred pounds per thousand words, and one can believe it.

So Bennett's life dragged on for its last decade. The Journal
still shows a keen enjoyment of the details of existence; *Imperial
Palace*, published only a matter of months before he died, shows
the undiminished strength of his interest in the minutiae of organization in a big hotel, and he seems to have enjoyed his visit to
Russia with Beaverbrook; but there is no doubt that he was tired
and overworked. Mental Efficiency had been an exacting Pros-
pero, and this Ariel was never granted his freedom. The disastrous step of moving into a huge and expensive flat in Baker
Street was the last straw; it broke his health completely, and

within six months, on March 27, 1931, he was dead. His death
was hastened, and some would say caused, by drinking water
from a carafe in a French restaurant while on holiday in an attempt to build up his strength.

In an essay of this length, it is impossible to survey Bennett's
output, book by book. Instead, we must see how his work as a
whole stands up in relation to one or two central issues. How
deeply did he understand the society, and the humanity, of his
day? Did he manage to comprehend and sympathize with the
forces that really moved them?

The world Bennett shows us is a world of personal relationships, historical changes, money, illness, politics, and religion. Let us pause to examine the last item here, if only because he began his career with virtually no understanding of
religion, and came to understand it better only as time deepened
his view of life. The early Bennett, having coolly rejected the
Sunday-school religion of his childhood, has a tendency simply
to leave religion out of account in his portrayal of human character. He presents people as simple organisms, propelled by this
pressure and that incitement, moved hither and thither by the
predictable demands of their appetites and what they take to be
their self-interest. What we miss in them is that streak of the
crazy, the unexpected, the fanatical, that makes ordinary people
pour energy and passion into things that might have been expected to leave them cold. In particular, we miss the religious
impulse: not necessarily a formal religious faith, but an assent to
the power of the dark and mysterious, the intangible, the unbid-
dable. It is true that in *Anna of the Five Towns* (1902), which
stands out among his novels for its unusually complete documentation of Potteries life both industrial and social, there is a
description of a revivalist religious meeting. But it is seen en-

tirely from the outside: photographed in words, not imagined. This cold objectivity was, so far, all he could manage. Thus, in *The Old Wives' Tale*, we find almost no mention of religious feelings. Of the entire roll-call of characters, there is hardly one who is motivated by them. And when, at the end of the book, Constance contemplates the wreck of Sophia's life, and some faint religious reflex (it is hardly more) stirs in her mind, Bennett feels obliged to apologize for mentioning anything so vestigial and archaic.

Yes, Constance's heart melted in an anguished pity for that stormy creature. And mingled with the pity was a stern recognition of the handiwork of divine justice. To Constance's lips came the same phrase as had come to the lips of Samuel Povey on a different occasion: God is not mocked! The ideas of her parents and her grandparents had survived intact in Constance. It is true that Constance's father would have shuddered in Heaven could he have seen Constance solitarily playing cards of a night. But in spite of cards, and of a son who never went to chapel, Constance, under the various influences of destiny, had remained essentially what her father had been. Not in her was the force of evolution manifest. There are thousands such.

In other words, Constance feels this touch of numinous awe, this sense that "God is not mocked," because she is old-fashioned and incapable of moving on from the position held by her parents and grandparents. That such feelings might be permanent in the human animal, that Divine retribution for mockery might be something perpetually present to the human consciousness despite all the modifications wrought by "evolution," simply does not occur to him. It is a curious blankness, an Edwardian blankness that dates the novel somewhat. But Bennett moved on from this to a deeper and more sympathetic awareness. In *Clayhanger* (1910) we have the famous set piece of the Sunday School Centenary. The main function of this scene

in the novel is that Edwin takes Hilda to witness it, and certain
features of Hilda's character are thrown into relief by the experience. But it also has considerable thematic importance.
Throughout the novel, Edwin is shown as belonging to a fragile
social layer, a thin, delicate shell of middle-class refinement
which supports itself, somehow, over the dark and seething
mass of the populace. This mass, which is too dangerous to
explore, pulses with a rich and violent life of its own; Edwin is
excluded from it, though Darius, by virtue of his origins, knows
it from the inside. Once or twice, Edwin catches a glimpse of
some of the dangerous, forbidden richness, as when he watches
the clog dance in the public house, or hears Big James and his
friends sing "Loud Ocean's Roar," or gazes wistfully at the outside of the "Blood Tub." But his place is with the Orgreaves,
and his sisters, and Auntie Hamps. The people have their own
life, from which he must be excluded, sharing it no more than
Constance and Sophia shared it. And the people also have their
own religion, from which Edwin, being thoughtful and to some
extent educated, is also excluded. This religion is violent, orgiastic, absurd, but it is powerful. Its sheer emotional force sweeps
Edwin off his feet:

> And the conductor of the eager massed bands set them free with a
> gesture, and after they had played a stave, a small stentorian choir at
> the back of the platform broke forth, and in a moment the entire multi-
> tude, at first raggedly, but soon in good unison, was singing—

> Rock of Ages, cleft for me,
> Let me hide myself in Thee;
> Let the water and the blood
> From Thy riven side which flowed,
> Be of sin the double cure:
> Cleanse me from its guilt and power.

> The volume of sound was overwhelming. Its crashing force was
> enough to sweep people from barrels. Edwin could feel moisture in his

eyes, and he dared not look at Hilda. "Why the deuce do I want to cry?" he asked himself angrily, and was ashamed. And at the beginning of the second verse, when the glittering instruments blared forth anew, and the innumerable voices, high and loud, infantile and aged, flooded swiftly over their brassy notes, subduing them, the effect on Edwin was the same again: a tightening of the throat, and a squeezing down of the eyelids. Why was it? Through a mist he read the words "The Blood of the Lamb," and he could picture the riven trunk of a man dying, and a torrent of blood flowing therefrom, and people like his Auntie Clara and his brother-in-law Albert plunging ecstatically into the liquid to be white. The picture came again in the third verse—the red fountains and the frantic bathers.

A little later, Edwin's attention is caught by a line from one of Cowper's hymns, about "India's coral strand."

In thinking upon it he forgot to listen to the speech. He saw the flags, banners and pennons floating in the sunshine and in the heavy breeze; he felt the reverberation of the tropic sun on his head; he saw the crowded humanity of the Square attired in its crude, primary colours; he saw the great brass serpentine instruments gleaming; he saw the red dais; he saw, bursting with infancy, the immense cars to which were attached the fantastically plaited horses; he saw the venerable zealots on the dais raving lest after all the institutions whose centenary they had met to honour should not save these children from hopeless and excruciating torture for ever and ever; he saw those majestic purple folds in the centre embroidered with the legend of the blood of the mystic Paschal Lamb; he saw the meek, stupid, and superstitious faces, all turned one way, all for the moment under the empire of one horrible idea, all convinced that the consequences of sins could be prevented by an act of belief, all gloating over inexhaustible tides of blood. And it seemed to him that in the dim cellars under the shambles behind the Town Hall, where he had once been, there dwelt, squatting, a strange and savage god who would blast all those who did not enter his presence dripping with gore, be they child or grandfather. It seemed to him that the drums were tom-toms, and Baines's a bazaar. He could fit every detail of the scene to harmonize with a vision of India's coral strand.

Under the influence of these images, he turns to Hilda with the remark, "It only wants the Ganges at the bottom of the

Square." And Hilda, of course, overwhelms him with her passionate defense of religious belief, religious passion, simply because they *are* belief and passion. The whole scene is brilliantly done, and we are left with the impression that while Bennett's judgment on religious emotions is as harsh and as external as ever, he has been forced into a more sympathetic perception of their nature, simply by dwelling on the lives of those who are moved by them. The faces of the massed fanatics are "stupid and superstitious," but at least Bennett does not apologize on their behalf for the way they are lingering on the stage instead of making way for more modern attitudes. In this orgiastic rite, he seems to be acknowledging, there is something permanent in humanity, however regrettable we may find it. The forms of religious belief may be altered, but the impulse to believe will remain; common sense will not, after all, prevail, at any rate among the populace.

This awareness must have readied Bennett for the explosion of 1914–18, when it was finally demonstrated that neither men nor nations could be trusted to act in accordance with enlightened, or even unenlightened, self-interest. And Bennett's reaction was to write a novel in which the central character is a religious believer, however tainted and however lapsed.

This was *The Pretty Lady* (1918). It was a courageous book to write, not only because it dealt with the life of a prostitute (the wartime relaxation of taboos no doubt made the subject less dangerous than it would have been a few years earlier), but because of the imaginative boldness it required. To project himself imaginatively into the life of a woman is always a risk for the male novelist; Bennett had taken this risk successfully in *The Old Wives' Tale* and more or less successfully in *Anna, Leonora,* and *Hilda Lessways,* but there still remained the problem that Christine was a Frenchwoman, and with all his long experience of

France Bennett had, understandably, never so far ventured to introduce French characters in other than tangential roles. That he succeeded so well (for *The Pretty Lady* is the most unfairly neglected of all his novels, and should be reprinted) is very largely due, I think, to his newly increased insight into the nature of the religious emotions.

Christine, being an ordinary Frenchwoman (the fact of her being a prostitute only intensifies her ordinariness, confining her as it does in a narrow, stuffy little world), is naturally a Catholic. In drawing her character, Bennett could not in any case have avoided this element, but in fact he chose to make it central to the book, and the action pivots on it.

Christine is a second-generation Parisian prostitute who finds herself in London at the beginning of the war. (Conscientious as ever, Bennett provides a labored but plausible explanation of how this came to be.) Plying her trade, she deals with many men, but there are two with whom her involvement is genuine. One, who shares the central spotlight of the novel, is G. J. Hoape, an aging bachelor of settled habits and materialistic, rational, benevolent attitudes. Hoape in fact represents the old steady Edwardian England, trying to keep its coarse-grained sanity in this new apocalyptic world. He lives the kind of life that the young Bennett, twenty years earlier, had planned for himself as he grew older; his flat in Albany is irreproachable, his books and china enviable, his life selfish and secure. One theme of the book, and very ably Bennett handles it, is the ruthless destruction of these habits of mind. By the end, Hoape has realized that the world in which he must live out the rest of his life has no place for the old certainties of a prosperous bachelorhood. He is friendly with two young women of the Mayfair world, one of whom willfully exposes herself to danger from air raids until she is duly killed in one, and the other, a war widow, undergoes a

violent nervous breakdown in the course of which she involves
Hoape in sharing and understanding her suffering, to his spiritual betterment. At the end, Hoape reflects, "Perhaps the frame
of society was about to collapse. Perhaps Queen, deliberately
courting destruction, and being destroyed, was the symbol of
society. What matter? Perhaps civilisation, by its nobility and
its elements of reason, and by the favour of destiny, would be
saved from disaster after frightful danger, and Concepcion was
its symbol."

Hoape's commerce with Christine is in fact a relic of his
former life; he has found this the best method of satisfying his
sexual nature without becoming involved in family life and thus
having to revolutionize his habits. At nearly fifty years of age
(the same age as Bennett during the writing of the book), Hoape
"had casually known hundreds of courtesans in sundry capitals,
a few of them very agreeable; also a number of women calling
themselves, sometimes correctly, actresses. . . . But he had
never loved—unless it might be, mildly, Concepcion, and Concepcion was now a war bride."

To have gone fifty years without being in love with a woman
argues a detachment from emotion, an ability to take life skillfully on the level of satisfaction and self-interest, that the
younger Bennett might, in some moods, have admired and
wished to emulate. The older Bennett did not. Hoape's position
is described with an irony, and demolished with a completeness,
that leave us in no doubt of the author's standpoint. Starting
from this premise, it is inevitable that Hoape's dealings with
Christine will come to an end; they are too mechanical, too shel-
tered from the rough and prodigal winds of real love. In fact,
the debacle comes because of her involvement with the second
man in the story, the officer whose name is given simply as
Edgar.

Edgar, though also a mature man, is sharply contrasted with Hoape. He is doomed, mystical, tragic, an inhabitant of the apocalyptic landscape of the war. What binds Christine to Edgar is precisely that she has religious emotions and that he becomes the focus of these emotions. He comes into her life just after she has paid a Sunday morning visit to Brompton Oratory; there, she experiences a renewal of devotion for the Virgin Mary; Chapter 16, "The Virgin," is devoted entirely to this visit and should be studied carefully by anyone concerned with Bennett's development. For all his long experience of French Catholicism, he could not have written that chapter at any earlier point in his career. The attitude to Christine's religion is as skeptical and detached as the attitude to Nonconformism in *Clayhanger;* Bennett sees it as a complex and interesting form of superstititon, a faith but hardly a philosophy; the difference, however, is that this time the religious feelings are a central motivation in a central character, and accordingly the novelist makes the effort of seeing them from the inside.

Christine enters the Oratory in a state of nervousness. She has had, the night before, the kind of experience she never ceases to dread: a public brawl in which she was involved. Vaguely but powerfully, she feels that her luck is going wrong and that the reason may be that she has offended the Virgin by transferring her worship, of late, to the infant Jesus. Determined to remedy this, she hurries past the Miraculous Infant Jesus of Prague, not daring to stay long enough to mutter the appropriate prayer, and hastens to renew her allegiance to the Virgin:

Christine cast herself down and prayed to the painted image and the hammered heart. She prayed to the goddess whom the Middle Ages had perfected and who in the minds of the simple and the savage has survived the Renaissance and still triumphantly flourishes; the Queen of heaven, the Tyrant of heaven, the Woman in heaven; who was so

venerated that even her sweat is exhibited as a relic; who was softer
than Christ as Christ was softer than the Father; who in becoming a
goddess had increased her humanity; who put living roses for a sign
into the mouths of fornicators when they died, if only they had been
faithful to her; who told the amorous sacristan to kiss her face and not
her feet; who questioned lovers about their mistresses: "Is she as pretty
as I?"; who fell like a pestilence on the nuptial chambers of young men
who, professing love for her, had taken another bride; who enjoyed
being amused; who admitted a weakness for artists, tumblers, soldiers
and the common herd; who had visibly led both opponents on every
battlefield for centuries; who impersonated absent disreputable nuns
and did their work for them until they returned, repentant, to be forgiven by her; who acted always on her instinct and never on hèr reason;
who cared nothing for legal principles; who openly used her feminine
influence with the Trinity; who filled heaven with riff-raff; and who
had never on any pretext driven a soul out of heaven. Christine made
peace with this jealous and divine creature. She felt unmistakably that
she was forgiven for her infidelity due to the Infant in the darkness
beyond the opposite aisle. The face of the Lady of VII Dolours miraculously smiled at her; the silver heart miraculously shed its tarnish and
glittered beneficent lightnings. Doubtless she knew somewhere in her
mind that no physical change had occurred in the picture or the heart;
but her mind was a complex, and like nearly all minds could disbelieve
and believe simultaneously.

On returning home, calmed and comforted, Christine finds to
her consternation that the very man who started the brawl, an
officer the worse for drink, is in her flat, and that he has been
drinking again in the meantime and is now insensible. At first
she wonders "what the very clement Virgin could be about,"
but when he regains consciousness their relationship develops
and his personality becomes fused, in her mind, with her feelings toward the Virgin. She feels a distinct *frisson* on learning
from her maid that he must have been entering her flat at the
very moment when she was kneeling to the Virgin, and was thus
"part of the miracle" of her renewed strength for life. Clearly

"the Virgin had sent this man to her." Hoape, on whom her attention has up to now been mainly fixed, telephones at this
point, and, though she goes briefly to visit him, she disappoints
him and returns to Edgar, whom she feels the need to protect
and comfort. Later, when Hoape and a friend of his, who is on
leave from the Front, have arranged an evening out with some
women of the town, and Christine is of the party, she suddenly
gets up and leaves the party without explanation on hearing her
name called several times in Edgar's voice. This phenomenon is
never explained; Christine herself regards it as a miracle, and
Bennett offers no counterexplanation; she hurries out into the
night, and there, her faith in the miracle ebbing away, wanders
gloomily about until she is suddenly confronted by a private
soldier just back from the Front, who "in a fatigued, gloomy,
aristocratic voice" asks her the way to the Denman Street Hos-
tel. It is Edgar. He has been reduced to the ranks for drunkenness. The effect on Christine is electrifying: "A sacred dew suf-
fused her from head to foot. She trembled with an intimidated
joy. She felt the mystic influences of all the unseen powers. She
knew herself with holy dread to be the chosen of the very clement Virgin, and the channel of a miraculous intervention."

Taking Edgar back to her flat, she tends him devotedly, once
again rejecting Hoape in the process (he rings the bell and is not
admitted), and once again experiencing what she takes to be a
mystical joy. "She was mystically happy in the incomparable
marvel of the miracle, and in her care of the dull, unresponding
man. Her heart yearned thankfully, devotedly, passionately to
the Virgin of the VII Dolours."

Edgar makes no further reappearance in the story. He is, presumably, killed on the battlefield. We have, however, seen
enough of him to realize that the contrast between him and
Hoape is one of the chief polarities of the book. Like Christine,

he has powerful religious emotions. On his first visit to her flat, he shows her his talisman: "an oval piece of red cloth with a picture of Christ, his bleeding heart surrounded by flames and thorns and a great cross in the background."

"That," said the officer, "will bring anybody safe home again." Christine was too awed even to touch the red cloth. The vision of the dishevelled, inspired man in khaki shirt, collar and tie, holding the magic saviour in his thin, veined, aristocratic hand, powerfully impressed her, and she neither moved nor spoke.

"The magic saviour"; Bennett's view of religion, any religion, is evidently that it is magic, an affair of lucky charms and talismans. But at least he realizes, as in the old comfortable days he did not, that human beings can use this magic as a means of keeping on going in impossible situations. Christine's situation is impossible; so, for different reasons, is Edgar's. Hoape, who is still clinging to the middle of the road, can do without magic; they know that they need it, and the knowledge brings them together. In the end, Christine's downfall is the direct result of her attachment to Edgar. Forced out of her flat by some wartime requisitioning order, she is in despair when Hoape, who has been toying with the idea for some time, decides to "put her among her own furniture," as the decorous French phrase has it, and set her up as his permanent mistress. Both of them are immensely pleased at the prospect of this arrangement, which promises to solve all their problems at one blow. But, with the happy ending in sight, disaster strikes Christine. She hears Edgar's voice once more inside her head: driven by the need to find him and by a hysterical desire to show loyalty to the Virgin—exacerbated by contrition over a recent temporary lapse into Protestantism—she goes out into the street at night and approaches soldier after soldier, scrutinizing each man's face.

Hoape sees her, draws the obvious conclusion, and in a rush of shame and revulsion resolves never to set eyes on her again. *The Pretty Lady* is Bennett's principal war-novel. It is his agonized response to the insensate violence and cruelty of those years, and his intuitive acknowledgment that the old settled Europe had gone for ever. With a prostitute as its heroine, the dismembering of a comfortable man's life as its main theme, it is a lurid story, lit by the flames of burning cities; it is full of images of horror—a child's arm found in the street after a bombing raid, a factory-girl's scalp torn off by a machine—and its vision of life is very much in consonance with that of "The Waste Land" or "The Second Coming." Looking ahead in Bennett's work, we see that his best stories will, from now on, mirror this jaded civilization that has looked too much on death: we think of *Accident,* which finds a savage delight in taking a haughty Continental express train, full of rich Anglo-Saxons on their way to a midwinter holiday, and sweeping it from the rails in a terrifying mishap; or of the disillusion with worldy success in *Lord Raingo;* or of Mr. Earlforward in *Riceyman Steps,* dying of cancer among his hoarded bric-a-brac. "These fragments I have shored against my ruins."

So much for the general outline. We have taken a walk round Bennett's achievement, surveyed the circumstances of his life and time, ventured on some generalizations. But in criticizing an author we must, finally, put the question: Where is his masterpiece?

I suggested earlier that it was an artistic necessity, for a writer of Bennett's epoch, to see provincial life with a metropolitan eye. As Henry James was able to see America both as an American and as a European, as Conrad was able to write of his En-

glish characters from both a British and a Continental point of
view, so it was essential for Bennett to see the Five Towns from
the inside and the outside simultaneously. Only this balance
would provide the necessary richness.

In *The Old Wives' Tale* Bennett has exactly the right blueprint.
The Paris sections are designed to provide the external angle on
Bursley. Of course the whole book is "about" Bursley; it is
about the spirit of St. Luke's Square, and what happens to that
spirit when it faces the ordeals of life, whether on its own
ground or in alien circumstances. When Sophia, after her almost
fatal fever, comes to herself in the apartment of Madame Fou-
cault, she gets out of bed and, finding herself alone in the place,
takes a critical look at her surroundings and unhesitatingly condemns them "with the sharp gaze of a woman brought up in the
traditions of a modesty so proud that it scorns ostentation." At
once we are back in the Baines parlor in St. Luke's Square; indeed, we have never, in spirit, left it.

The blueprint, then, is perfect. But the book itself falls just
short of perfection. The gap in tone between the Bursley and
Paris sections is too marked. The Parisian focus, instead of adding richness to the picture of Bursley, makes it seem more external. It does not illuminate: it dims. By comparison with the
great set pieces—the execution, the Siege of Paris, Chirac's as-
cent in the balloon—life in Bursley seems little and cluttered.
And this obscures the book's main point, which is that Constance and Sophia, both formed in St. Luke's Square, live the
life of St. Luke's Square wherever they go, and that in consequence the two lives, outwardly contrasting, are inwardly identical.

In *Clayhanger*, Bennett attempted the Bursley theme again,
this time on a huge canvas. The external focus was postponed for
later volumes; the idea of a trilogy seems to have occurred to

him during the writing of *Clayhanger* itself, and Hilda Lessways, whose motivation in so many episodes remains opaque, and who comes into the Five Towns scene from outside, was partitioned off in a volume to herself which, though it is an essential series of footnotes to *Clayhanger*, does not stand anywhere near it in interest and breadth. As a result, *Clayhanger*, like *The Old Wives' Tale* but for different reasons, suffers from a lack of that nicely adjusted duality of vision so essential to an art like Bennett's. It is too heavily absorbed in its own subject matter; the Five Towns are seen from the inside but not from the outside; the provincial vision is there, but the metropolitan is not. The novel abounds in good, and sometimes wonderful, things: the retrospect of Darius's boyhood; the portrait of Mr. Shushions; the relationship of Darius and Edwin; the beautiful understanding delineation of adolescence in Edwin himself. But it is not the masterpiece we are looking for. It is too incomplete; the decision to wait for a second volume before looking at Edwin and his family through Hilda's eyes, understandable enough in a novelist who liked elbowroom, was probably a mistake.

Where is it, then? *Lord Raingo?* A fascinating study of worldy success and personal tragedy, but not a great novel. *Riceyman Steps?* A wonderful piece of observation, set in one of those huge dingy areas of London that are provincial in all but name, and showing the spirit of St. Luke's Square, at the end of its historical life-span, turning in on itself in mania, illness, and self-destruction; but a coda to his life's work rather than a masterpiece.

Where then? My own opinion is that we must go back to that fresh and vital period of Bennett's life just before the publication of *The Old Wives' Tale*, and examine the two stories "The Death of Simon Fuge" and "The Matador of the Five Towns." The first and more important of these occurs in *The Grim Smile of the*

Five Towns (1907), the second is the title story of a volume published in 1912.

Both stories employ the device of bringing a highly cultivated Londoner down into the Five Towns and having him experience things there that enlarge his knowledge of life, open his eyes, and in general improve his education. "The Matador" is the more obvious; it throws the sensitive outsider into the violent and passionate world of professional football, at that time just beginning to be a mass spectator sport and the focus of intense emotions for an urban working class. It is brilliant; but the earlier story, written during that Paris period when Bennett was on the whole at his happiest and most creative, is finer, and contains more of the truth.

Loring, a British Museum authority on ceramics and a gentle, tolerant, accomplished aesthete, is on his way down to the Five Towns to arbitrate some question concerning his particular field. In the train he reads of the death of Simon Fuge, a flamboyant painter, a minor master, a man given to highly colored living and more highly colored reminiscing, a kind of Frank Harris but with genius. The story concerns Loring's confrontation with his host, Brindley, and Brindley's friends: the cultivated class of the Five Towns. And also with the spirit of Simon Fuge, a Five Towns native, long self-exiled.

There is no "plot"; in method, the story probably reflects Bennett's enthusiasm for Chekhov, whom he had read in French before an English translation was made. The characters go from house to house: they have a drink in a bar, they meet people, and they talk. And over all broods the idea of Simon Fuge. A romantic legend about the painter and two beautiful girls, on a lake at night, is exposed to the withering realism of the Five Towns. The two women, sisters, are produced; one is serving in the bar, the other is married to one of Brindley's friends. Music

is played, books are discussed. Loring, who had expected nothing but uncouthness, becomes aware that he has stumbled on a
civilization. Only in one respect are these people less than civilized. They cannot, except in their inmost hearts, give Simon
Fuge his due. They may be fully alive to the importance of his
work, but they must pretend to ignore him, to be unimpressed.

"By the way" [says Brindley, referring to the doctor], "I wonder
whether he knows that Simon Fuge is dead. He's got one of his etch-
ings. I'll go up."

"Who's Simon Fuge?" asked Mrs. Brindley.

"Don't you remember old Fuge that kept the Blue Bell at Cauldon?"

"What? Simple Simon?"

"Yes. Well, his son."

"Oh! I remember. He ran away from home once, didn't he, and his
mother had a port-wine stain on her left cheek? Oh, of course. He came
down to the Five Towns some years ago for his aunt's funeral. So he's
dead. Who told you?"

It is all very deftly done. But Loring, as his train pulls out,
reflects that Fuge can afford to wait. His art, even though it is
represented in his birthplace only by one minor canvas, will
speak for him. "And one day the Five Towns will have to 'give
it best.' They can say what they like! . . . What eyes the fellow
had, when he was in the right company!"

And so the story ends. Its importance in the total picture of
Bennett's work is very considerable. It is the only example of a
portrait of the Five Towns which achieves the perfect balance
between internal and external vision. It is also the most admiring portrait. Perhaps the only really crucial question about any
society is, "Could a decent, good-hearted person, who was also
gifted and intelligent, be happy there?" By this test, most socie-
ties fail. In a frivolous society, only the frivolous can be happy;
in a cruel society, only the cruel; in a stupid society, only the
stupid. Where do we find the place in which a man of energy

and sensibility, an exceptional man who is yet without ruthless egotism, can be happy? In "The Death of Simon Fuge" Bennett shows the Five Towns as such a place. The picture is not without irony, and it is not without critical reservations; but Mr. Brindley, Mr. Colclough, and their friend the doctor are happy men, living useful and fulfilled lives; free of the fripperies of metropolitan fashion, yet in touch with what is genuinely new.

This is Bennett's picture of happiness. It was a happiness that became, for him personally, increasingly unattainable. At the time when he published that story, he might still have attained it; but a year later he published *The Old Wives' Tale*, and after that he was too rich, too famous, to be at ease in a provincial society. But a writer's positive values only emerge clearly when he is writing about happiness; and "The Death of Simon Fuge" is not only the most delicate product of Bennett's art, it is also his most serene and optimistic picture of human life. It came at the beginning; but the statement it made was final.

DAVID LODGE

Evelyn Waugh

It may happen in the next hundred years that the English novelists of the present day will come to be valued as we now value the artists and craftsmen of the late eighteenth century. The originators, the exuberant men, are extinct and in their place subsists and modestly flourishes a generation notable for elegance and variety of contrivance. . . . . Among these novelists Mr. Gilbert Pinfold stood quite high.

Thus begins Evelyn Waugh's *The Ordeal of Gilbert Pinfold* (1957), a work so transparently autobiographical that we must regard the passage as some kind of exercise in self-definition. Out of context, "the originators, the exuberant men" might be taken to refer to writers like James Joyce and D. H. Lawrence. Read this way, the passage confirms the orthodox view of literary critics, that a reaction occurred in English fiction of the thirties and subsequent decades, against the "modern" or "experimental" novel, leading to a certain decline in creative ambition and achievement. Readers aware of Mr. Pinfold-Waugh's well-advertised distaste for the modern in life and art will, however, suspect that in this passage he was more likely to be thinking of Dickens than Joyce, and that it was against the nineteenth-century masters rather than their twentieth-century successors that he modestly measured himself. In fact, either interpretation would be somewhat misleading. It is true that, in 1962, Waugh replied to an interviewer's question: "Experiment! God forbid! Look at the results of experiment in . . . Joyce. He started off writing very well, then you can watch him going mad with vanity." And it is true that the salient characteristics of Waugh's own work—his carefully constructed plots, his lucid, classically correct prose, his abundant and instantly accessible humor—seem to have little in common with the tortured and tortuous products of modernism. Nevertheless, Evelyn Waugh's fiction, particularly his early fiction, has a definable, though oblique, continuity with the modern movement in literature. To try and define it is to risk taking up an incongruously solemn stance toward a writer chiefly—and rightly—admired for his comic gifts; but the risk is worth taking if it helps to explain the difference between Waugh and, say, P. G. Wodehouse. Waugh is indeed wonderfully entertaining, but he is more than an entertainer.

In an early (1929) uncollected essay on Ronald Firbank, that late-flowering bloom of the Decadence whose satirical romances of aristocratic and ecclesiastical manners influenced him deeply, Waugh commended Firbank for never forgetting that "the novel should be directed for entertainment"; but the burden of his argument is Firbank's importance as a technical innovator:

He achieved a new, balanced interrelation of subject and form. Nineteenth-century novelists achieved a balance only by complete submission to the idea of the succession of events in an arbitrarily limited period of time . . . the novelist was fettered by the chain of cause and effect. . . . [Firbank's] late novels are almost wholly devoid of any attributions of cause to effect; there is the barest minimum of direct description; his compositions are built up, intricately and with a balanced alternation of the wildest extravagances and the most austere economy, with conversational *nuances*.

The relevance of this account to Waugh's own early novels will
be apparent to anyone familiar with them. In the novels Firbank
published through the twenties, the young Waugh found the
model for a kind of fiction that could be distinctively modern
without surrendering to what has been called "the fallacy of
expressive form." Since modern man inhabits a universe that
seems confused, fragmented, lacking in order and stability,
therefore it is inevitable that his art should display equivalent
formal characteristics: so runs the orthodox defense of modern
art. Waugh, while sharing this view of modern secular civilization, declined, for reasons that were partly aesthetic, partly tem-
peramental, and partly philosophical, to follow the advice of
Conrad's Stein, "In the destructive element immerse," or to pursue, as did Eliot, Pound, Joyce, and Virginia Woolf, the verbal
imitation of a disorderly universe. It is clearly of these latter
writers that Waugh is thinking when he writes, of "other solu-
tions" to the problem Firbank solved, that "in them the author
has been forced into a subjective attitude to his material; Firbank
remained objective." So did Waugh. The disorderliness, the
contingency, the collapse of value and meaning in contemporary
life, are rendered dramatically through conversational nuances
and ironic juxtaposition of scenes; narratively through the elimi-
nation or parody of cause and effect (events in Waugh's novels
are either gratuitous or grotesquely disproportionate to their
causes). But the implied author mediating this vision of comic
anarchy remains objective—morally, emotionally, and (perhaps
most important) stylistically. He does not, except in passages of
obvious pastiche, bend his verbal medium to fit the contours of
his characters' sensibility, nor dissolve the structure of formal
English prose to imitate subconscious or unconscious processes.
He retains always a classical detachment, lucidity, and poise.
This is the source of Evelyn Waugh's distinctive tone, and of his

most characteristic comic effects; it is also what troubles the critics who have accused him of being cruel, snobbish, and nihilistic.

For contemporary readers the modernity of Waugh's early novels was partly a function of his instinct for the symptoms of social and cultural change, particularly as it affected the upper classes. His crystalline comedies reflected back to them images, at once glamorous and grotesque, of what was distinctively new in their experience: air travel and fancy dress, cocktails and chromium plating, motor-racing and movie-making. He was one of the first novelists to grasp the significance of the telephone in modern life and to exploit it extensively in fiction. In at least one case he created rather than imitated fashion, putting the "sick-making," "shy-making" slang of his own coterie into general currency with *Vile Bodies* (1930). Yet these early novels have not seemed, in the pejorative sense, "dated" to subsequent generations of readers, partly because the topical detail is handled with such wit and economy, and partly because it is made to serve a larger literary meaning. For this last I should like to adopt a term used by Professor Northrop Frye in his monograph on T. S. Eliot: the "myth of decline."

The myth of decline is as old as man's nostalgia for a pastoral paradise lost, but it acquires a special importance in nineteenth- and twentieth-century literature, which, as Frye points out, has tended to invert the Enlightenment graph of human history as an upward curve of inevitable Progress, and to point instead to an accelerating deterioration in the quality of life. The beginning of the decline (or Second Fall) is variously located in the Industrial Revolution, the English Civil War, the Reformation, the birth of Christianity, or man's first departure from primitive tribal life, but the historical provenance of the idea is less important than its imaginative power—hence the appropriateness of the term "myth."

That Evelyn Waugh nourished his own version of this myth was signaled by the title of his first novel, *Decline and Fall* (1928). Clearly inapplicable to the hero, Paul Pennyfeather, whose fortunes follow a circular rather than a vertical trajectory, the title conveys a judgment on the society which shocks, seduces, dazzles, and exploits him during his hectic sortie beyond the walls of Scone College. Obviously, it echoes Gibbon's *Decline and Fall of the Roman Empire*, a work which Waugh perhaps read as a student of History at Oxford, and with which he seems to have had a kind of negative identification. As sly allusions to Gibbon in *Helena* (1950) make clear, Waugh deplored the historian's Enlightenment skepticism and anticlericalism, but admired his style—an elegant, urbane, sardonic style that was evidently one of the models for his own. Thus we may speculate that Evelyn Waugh saw himself as chronicling—not discursively, but imaginatively, not retrospectively, but immediately—the decline and fall of another great Empire and the culture associated with it. Certainly the title "Decline and Fall" would be as appropriate to any of his other novels as it is to his first.

" 'Change and decay in all around I see,' " sings Uncle Theodore, in *Scoop* (1938), gazing out of the morning-room window of Boot Magna Hall at the immense trees that

had suffered, some from ivy, some from lightning, some from the various malignant disorders that vegetation is heir to, but all principally from old age. Some were supported with trusses and crutches of iron, some were filled with cement; some even now, in June, could show only a handful of green leaves at their extremities. Sap ran thin and slow; a gusty night always brought down a litter of dead timber.

The trees in the park reflect the state of the human inhabitants of the Hall, a family of ancient and noble lineage now enjoying neither modern comforts nor traditional dignity, its energy and resources almost entirely absorbed by the lavish maintenance of an army of aged and bedridden servants. The country house as an image of decline and decay can be traced right through Waugh's *œuvre:* King's Thursday in *Decline and Fall*, demolished to make way for Dr. Otto Silenus's "surprising creation of ferro-concrete and aluminium"; Doubting Hall in *Vile Bodies*, dilapidated seat of Colonel Blount, whose footmen were killed in the war and whose butler suffers terribly in his feet; obsolescent Hetton Abbey in *A Handful of Dust* (1934), itself a Victorian supplanter of a genuine old house; and all the fine houses, including Brideshead, of *Brideshead Revisited* (1945) that are despoiled, abused, or demolished almost before the narrator has time to record them in "Ryder's English Homes."

In *Edmund Campion* (1935), a biography of the English recusant martyr published five years after Waugh's conversion to the Roman Catholic faith, he expounded a historical version of his myth of decline which can be traced back through Chesterton, Belloc, and Tawney to Cobbett and Lingard. In this perspective, the Reformation was a catastrophe which stifled at birth the "spacious, luminous world of Catholic humanism" personified in Thomas More, and left England, at the end of the Tudor dynasty, with a future of "competitive nationalism, competitive industrialism, competitive imperialism . . . the power and the weakness of great possessions." It is significant, however, that this Catholic humanism, the union of all that is best in religious and secular culture, was admittedly a possibility rather than a fact: in Waugh's historical scheme there is no point at which all was right with the world. Perfection exists outside time and space altogether, in the Kingdom of God.

Translated into political terms, such a view can only be described as conservative and reactionary; and Waugh's qualified support of Mussolini and Franco in the thirties was predictable, if ill-judged. In time, Waugh recognized that his values and beliefs had no place in the field of practical politics. Mr. Pinfold is described as professing "an idiosyncratic toryism which was quite unrepresented in the political parties of his time," and Waugh himself advertised the fact that he had never voted in a Parliamentary election, once parrying a challenge on this point by saying that he did not presume to advise his Sovereign on her choice of ministers. The riposte was characteristic and revealing. There is an element of self-indulgent fantasy, of role-playing, in Waugh's myth of decline, as he seems to concede on occasion— in, for instance, John Plant's comment, in *Work Suspended* (1942), on his generation's cult of domestic architecture:

When the poetic mood was on us, we turned to buildings and gave them that place which our fathers accorded to Nature—to almost any buildings, but particularly those in the classical tradition, and, more particularly, in its decay. It was a kind of nostalgia for the syle of living which we emphatically rejected in practical affairs.

In a similar way, Evelyn Waugh's imagination is more quickly fired by institutions in an advanced stage of decay than in their putative prime. The artist in Waugh seizes with glee upon what the educated Catholic gentleman most deplores, a process perfectly exemplified by Dennis Barlow's rapturous exploration of Hollywood's monstrous cemetery in *The Loved One* (1948): "His interest was no longer purely technical nor purely satiric. In a zone of insecurity in the mind where none but the artist dare trespass, the tribes were gathering." Not surprisingly Evelyn Waugh was one of the earliest and most sophisticated exponents of that form of taste known as "camp" (see, for instance, his deliciously ambivalent appreciation of Gaudi's architecture in *Labels* [1930]).

When culture is seen as a process of continual decline, nothing is invulnerable to irony. The modern is ridiculed by contrast with the traditional, but attempts to maintain or restore the traditional in the face of change are also seen as ridiculous; and in any case the traditional usually turns out to be in some way false or compromised. This can be clearly seen by retracing the "house" motif in Waugh's work. Consider, for example, Paul Pennyfeather's approach to King's Thursday:

> "English spring," thought Paul. "In the dreaming ancestral beauty of the English country." Surely, he thought, these great chestnuts in the morning sun stood for something enduring and serene in a world that had lost its reason and would so stand when the chaos and confusion were forgotten? And surely it was the spirit of William Morris that whispered to him in Margot Beste-Chetwynde's motor-car about seed-time and the harvest, the superb succession of the seasons, the harmonious interdependence of rich and poor, of dignity, innocence and tradition? But at a turn in the drive, the cadence of his thoughts was abruptly transected. They had come into sight of the house.
>
> "Golly," said Beste-Chetwynde. "Mamma has done herself proud this time."

Obviously Paul's reverie has the effect of highlighting the incongruity and perversity of the new Bauhaus-style King's Thursday. But the joke rebounds upon Paul's reverie, which is exposed as a sentimental illusion, compromisingly enjoyed from the comfort of a modern motor-car, derived secondhand from literary sources and revealing an immature desire to escape chaos and confusion. The case of Hetton in A Handful of Dust is similar: though its Victorian neo-Gothic is marginally preferable to the white chromium-plating and natural sheepskin in which Mrs. Beaver proposes to "do over" one of its rooms, we are left in no doubt that it is a hideously ugly fake. Tony Last's devotion to it, though touching, is misdirected, a symptom and a symbol of his innocence and immaturity. In Brideshead Revisited, it is true, we find something more like an orthodox conservationist attitude—the myth of decline has become more rigid and polemical here—but at the very end, the narrator recognizes that the disfigurement of Brideshead by its military occupants and the dispersal of the aristocratic family that once occupied it matter less than the fact that the sanctuary lamp continues to burn in the ugly little *art nouveau* chapel.

The myth of decline provided Evelyn Waugh with a sliding scale of value on which almost everything is found in some way defective. The only absolute to which he appeals—the ideal of Christian perfection—is not on the scale of secular history at all. Thus he was being quite consistent, though no doubt deliberately provocative, when he said late in life that he saw nothing objectionable in the total destruction of the world providing it came about, as seemed likely, accidentally (that is, without sin being committed). He has been accused of being less consistent in his later fiction—of speciously identifying the eternal verities with a particular human social group, the English Catholic aristocracy and gentry. Of his earlier novels, where the absolute values of Christianity are not explicitly invoked, it has been said that they lack a moral center: that the modern and the traditional, civilization and barbarism, and every shade of political thought and racial prejudice are rendered absurd by being played off against each other rather than measured against positive norms. Waugh himself has encouraged this view by disowning the title of satirist in these terms:

Satire is a matter of period. It flourishes in a stable society and presupposes homogeneous moral standards—the early Roman Empire and eighteenth-century Europe. It is aimed at inconsistency and hypocrisy. It exposes polite cruelty and folly by exaggerating them. All this has no place in the century of the Common Man, where vice no longer pays lip service to virtue.

This remark is as confusing as it is revealing. There is indeed satire written from clear, commonly shared principles, but we do not have to look beyond the eighteenth century to find quite another kind of satire. No one has satisfactorily identified the positive principles behind *The Tale of a Tub* or the Fourth Book of *Gulliver's Travels*. Yet these works certainly have the motives and effects attributed to satire by Waugh—and so do his own early novels. It would seem that when the satiric impulse is joined to the fictive imagination and the comic spirit, as it is in Swift and Waugh, an imaginative energy is released too strong to be contained within a simple didactic framework. The artist begins almost playfully to explore the possibilities of his *donnée*, and the reader is invited to respond to a mosaic of local comic and satiric effects rather than laboriously to decode a consistent message. The anchor of the reader's response will in this case be, not an abstractable set of positive values, but the intelligence and poise of the implied author as conveyed by his style and management of events. There *is*, in fact, behind Waugh's fictional world, a consistent point of view—that of a dogmatic Christian antihumanism; but it is not one with which the reader has to identify in order to enjoy the satirical comedy.

Evelyn Arthur St. John Waugh was born on October 28, 1903, in a modest villa in the London suburb of Hampstead, and died in 1966, the owner of Combe Florey House, near Taunton in Somerset. Both his parents came from respectable upper-middle class families of professional standing. His father, Arthur Waugh, was a publisher (director, in fact, of Evelyn's own publishers, Chapman and Hall), a journalist, and a minor critic. In the readable but somewhat guarded autobiography of his early years, *A Little Learning* (1964), Evelyn described his father as "a Man of Letters . . . a category, like the maiden aunt, that is now almost extinct." If the portraits of Mr. Plant, Sr. and Mr. Ryder, Sr. are any guide, Arthur Waugh cultivated his own obsolescence with a certain relish, and thus indirectly nourished his son's myth of decline.

Evelyn seems to have enjoyed a tranquil, happy childhood, overshadowed in more ways than one by his elder brother, Alec. After leaving Sherborne, Mr. Waugh's beloved old school, under something of a cloud, Alec precociously dashed off a novel about his experiences there. *The Loom of Youth*, published in 1917 when its author was serving in the trenches of Flanders, attracted considerable attention, particularly for the (then) startling candor with which it treated adolescent homosexuality. Such was the notoriety of this book that Evelyn was unable to follow his brother to Sherborne, and was sent instead to Lancing, a school of Anglican ecclesiastical temper that his parents thought suitable for a child of rather exceptional piety. It was at Lancing, however, that Evelyn became an agnostic; he was better known there as the founder of the Dilettanti Society and the Corpse Club. In 1922 he went up to Hertford College, Oxford, to read history.

To be a child or adolescent during a major war is inevitably to feel diminished and frustrated, and for Evelyn this feeling must have been personalized in the glamorous figure of his brother, Alec (who went on to become a writer of popular novels and travel books). It is not surprising, therefore, that at Oxford Evelyn felt, in his own words, "reborn into full youth." By 1922, the sober veterans of the war had departed, and the university was "re-possessed by the young." The manner of their repossession—the drinking, the ragging, the dandyism, the defiance of authority, the experimentation with every style of life and art—is unforgettably evoked, for all its nostalgic idealization, in the long first section of *Brideshead Revisited*. Waugh later described his own undergraduate career as "idle, dissolute and extravagant." It ended inauspiciously in 1924 with a third class result in his final examinations. "My education, it seems to me," he wrote, "was the preparation for one trade only, that of an English prose writer," but it was six years before he discovered his vocation. In the intervening time he enrolled for a while at an art school, took teaching posts in two private schools, was a probationary reporter on the *Daily Express*, and even, bizarrely, contemplated apprenticeship to a carpenter. All this experience was to yield fruit later, but at the time Waugh was far from happy: *A Little Learning* leaves him in 1925 lugubriously contemplating suicide on a Welsh beach. In 1927, however, he obtained a commission from Duckworth's to write a biography of Dante Gabriel Rossetti, and became engaged to Evelyn Gardner, daughter of Lord Burghclere. He seems to have written *Decline and Fall* in a desperate attempt to convince his fiancée's skeptical parents that he was capable of earning his living as a writer. *Rossetti*, published in May, 1928, was kindly received, and was indeed a very creditable first book, displaying the elegance, economy, and wit that were to mark Waugh's subsequent writing. *Decline and Fall*, published by Chapman and Hall in the autumn of 1928, after Duckworth's had rejected it as being too risqué, was a definite success. The two Evelyns were married clandestinely that summer, and the following winter accepted, as a delayed honeymoon, the offer of a free Mediterranean cruise in return for discreet advertisement of the shipping line in the resulting travel book, *Labels* (1930). On their return to England in the spring of 1929, Waugh retired to the country to write *Vile Bodies* in solitude. In the summer, his wife informed him that she was in love with another man, and the couple separated. Civil divorce proceedings were begun, and Waugh resumed *Vile Bodies*. It was published in January, 1930, and at the same time Waugh informed his friend Christopher Hollis that he was receiving instruction in the Roman Catholic faith from the Jesuits. He was received into the Church in the summer of that year. Thus, the years between 1927 and 1930 encompassed three fateful and closely connected events in Waugh's life: his self-discovery as a literary artist, the breakdown of his first marriage, and his conversion to Catholicism.

In *Labels*, Waugh describes the experience of "looping the loop" in one of the early aircraft:

In "looping," the aeroplane shoots steeply upwards until the sensation becomes unendurable and one knows that in another moment it will turn completely over. Then it keeps on shooting up and does turn completely over. One looks down into an unfathomable abyss of sky, while over one's head a great umbrella of fields and houses has suddenly opened. Then one shuts one's eyes. My companion on this occasion was a large-hearted and reckless man; he was President of the Union, logical, matter-of-fact in disposition, inclined towards beer and Ye Olde Merrie Englande. . . . He had come with me in order to assure himself that it was all really nonsense about things heavier than air being able to fly. He sat behind me throughout, muttering, "Oh, my God, oh, Christ, oh, my God." On the way back he scarcely spoke, and two days later, without a word to anyone, he was received into the Roman Church.

This is not merely a funny story, told with Waugh's usual finesse. It is also a parable. Twenty years later, writing about his conversion to Catholicism, Evelyn Waugh said: "Those who have read my works will perhaps understand the character of the world into which I exuberantly launched myself. Ten years of that world sufficed to show me that life there, or anywhere, was unintelligible and unendurable without God." Stephen Greenblatt has shrewdly observed the occurrence in Waugh's fiction of the demonic imagery of circles, wheels, and spirals that Northrop Frye associates with satire and irony, pointing to the circular construction of many of Waugh's plots, and to such motifs as the "Great Wheel at Luna Park" in *Decline and Fall*,

and Agatha Runcible's nightmare as she is dying from her
motor-racing exploit ("I thought we were all going round and
round in a motor race and none of us could stop") in *Vile Bodies*.
To these examples we may add the "unendurable" sensation of
looping the loop. All are images of the accelerating collapse of
order and meaning which many artists perceived in Western culture and society after the trauma of World War I.

> Things fall apart; the centre cannot hold;
> Mere anarchy is loosed upon the world.

The traditional resources of Merrie England were clearly inadequate to this sense of crisis. Many of Waugh's contemporaries
turned for salvation to Marx and political commitment; he followed the example of his fellow passenger and joined the most
uncompromisingly dogmatic Christian church, still, in those
days, unshaken by the winds of secular change. No doubt the
decision was precipitated by the abrupt breakdown of his marriage. This is the opinion of his brother, Alec, to whom he said
at the time, "The trouble about the world today is that there's
not enough religion in it. There's nothing to stop young people
from doing whatever they feel like doing at the moment." The
experience was obviously bitter and profound in its effects: in
novel after novel the theme of sexual infidelity—usually of a
woman, usually revealed with shattering unexpectedness—
recurs. Yet the flat, if understandable moralism of Evelyn's remark to his brother rarely intrudes into the fiction, not even into
Vile Bodies, written in the midst of this domestic crisis. In *Decline
and Fall*, written two years earlier, we find only hints of the way
his mind was beginning to turn, hidden beneath the surface of
what is in many ways his most stylized and high-spirited essay
in comedy.

It begins with two Oxford dons cowering in their rooms, anticipating with relish the fines they will be able to impose as a result of the celebrations of the Bollinger Society that are in progress.

A shriller note could now be heard rising from Sir Alastair's rooms: any who have heard that sound will shrink at the recollection of it; it is the sound of the English county families baying for broken glass. . . . "It'll be more if they attack the Chapel," said Mr Sniggs. "Oh, please God, make them attack the Chapel."

The comic inversion of natural or traditional order implied in the transmutation of huntsmen into hounds and prayers offered for sacrilege is unflaggingly sustained in the sequel. The Bollingerites escape lightly compared to Paul Pennyfeather, an earnest and respectable scholar whom they intercept cycling home from a meeting of the League of Nations Union and deprive of his trousers, in consequence of which he is expelled from the college. The episode and its aftermath are related in a few rapid, cross-cut scenes in which everyone is very civil but entirely indifferent to the monstrous injustice suffered by Paul. Even Paul's own indignation is deliberately retarded till the very end of the chapter, when he tips the college porter; and then it is qualified by an unexpected adverbial phrase (a characteristic device of Waugh's):

"Well, goodbye, Blackall," he said. "I don't suppose I shall see you again for some time."
"No, sir, and very sorry I am to hear about it. I expect you'll be becoming a schoolmaster, sir. That's what most of the gentlemen does, sir, that gets sent down for indecent behaviour."
"God damn and blast them all to hell," said Paul meekly to himself as he drove to the station, and then he felt rather ashamed, because he rarely swore.

Paul, as has often been observed, is a Candide figure, whose innocence is used as a foil for the exposure of folly and vice in the

world at large. True to the porter's prediction, he is compelled
to take employment as a schoolmaster at Llanabba Castle, an
outrageously fraudulent establishment presided over by
Augustus Fagan, Esq., Ph.D. Here he meets three characters
each of whom, without being heavily symbolic, has something
to tell him about Life. His colleague Mr. Prendergast, an ex-
clergyman afflicted with Doubts, is a cautionary example of
what happens when spirituality is divorced from dogma. The
baffling lies and impostures of the butler, Philbrick, caricature
the bewildering social mobility of postwar society. Grimes, another teacher, is more complex, and his significance more of a
riddle. In one sense he embodies the decline of the public-school
code which he so brazenly exploits ("I should think," he says,
"I've been put on my feet more often than any living man"); in
another his infinitely elastic, totally amoral capacity for survival
compels respect, and under his tuition Paul becomes a little less
innocent.

   The Llanabba School Sports forms the backdrop to a hilarious
comedy of incompatible manners between the academic staff,
the uncouth Welsh natives, and the visiting parents, among
whom is the glamorous Mrs. Margot Beste-Chetwynde. Paul
falls in love with Margot, and eagerly accepts an invitation to ac-
company her son to King's Thursday. There, after a highly un-
conventional house party has dispersed, he is astonished and
delighted to find his affection reciprocated—and indeed consum-
mated. Margot proposes marriage, and while the arrangements
are being made employs Paul's assistance in running her business, "The Latin-American Entertainment Co. Ltd." This, unknown to Paul, is a prostitution agency, and through a complex
chain of circumstances he is arrested on the eve of his wedding.
Chivalrously shielding Margot, Paul is sentenced to seven years'
imprisonment.

Paul is surprisingly happy in prison. "Anyone," he reflects, "who has been to a public school will always feel comparatively at home in prison"—the truth of which is underlined by the reappearance of Prendergast as chaplain and Philbrick and Grimes as prisoners. The chief source of dissatisfaction is the prison governor, Sir Lucas-Dockery, and his cranky theories of penal reform. In the belief that "all crime is due to the repressed desire for aesthetic expression," he supplies a homicidal carpenter with a set of tools with which he beheads the unfortunate Prendergast. Typically, however, the satire on progressive penology is balanced by satire of traditional practice, as represented by the chief warder, a great believer in the Observation Cell.

"That brings out any insanity. I've known several cases of men you could hardly have told were mad—just eccentric, you know—who've been put under observation and after a few days they've been raving lunatics."

Eventually, Margot's friends conspire to move Paul out of prison on the pretext that he needs surgery. At a sanatorium run by Augustus Fagan, M.D., a fake death certificate is composed and Paul is sequestered for a time at Margot's villa on Corfu. There he reencounters Dr. Silenus, the architect of King's Thursday (and a caricature of Walter Gropius), who reads him a lecture on Life. It is, he explains, like the revolving floor of a fairground side show. The nearer you get to the middle the easier it is to keep your balance, and at the very center there is a completely still point, for which Silenus (type of the artist) is searching. Most people, however, are tumbled over and flung about on the perimeter. Some, like Paul, are obviously better off merely watching from a safe seat. Taking this tip, Paul returns, disguised, to resume his studies at Scone College. But he is not

quite the same Paul. We leave him studying the history of the
Early Church (Gibbon's period, incidentally) in a spirit of intransigent orthodoxy:

There was a bishop in Bithynia, Paul learned, who had denied the
Divinity of Christ, the immortality of the soul, the existence of good,
the legality of marriage, and the validity of the sacrament of extreme
unction! How right they had been to condemn him!

Vile Bodies is perhaps the most "modern" of all Waugh's novels, both in its fragmentary, *Waste Land*-like construction and in
the apocalyptic despair which underlies its brittle comedy.
There is a hero—Adam Fenwick-Symes, a slightly more knowing and sophisticated Paul Pennyfeather—but the story of his attempts to obtain enough money to marry his girl, Nina, is only
one of many that appear and disappear and reappear in the mosaic of dialogue and description. The brilliant opening chapter,
describing a rough Channel crossing, indicates that the novel
will distribute its attention widely over the social scene. In quick
succession we meet Fr. Rothschild, a caricature of the crafty
cosmopolitan Jesuit; the American evangelist Mrs. Melrose Ape
and her troupe of "Angels"; Agatha Runcible, Miles Malpractice, and the rest of the Younger Set; the Right Hon.
Walter Outrage, "last week's Prime Minister"; two Firbankian
dowagers; Adam, aspirant author; and a group of card-playing
commercial travelers sufficiently demoralized by the storm to
join Fortitude, Chastity, Creative Endeavour, and the rest of
Mrs. Ape's angels in her rousing hymn, "There ain't no flies on
the Lamb of God."

The novel is saturated in the myth of decline—the decline, for
instance, of the British aristocracy:

At Archie Schwert's party the fifteenth Marquess of Vanburgh, Earl
Vanburgh de Brendon, Baron Brendon, Lord of the Five Isles and He-

reditary Grand Falconer to the Kingdom of Connaught, said to the eighth Earl of Balcairn, Viscount Erdinge, Baron Cairn of Balcairn, Red Knight of Lancaster, Count of the Holy Roman Empire and Chenonceaux Herald to the Duchy of Acquitaine, "Hullo," he said. "Isn't this a repulsive party? What are you going to say about it?" for they were both of them, as it happened, gossip writers for the daily papers.

When Balcairn, excluded from Margot Metroland's party for Mrs. Ape, files a totally invented and outrageously libelous story and puts his head in a gas oven, Adam is offered his job on the *Daily Excess*. He contrives to hold it for a while, first by running a series on "Notable Invalids" and "Titled Eccentrics" (more images of decline), then by inventing fictitious celebrities with whom everyone is soon claiming acquaintance. But Nina, deputizing for him one day, goes too far, and Miles Malpractice becomes the next "Mr. Chatterbox." Opportunities are always circulating in this way in the novel, one man's failure meaning another man's success. Whereas the pattern of events in *Decline and Fall* approximates, eventually, to the benevolent providence of traditional comedy, *Vile Bodies* seems to illustrate the wry judgment expressed in *Labels*, that "Fortune . . . arranges things on the just and rigid system that no-one shall be happy for very long." Adam and Nina, always on the point of getting married, always foiled by some twist of fate, are obvious victims of this system. But the instability of their relationship is also a symptom of what Fr. Rothschild calls "a radical instability in our whole world-order." The Older Generation and the Younger Set are hopelessly alienated. The bankruptcy of politics is represented by Outrage; the bankruptcy of religion, by Mrs. Ape. Economic anarchy is vividly illustrated by Adam's up-and-down financial fortunes.

Returning penniless from France, Adam immediately wins £500 by solving a simple trick with halfpennies, but, being drunk at the time, gives the money to an anonymous Major (also drunk) to put on a horse. The Major places the bet and the horse wins, but though the Major is constantly crossing Adam's path he remains elusive until the very last, apocalyptic scene of the novel, when Adam sits "on a splintered tree stump in the biggest battlefield in the history of the world," by which time galloping inflation has deprived the winnings of any value. In the meantime, Adam is given a check for £1000 by Nina's eccentric father, Colonel Blount, but discovers belatedly that it is signed "Charlie Chaplin." To settle a bill, Adam "sells" Nina to his rival, "Ginger" Littlejohn, for £78.10.2, an episode in which the themes of moral and economic anarchy neatly coincide. The sequel is one of Waugh's most delicate and complex feats of irony. Nina marries Ginger, but he is recalled to his regiment at the end of their honeymoon, and Adam impersonates him when Nina visits her family home. It is Christmas, and to the ritual reception of the new bride is added the traditional celebration of a rustic Christmas. This nostalgic idyll is described appealingly, but is undercut not only by the presence of the adulterous young couple but by the rumors of impending war in the background. The effect of comedy tinged with a strictly controlled pathos is typical of the novel as a whole.

Between 1930 and 1937 Waugh had no permanent home, and traveled extensively, particularly in Africa and Central America. In 1930 he went to Abyssinia to report the coronation of Emperor Haile Selassie I; in 1933 he made an expedition through the hinterland of British Guiana; and in 1935 he returned to Africa to cover the opening phase of the Italian-Abyssinian War for the *Daily Mail*. The curious reader may readily discover for himself in the three travel books, *Remote People* (1931), *Ninety-Two Days* (1934), and *Waugh in Abyssinia* (1936), the sources of characters and incidents in the novels *Black Mischief* (1932), *A Handful of Dust* (1934), and *Scoop* (1938), respectively. *Robbery under Law: The Mexican Object-Lesson* (1939) was more of a political tract than a travelogue, but Waugh used his experience of Mexico in *Brideshead Revisited*.

The spectacle Waugh observed in Africa, of European colonialism and primitive tribalism striving mutually to exploit each other, fed his imagination in a number of ways. In the absurdities and incongruities produced by this collision of cultures, the satirist found half his work of distortion and caricature done for him. Only in *Alice in Wonderland* could Waugh find a "parallel for life in Addis Ababa . . . the peculiar flavour of galvanised and translated reality." More seriously, the primitivism of Africa appeared to Waugh as both a foil to and a portent for a "civilization" that was itself declining into a new, and less appealing, kind of barbarism. The racial snobbery of which Waugh has sometimes been accused may, perhaps, be found in his travel books, but not in the corresponding novels, where, if any group survives the author's impartial irony, it is the non-Europeans. The progressive reforms of the Azanian Emperor Seth (in *Black Mischief*) backfire not only upon himself but upon the civilization from which he derives them. His before-and-after posters advocating birth control, for instance, are ironically misconstrued by the natives as promoting a juju for the encouragement of fertility.

Seth personifies a misplaced faith in Western ideas of Progress. When his general, Connolly, defeats a rebel army at the beginning of the novel, Seth does not heed the assurance that the solitary tank on which he had placed all his hopes of victory was useful only as a punishment cell. "We are Progress and the New Age. Nothing can stand in our way." Seth thus falls an easy victim to the opportunism of Basil Seal, a new kind of

Waugh hero, or antihero: not the innocent Candide figure, but the innocent cad, a true child of *l'entre-deux-guerres*, so devoid of principle that deception and fraud are reflex responses to him and he is incapable of seeing through his own lies.

Basil collaborates with the Armenian entrepreneur, Mr. Youkoumian, to supply Seth with the apparatus of Progress at a fat percentage, while relaxing amorously with Prudence, the silly daughter of the even sillier English Ambassador. But Seth's delusions of civilized grandeur get out of hand, he is overthrown by a coup, and meets a dark, ambiguous death in the jungle he had despised. In accordance with the same pattern of black comic justice, the idle love-talk of Basil and Prudence ("You're a grand girl, Prudence, and I'd like to eat you." "So you shall, my sweet, anything you want") is gruesomely realized in the dénouement when Basil unwittingly consumes his mistress at a cannibal feast.

Black Mischief is clearly continuous with *Vile Bodies:* there is the same moral atmosphere of deception and corruption, a similarly wide range of representative characters wittily caricatured and deftly juxtaposed through a montage of short scenes, and the same cool, dispassionate irony in the narrator's tone. In *Scoop*, his second African novel, Waugh returned to the ingenuous hero and the circular plot of *Decline and Fall*, while the mainspring of the action—mistaken identity—is a very old comic device indeed. William Boot, the bachelor head of the Boot Magna household, and author of a nature column, "Lush Places," in the *Daily Beast*, is confused with his cousin John Boot, a fashionable novelist, and dispatched by the *Beast*'s proprietor, Lord Copper, to cover an impending war in the African state of "Ishmaelia." There follows much broad but effective satire on the mendacity of journalists and politicians. Though hopelessly unprofessional (while his colleagues are busy inventing spurious news stories, he is sending back long, chatty, and ruinously expensive cables about the weather), William manages to scoop the biggest story of the war and he returns home in triumph. Through a chain of confused circumstances, however, the knighthood and banquet planned for William go to his cousin John and Uncle Theodore, respectively, and William returns gratefully to the peace of Boot Magna and the unexacting composition of "Lush Places." As Europe is to Africa, so the metropolitan world of the *Beast* is to Boot Magna: in both pairings a sophisticated modern barbarism is discomfited by a more intransigent and deeply rooted primitivism. The story of William's expedition to Ishmaelia is bracketed by the baffled attempts of Lord Copper's lackey, Mr. Salter, to control and comprehend William and his rustic environment. Salter's visit to Boot Magna at the end of the novel, for instance, hilariously reenacts the trials and tribulations of jungle exploration.

Between *Black Mischief* and *Scoop* came *A Handful of Dust*, which many critics consider to be Waugh's best novel. What is most striking about it is, perhaps, the way in which the style and technique of Waugh's satirical comedies are effortlessly adapted to a more subtle and soberly realistic treatment of contemporary manners and morals. This is not to say that the novel lacks humor, but the opening line of dialogue, "Was anyone hurt?" strikes an ominous note: many people are to be hurt in this novel. The story is simple in outline. Tony and Brenda Last are apparently an ideally happy couple. She, however, shares halfheartedly in his enthusiasm for his huge, ugly, and expensive property, Hetton Abbey, and drifts into an affair with the vapid man-about-town, John Beaver. The accidental death of the Lasts' only son, also called John, precipitates a crisis, and Brenda asks for a divorce. Tony, after reluctantly cooperating in the undignified preliminaries, is shocked by the threat of losing

Hetton into canceling the divorce proceedings. He abruptly embarks on a journey into the Brazilian interior, where he meets a
gruesome living death—condemned to read aloud the novels of
Dickens to a mad and homicidal settler for the rest of his days.
Tony is reported as dead to the outside world; Brenda, suddenly
as poor as Beaver, marries Tony's friend Jock Grant-Menzies,
and Hetton is converted into a silver-fox farm by an impover-
ished branch of the family.

Behavior in Waugh's previous novels was the stylized shadow-
play of a general collapse of values. In *A Handful of Dust*, with
the abandonment of farce and a movement toward more
rounded characterization, the question of individual guilt is
raised. Who, then, is responsible for the domestic tragedy it
chronicles? There are three principal centers of guilt: John
Beaver and the social set to which he parasitically clings, Brenda
Last, and Tony himself. Beaver, who "got up at ten and sat near
his telephone most of the day, hoping to be rung up," personifies the moral as well as the economic effects of the Great
Depression (or Slump, as it was called in Britain), but he is
perhaps not as guilty as Brenda's female friends. Her sister,
Marjorie, for instance, who encourages the affair at first, disapproves too late and for the wrong, purely snobbish, reasons.
Still more sinister is Polly Cockpurse, whose solution to
Brenda's problem is to offer Tony a mistress in compensation—
the appalling Princess Abdul Akbar. "What *does* the old boy expect," she complains when this experiment fails. "It isn't as
though he was everybody's money." The narrator scrupulously
avoids comment, allowing these people to condemn themselves
out of their own mouths.

Brenda's mixture of adult sophistication and childlike irre-
sponsibility is convincingly presented as both charming and destructive. Her betrayal of Tony is complete and unhesitating,

yet curiously devoid of passion or remorse. Tony is the last person to understand what is going on. Even after receiving the letter asking for a divorce, "it was several days before Tony fully realised what it meant. He had got into the habit of loving and trusting Brenda." Yet Waugh skilfully manipulates the reader's sympathies, so that compassion is never entirely withdrawn from Brenda, and Tony's responsibility for the breakdown of the marriage is not overlooked.

Waugh himself said cryptically of A Handful of Dust that "it was humanist and contained all I had to say about humanism." What he had to say was largely negative, but entirely implicit. Though Tony is a conscientious churchgoer, religion is, for him, a purely social function, and he is embarrassed by the vicar's condolences on the death of his son: "after all, the last thing one wants to talk about at a time like this is religion." Instead, in a scene of painful comedy, he turns for distraction in this crisis to a game of Animal Snap—one of many examples in Waugh's work of adults regressing to childhood rituals under stress. Tony's real religion is a feudal myth as artificial, as literary, as that of Tennyson's Idylls of the King, from which the bedrooms of Hetton are named (Brenda, of course, sleeps in "Guinevere," and Beaver in "Lancelot"). Tony's cult of Hetton is an index of his culpable ignorance of objective good and evil. When he finally grasps the nature of the world he lives in, "A whole Gothic world had come to grief. . . . There was now no armour glittering through the forest glades, no embroidered feet on the green sward; the cream and dappled unicorns had fled." Yet still Tony is haunted by his myth. The Lost City which he seeks in the depths of Brazil is not a real city, still less the City of God, but a transfigured Hetton: "He had a clear picture of it in his mind. It was Gothic in character, all vanes and pinnacles." At last, in the delirium of fever, he tells the settler, Mr.

Todd, "what I have learned in the forest. . . . There is no City,
Mrs Beaver has covered it with chromium plating and converted
it into flats." There are, however, in the forest the "Victorian
Gothic" novels of Dickens.

The title is, of course, taken from *The Waste Land:* "I will
show you fear in a handful of dust." The novel depicts a sick society whose hedonism disintegrates at the first touch of mortality. Crucial, here, is the bitterly ironic scene in which Brenda,
informed of her son's death, confuses his name with Beaver's.
But Waugh does not, in the cause-and-effect style of the Victorian novel, logically connect the child's death with the mother's
wrongdoing. "Every one agreed that it was nobody's fault." It
was nobody's fault, we are made to feel, because, like the
broken marriage, it was everybody's fault.

In 1936 Waugh's own marriage was annulled by Rome and he
was free to marry again. He did so in the following year, and
settled down with his wife Laura in a sixteenth-century Glou-
cestershire manor where, in due course, he raised a family of six
children. The advantages of domestic stability, however, seem,
as far as Waugh's writing was concerned, to have been more
than offset by the unsettling political climate of the late thirties,
and by certain changes within Waugh himself. The unfinished
Work Suspended (1942), the principal product of these years,
seems suggestive in this respect. It is the first-person narrative of
John Plant, an expatriate writer of successful detective stories
who, returning to England on the death of his father, finds he
no longer has any inclination to finish the book he is working
on. Instead he desultorily searches for a house in the country
and develops an obsessive but undeclared passion for the pregnant wife of a friend. We are given a delightful, affectionately
ironic portrait of John's father, a studiously unfashionable

painter, and glimpses of a promising comic character called Atwater, before the first air-raid sirens of World War II bring the story, and "an epoch—my epoch," to an abrupt and inconclusive end. Several features of *Work Suspended* anticipate later developments in Waugh's fiction, especially in *Brideshead Revisited:* the autobiographical convention, the slower, more ruminative tempo of the prose, inclining toward long and elaborately constructed analogies, and the pervasive tone of a narrator who feels sardonically alienated from his society and threatened by apathy and ennui within himself.

In his next novel, however, Waugh returned to the mode and the cast of his earlier comedies, following the fortunes of Basil Seal and a host of other familiar figures through the first year of the war, "that odd, dead period before the Churchillian Renaissance," as the Dedication says, "which people called at the time the Great Bore War." Though *Put Out More Flags* (1942) certainly has its moments (Basil Seal's racket with evacuees, for instance, or the bomb-carrying lunatic in the War Office) the novel has neither structural nor thematic unity. The satirical impulse pulls against a patriotic one, in accordance with which the aging Bright Young Things—even Basil Seal—are shown as finally undergoing, in the national emergency, an implausible change of heart (an organ which, in the past, they showed few signs of possessing). But one should not judge *Put Out More Flags* too harshly, for it was written on a troopship, partly to relieve the author's own boredom.

It was entirely characteristic of Waugh that at the outbreak of war he enlisted in the Royal Marines, subsequently joining the first Commandos. He was thus one of the few important British writers of his generation to have firsthand experience of regimental life and active service, and this was to bear fruit in his trilogy about the war. Fortunately, perhaps, for English letters, an injury sustained late in 1943 prevented him from taking part in the Normandy landings; and it was during the ensuing convalescent leave that he wrote *Brideshead Revisited*, published in 1945.

This novel, he drily remarked in the Preface to the revised edition of 1960, "lost me such esteem as I once enjoyed among my contemporaries, and led me into an unfamiliar world of fan mail and press photographers." It was his first really popular success, especially in America, where sales reached three quarters of a million copies; but in the more select circles of literary opinion it dismayed admirers of his early work, such as Edmund Wilson. The most just assessment of the novel is Waugh's own Preface, where he shows himself fully aware of its structural faults and the excesses and false notes of its language. The latter he attributes partly to the time and place of the novel's composition:

It was a bleak period of present privation and threatening disaster . . . and in consequence the book is informed with a kind of gluttony, for food and wine, for the splendours of the recent past, and for rhetorical and ornamental language, which now with a full stomach I find distasteful. . . . It is offered to a younger generation of readers as a souvenir of the Second War rather than of the twenties or of the thirties, with which it ostensibly deals.

Brideshead Revisited is indeed a classic example of the literary taste of the forties, and for this reason one may doubt the wisdom of Waugh's attempts to temper its "gluttony" in the revised edition. It was also Waugh's first—and, essentially, his last—contribution to the "Catholic Novel." This fictional tradition, which goes back to the French Decadence, is characteristically concerned with the operation of God's grace in the world, with a conflict between secular and divine values in which the latter are usually allowed an ironic and unexpected triumph. The theme which François Mauriac explored in his bleak French provinces, and Graham Greene in various seedy backwaters of civilization, Waugh embodied in the story of an English aristocratic family, filtering it through a narrator whose humbler background dramatizes the glamorous appeal—even in its decline—of hereditary privilege, and whose gradually eroded agnosticism acts as a buffer between the skeptical reader and the religious values endorsed by the author. The double-sidedness of the novel's concern is indicated by its deliberately old-fashioned subtitle: "The Sacred and Profane Memories of Captain Charles Ryder."

The frame of the main narrative is a completely convincing account of how Charles Ryder, an embittered regimental officer who has already resigned himself to a war of inglorious tedium, moves one night into a new billet which, by morning, reveals itself as the house of Brideshead, a place associated with the most thrilling and painful moments of his past. His memory released by this spring (the whole novel is heavily Proustian in feeling), Ryder begins to recall the history of his connections with the Brideshead family: Lord Marchmain, who adopted the Catholic faith of his wife, then apostasized and deserted her to live in sin and social disgrace with his Italian mistress; Lady Marchmain, a woman of great piety, but destructive possessiveness; and their children—"Bridey," the dull, dim eldest son; the exquisite and enigmatic Julia; the feckless and charming Sebastian; and plain, loyal Cordelia. It is through Sebastian that Ryder first becomes involved with this family, when they are both gay, irresponsible undergraduates at Oxford in the early twenties.

Oxford—submerged now and obliterated, irrecoverable as Lyonnesse, so quickly have the waters come flooding in—Oxford, in those days was still a city of aquatint. In her spacious and quiet streets men walked and spoke as they had done in Newman's day; her autumnal mists, her grey springtime, and the rare glory of her summer days—such as that day—when the chestnut was in flower and the bells rang out high and clear over her gables and cupolas, exhaled the soft vapours of a thousand years of learning.

Clearly, through the medium of Ryder, Waugh's style has lost some of its classical control and modern terseness, and a certain relaxation and lushness has crept in: semicolons and parentheses break up the syntactical structure to make room for adjectival and adverbial phrases heavy with sensation, with aesthetic and emotive self-indulgence. "This was my conversion to the baroque," says Ryder, of his introduction to the house of Brideshead, and the conversion is reflected in his prose.

A nostalgic lyricism permeates the first, long section of the novel, "Et in Arcadia Ego"; but two finely drawn characters, Mr. Ryder, Sr. and the homosexual aesthete Anthony Blanche, who vainly warns Charles against the fatal "charm" of the Brideshead family, strike a welcome note of skepticism and irony. The narrative is mainly concerned with Sebastian's decline from youthful dissipation to a deliberate and rather obscurely motivated alcoholism, so that Ryder finds himself painfully divided between his loyalty to his friend and his attachment to the rest of the family. Eventually Sebastian is abandoned as a hopeless case and left to live in exile; but Charles, rather unfairly, is also banished from Brideshead by Lady Marchmain. She now has another cross to bear in the marriage of Julia to the Canadian Rex Mottram, a brash and vulgar man-on-the-make whose instruction in the Catholic faith (the occasion of some amusing theological farce) is abruptly terminated by Bridey's discovery that he is a divorcé. Lady Marchmain dies, the family's London home is sold and demolished to make way for an apartment block, and Brideshead itself is almost deserted.

Ryder picks up his story ten years later, when he is returning to England from a painting tour of Mexico. In the meantime he has married and become a successful, though unfashionable, artist, best known for his portfolios of fine domestic architecture. His wife, who, we gather, has been unfaithful to him, and for whom he no longer feels any affection, joins him in New York for the voyage to England. On the same liner is Julia, now quite disillusioned in her own marriage, and in the course of a violent storm, which incapacitates nearly all the other passengers, she and Charles become lovers. Ryder's quiet but deadly hatred of his wife and the world of false, vulgar luxury (epitomized by the liner) which she inhabits is extremely well rendered; and so, in its way, is the high romance of the storm. Charles and Julia set about getting divorced preparatory to marriage, and when the ailing Lord Marchmain hints that he may bequeath Brideshead to them the ultimate "profane" dream of Charles Ryder seems about to come true. The sacred, however, has already disturbed the even tenor of his relationship with Julia, when a casual remark of Bridey's reawakens her Catholic sense of sin; and when Lord Marchmain returns to Brideshead to die and, against all expectation, is reconciled to the Church with his last breath, Julia returns to her faith and separates from Charles. There are several hints that Ryder himself is later converted in consequence of these events; and, as so often in modern Catholic literature (one thinks, for instance, of Francis Thompson's *The Hound of Heaven*), the descent of God's grace, because of the human sacrifice it demands, has an aspect of catastrophe—here conveyed through the iterative image of an avalanche.

The flaws of style and structure Waugh himself noted become more obvious the more often *Brideshead* is revisited. The book is quite unbalanced by the long and leisurely treatment of the young Sebastian, who then drops almost entirely out of the picture. Rather clumsy secondhand reports of his progress to an

unorthodox kind of sanctity, and the attempt to identify him as
the "forerunner" of Charles's passion for Julia, do not solve this
problem. The elegiac realism that is the narrator's staple style is
disturbed at times by passages written in quite different and dis-
cordant registers—for instance, the stylized caricature of Rex's
circle, or Julia's long aria on the subject of sin. The extended
images—the avalanche of grace, Sebastian as a Polynesian Is-
lander—though elaborated with elegance and beauty, seem
drawn from literary stereotypes rather than experience. But
what has most offended readers hostile to *Brideshead Revisited* is
the narrator's generously indulged spleen against the democrati-
zation of English society in his lifetime, a development epitomized for him by his plebeian brother-officer, Hooper. Ryder's
reflection on Lady Marchmain's three gallant brothers,
killed in World War I, has become notorious:

> These men must die to make a world for Hooper; they were the aborig-
> ines, vermin by right of law, to be shot off at leisure so that things
> might be safe for the travelling salesman, with his polygonal pince-nez,
> his fat wet handshake, his grinning dentures.

As I indicated earlier, the epilogue leaves Ryder resigned, in his
adopted faith, to the passing of Brideshead as he knew it, but
this comes too late to erase the impression that in this novel
Waugh's myth of decline has become damagingly fixed and limited to a particular phase and a partial view of modern social history.

In his next full-length novel, Waugh turned to a quite new
subject, potentially a much more affirmative one than anything
he had attempted previously; but the interesting thing is how
little difference it seems to make. *Helena* (1950) is a fictionalized
biography of the saint who, according to the legend Waugh
chooses to follow, was the daughter of a British chieftain

(Waugh makes him King Coel, or Cole, of nursery rhyme fame) and the mother of the Emperor Constantine, before she discovered, in her old age, the relics of the True Cross in Jerusalem. The overt purpose of the novel is to honor St. Helena, and through her to emphasize the historicity of the Incarnation and the common-sense reasonableness of Christian revelation; yet this message comes across less forcefully than the oblique comments on modern life. Though the novel was obviously thoroughly researched, the characterization and dialogue are deliberately, anachronistically modern, thus underlining the thinly disguised parallels between the fourth and twentieth centuries: both periods in which a great Empire began to crumble and confusion reigned in politics, manners, and morals. Waugh even contrives to insert satire on modern architecture and nonrepresentational art into this historical novel.

Since the period was one in which Christianity emerged from the catacombs and began to impose its values on European civilization, it might have been expected that in *Helena* Waugh would at last put aside his myth of decline. There is, indeed, a passage celebrating the "springtide" of Christianity: "New green life was pricking and unfolding and entwining everywhere among the masonry and ruts." Yet almost at once the narrator qualifies this optimistic note, undercutting the enthusiasm of the Christians, questioning the significance of Constantine's "conversion," and pointing out that subsequently "the oblivious Caesars fought on." The perfect union of the sacred and profane is as far from historical realization as it ever is in Waugh's vision. Even Helena's discovery of the Cross carries with it the penalty of inevitable human abuse:

She saw the sanctuaries of Christendom become a fairground, stalls hung with beads and medals, substances yet unknown pressed into sacred emblems; heard a chatter of haggling in tongues yet unspoken.

She saw the treasuries of the Church filled with forgeries and impostures. She saw Christians fighting and stealing to get possession of trash.

Between *Brideshead Revisited* and *Helena* Waugh published two short satirical novels. In *Scott-King's Modern Europe* (1947), a classics teacher at an English public school makes an uncomfortable visit to a corrupt central European republic and is confirmed in his opinion that "it would be very wicked indeed to do anything to fit a boy for the modern world." There are some amusing episodes, but on the whole it is a rather tired piece of work. *The Loved One* (1948) is a much more effective attack on the modern world—a world that was becoming increasingly Americanized. When Waugh went to Hollywood in 1947 to discuss the filming of *Brideshead Revisited*, the project was abandoned because of his intransigence over the script, but he found fresh inspiration in Forest Lawn, the great cemetery of Los Angeles. In "Whispering Glades" (thus, thinly disguised and with little exaggeration, Forest Lawn appears in the novel)—where the fear in a handful of dust is assuaged by vulgar ostentation and gross materialism, where the features of the "Loved Ones" are improved by cosmetics and wrenched into consoling expressions before they are expensively entombed among debased replicas of classical art and architecture—Waugh found a rich and many-faceted symbol for the denaturing of human life in the twentieth century. The novel is packed with images of natural order inverted or perverted: "the poulterer's pinch" the mortician Mr. Joyboy gives to his corpses, the empty beehives humming electronically on the "Lake Isle of Innisfree," Kaiser's Stoneless Peaches. Whereas the buildings on the movie-lots look solid and are in fact two-dimensional, those in Whispering Glades have the reverse, but equally unnatural effect.

The plot is a black comic variation on Henry James's Interna-

tional Theme: European Decadence, in the person of Dennis
Barlow, a young British poet, is allowed to triumph over an innocent but depraved America, represented by Mr. Joyboy and,
in part, by his assistant Aimée Thanatogenos. When Dennis's
career as a scriptwriter is abruptly terminated, he takes a job at
the Happier Hunting Ground, a pets' mortuary modeled on
Whispering Glades. The suicide of another expatriate Englishman brings him to the great original in a mood of ironic homage.
Here he meets Aimée, a girl in whom, though she has the same
mass-produced good looks as all the other girls Dennis meets, he
recognizes a hidden kindred spirit: "sole Eve in a hygienic Eden,
this girl was a decadent." While feeding his imagination on the
sublime absurdities of Whispering Glades, Dennis courts Aimée
with poems copied unscrupulously from the *Oxford Book of English Verse*. Mr. Joyboy asserts his rival claims on her affections.
Hopelessly divided between an atavistic attraction to the "uneth-
ical" Dennis and her conditioned respect and admiration for
Joyboy, Aimée Thanatogenos (whose name, of course, signifies
love and death) commits suicide in circumstances highly com-
promising to Joyboy. For a financial consideration Dennis cre-
mates Aimée's corpse in the ovens of the Happier Hunting
Ground. No tincture of emotion clouds the distilled irony of
this novella.

He entered the office and made a note in the book kept there for that
purpose. Tomorrow and on every anniversary as long as the Happier
Hunting Ground existed a postcard would go to Mr Joyboy. *Your little
Aimée is wagging her tail in heaven tonight, thinking of you.*

In 1952 Waugh published *Men at Arms*, the first volume of a
projected trilogy about World War II. The second volume,
Officers and Gentlemen, followed in 1955, with a note that the
work was concluded. Fortunately, however, Waugh reverted to

his original scheme and published the third volume, *Uncondi-tional Surrender*, in 1961. In the intervening years he wrote a conscientious, but rather low-spirited biography of his friend Mgr. Ronald Knox (1959) and a travel book, *A Tourist in Africa* (1960). *The Ordeal of Gilbert Pinfold* (1957) is easily the most inter-esting product of these years, which were evidently difficult ones for its author. This highly confessional novella was quite unexpected, coming as it did from a writer notorious for the fierce defense of his privacy, who rebuffed research students, sued journalists, and liked to be photographed at home standing defiantly beside the notices *Entrée Interdite aux Promeneurs* and "No Admittance on Business." It describes, essentially, a ner-vous breakdown, exacerbated by the imprudent use of drugs. Just how close the story was to Waugh's own experience can be verified from Frances Donaldson's memoir, *Evelyn Waugh: Por-trait of a Country Neighbour;* but no reader could fail to see in the opening chapter, "Portrait of the Artist in Middle Age," a re-vealing and far from uncritical self-portrait.

Mr. Pinfold, finding that increasing doses of chloral and bro-mide are not arresting the deterioration of his health and spirits, or loosening his writer's block, embarks on a ship bound for Ceylon. In his cabin he is disconcerted to overhear, apparently by an acoustic freak, the voices of some other passengers abus-ing his good name and plotting his humiliation. Mr. Pinfold is unable to trace these voices, but he finds them totally, ap-pallingly authentic even when their activities take a wildly melo-dramatic turn, involving murder, torture, and conspiracy. Pin-fold is, of course, the victim of hallucinations; but he does not concede this possibility until the end of the story when, refusing a bargain of peace in return for secrecy offered by his torment-ing voices, he dicusses them openly with his wife and doctor. What is fascinating about the hallucinations is that they are "displaced" and distorted projections of Mr. Pinfold-Waugh's public and private life. Some of the accusations he receives are absurd, some have a specious plausibility, and some—perhaps the majority—are criticisms Mr. Pinfold-Waugh has, on occasion, directed at others; for example, "Mr Pinfold typified the decline of England, of rural England in particular. He was a reincarnation . . . of the 'new men' of the Tudor period who had despoiled the Church and the peasantry." The "ordeal" is therefore a kind of identity crisis and the writing up of the experience a therapeutic exercise in self-analysis. That the myth of decline should be so pointedly turned upon its author is a measure of the detachment Waugh achieved, and the gain can be clearly seen in the completion of the war trilogy, where the somewhat affected and irritable toryism of Waugh's later years is tempered by a mature irony and compassion.

Nearly all novels about World War II are antiwar novels, but the note of protest is rarely supported by any coherent structure of ideas, and is usually compromised by the atavistic gusto with which bloodshed and combat are described. *Sword of Honour* (as Waugh's trilogy is collectively entitled) makes a political and moral judgment on the war which, though debatable, is thoughtful and telling; and its treatment of soldiering is consistently ironic and antiheroic. The story is long and complicated, but more than narrative continuity binds the three novels together: each has a dominant comic antihero who parodies or inverts the hero's stance, and each ends with an anticlimactic "battle" which confirms the hero's disillusionment.

The hero is Guy Crouchback—a name that combines associations of the reckless and ineffectual Catholic conspirator, Guy Fawkes, of the stooped Don Quixote, and of Christ bowed under the Cross. The imitation of Christ, however, is more evident in Mr. Crouchback, Sr.; in Guy himself, though he is loyal to his Catholic faith, spirituality has dried up along with human emotion. It is partly to redeem his hollow life that, at the age of thirty-five, childless and deserted by his wife, he closes up his Italian *castello* and, in a mood of quixotic chivalry, returns to England to enlist in the war that is just beginning. There is also an ideological motive: for the deeply conservative Guy, the Nazi-Soviet pact of 1939 has suddenly simplified the complexities of interwar politics:

Now, splendidly, everything had become clear. The enemy at last was plain in view, huge and hateful, all disguise cast off. It was the Modern Age in arms. Whatever the outcome there was a place for him in that battle.

Guy's disillusionment begins almost at once. No one in England seems to share his indignation at the Russian invasion of Poland, and no one seems to want him in the Army. Eventually Guy obtains a commission in the unfashionable but proudly traditional regiment of Halberdiers. In the activity of training and the camaraderie of the mess, it seems to Guy that he is "experiencing something he had missed in boyhood, a happy adolescence." As the novel proceeds, this analogy is more and more ironically developed. Thus Guy's first "war-wound" is a wrenched knee sustained in the course of an improvised football game at a rowdy regimental dinner. The Halberdiers are later billeted in a school whose dormitories are named after battles in World War I, and here "the preparatory school way of life was completely recreated." Brigadier Ritchie-Hook, the hideously scarred, legendary veteran of that war ("where lesser men collected helmets, Ritchie-Hook once came back from a raid across no-man's-land with the dripping head of a German sentry in either hand"), arouses in Guy a hero worship whimsically nourished by memories of the intrepid Truslove, a military hero of his boyhood reading.

Guy's antitype, or Jungian "shadow," in *Men at Arms* is Apthorpe, a fine comic character in whom, as Frederick Stopp has shown, the traditional *miles gloriosus* is crossed with a whole line of pseudo-respectable good fellows in Waugh's fiction. Apthorpe, like Guy, is older than most of the recruits, and the two men naturally become companions and rivals. At first Apthorpe, who makes great play with his experience in the tropics, cuts an impressive figure, but the speciousness of his pretensions is amusingly betrayed by beautifully managed nuances of speech and gesture. Apthorpe becomes involved in an extended feud with Ritchie-Hook over the use of his treasured "thunderbox" (a portable field latrine), an object surrounded by such mystery and intrigue that a fascist spy reports it as a secret weapon. Guy is drawn into the feud, an action which underlines the approximation of his military career to schoolboy pranks rather than serious warfare. Real combat, when it comes, is scarcely less bathetic. After endless delays "Hookforce" sails to West Africa to mount an assault on the Vichy French in Dakar. The operation is canceled at the last moment, but Ritchie-Hook proposes a small night-reconnaissance expedition which Guy volunteers to lead ("This was the true Truslove spirit"). Unknown to Guy, Ritchie-Hook has concealed himself in the party and endangers their lives and the mission when he plunges into the jungle to decapitate a Negro sentry. Guy's reputation is unfairly blemished by this absurd escapade; and when, a little later, he imprudently takes the hospitalized Apthorpe, a bottle of whisky with which the old fraud finally kills himself, Guy is sent back to England in some disgrace. Thus ends *Men at Arms*.

Two other characters must be mentioned. One is Virginia Troy, Guy's wife, but twice remarried and now again on the loose. Guy, in a passing mood of lechery, turns to Virginia on the casuistical grounds that she is still his wife in the eyes of

God, and is quite rightly rebuffed. The other character is Trimmer, hairdresser on a transatlantic liner in prewar days, a disreputable opportunist who is commissioned in the Halberdiers
but quickly transferred. In *Officers and Gentlemen* circumstances
bring both Guy and Trimmer together again on the remote Scot-
tish isle of Mugg, where a commando unit is being rapidly
decimated by the rigors of its training. Posing as a major, Trimmer has a brief affair with Virginia at a Glasgow hotel, and develops a maudlin passion from which Virginia finds it difficult to
free herself. For Trimmer, grotesquely, is chosen to lead Operation Popgun, a mission designed by the press officer Ian Kilbannock to provide the nation with a proletarian hero. The objective—a disused and unguarded lighthouse off the island of
Jersey—is entirely pointless. Because of a navigation error, however, the party lands on the mainland of occupied France, and in
a scene of fine burlesque the terrified Trimmer and the
eloquently drunk Kilbannock stumble around in the dark while
their men contrive to blow up a railway line. This fiasco is converted by Kilbannock's invention into a feat of great daring, and
Trimmer finds himself the hero of the British public. By enjoying Guy's wife and travestying his dreams of military glory,
Timmer thus takes over from Apthorpe the function of ironic
antihero. Guy, meanwhile, has had a long and tedious journey
round the Cape to Egypt, arriving just in time to participate in
the British withdrawal from Crete. The ignominy, misery, and
confusion of this debacle, which Waugh himself experienced,
are rendered in his finest piece of realistic writing. "Hookforce"
is left to surrender to the Germans, but at the last moment Guy
jumps into a small open boat from which, after many days, he is
carried to safety by another escaper, Corporal Major Ludovic.
This, in every sense of the word, queer man is compiling a book
of Pensées, some of which are disconcertingly apt: "Captain

Crouchback . . . would like to believe that the war is being fought by [gentlemen]. But all gentlemen are now very old." He is also the batman of Ivor Clare, a dashing young Commando officer who has seemed to Guy to represent "quintessential England, the man Hitler had not taken into account." Recovering from his ordeal in Alexandria, however, Guy learns that Clare deserted his men in Crete, though the intriguing socialite Julia Stitch (an old face from *Scoop*) is successfully covering his traces. This betrayal, combined with an earlier unpleasant experience in the confessional and the news of Germany's invasion of Russia (which, by the unprincipled logic of war, makes Britain the ally of Communist tyranny), completes Guy's disillusionment in his crusade:

> He was back after less than two years' pilgrimage in a Holy Land of illusion in the old ambiguous world, where priests were spies and gallant friends proved traitors and his country was led blundering into dishonour.

The sequel, *Unconditional Surrender*, does not modify—if anything, it deepens—Guy's skepticism about the aims of the war; but he does attain a more positive, mature, and humble perspective on his own part in it. Guy is selected, in droll circumstances, to join a British military mission to the Yugoslavian partisans. First he is sent for parachute training to an establishment weirdly administered by Ludovic, now promoted Major for his apparent heroism in the escape from Crete. Crazed with guilt about two murders committed on that occasion, which he mistakenly thinks Guy knows about, Ludovic emerges in this novel as the comic shadow of the hero. Eventually he publishes a successful romantic novel about the aristocracy (which incidentally bears a parodic resemblance to *Brideshead Revisited*) and with the royalties buys Guy's Italian *castello*. Guy is injured in a practice

parachute drop and, while convalescing in London, is sought
out by Virginia, now horrified to discover that she is pregnant
by Trimmer. To legitimatize the child, Guy takes Virginia back
as his wife, and both find the arrangement unexpectedly comfortable. Guy's generous gesture, condemned by his friends as
quixotically chivalrous, is in fact of all his actions the least deserving of such a criticism. In Yugoslavia, Guy learns that
Virginia has been killed by a flying bomb, but the child lives on,
a living symbol of Guy's (and Waugh's?) modified class consciousness.

In the Yugoslavian episode (closely based, like most of the
others, on Waugh's personal experience) the critique of Allied
policy as cooperation in the "dismemberment of Christendom"
is forcefully underlined. The Communist partisans are por-
trayed as crafty, repressive, and not particularly effective. A
rather specious "battle" is arranged to impress a visiting team of
Allied top brass, amongst whom Ritchie-Hook reappears. Of
course he cannot resist the opportunity to "biff the enemy" and
dies a grotesque, vainglorious death, useless to all except the
partisans, whose faces he saves. Impotent in matters of large
policy, Guy takes a small stand on behalf of a group of Jewish
displaced persons who are being ill-treated by the partisans. He
has very moderate success, and unknowingly contributes to the
judicial murder of their leader, Mme Kanyi. In his last interview
with her there is a very moving moment of truth which casts a
piercing illumination back upon the whole story of Guy Crouchback's war. "Is there any place that is free from evil?" Mme
Kányi asks.

"It is too simple to say that only the Nazis wanted war. These com-
munists wanted it too. . . . Many of my people wanted it. . . . It
seems to me that there was a will to war, a death wish, everywhere.
Even good men thought their private honour would be satisfied by war.

They could assert their manhood by killing and being killed. They would accept hardship in recompense for having been selfish and lazy. Danger justified privilege. I knew Italians . . . who felt this. Were there none in England?"

"God forgive me," said Guy. "I was one of them."

I have given only a skeletal outline of *Sword of Honour*, omitting dozens of memorable characters and episodes. At first, it seems to have the structure of picaresque fiction, in which the only principle of unity is the hero, moving through a linear sequence of diverse adventures. But on closer acquaintance one is impressed by the way in which Waugh contains the proliferating growth of his story within a fine mesh of cross reference and recurrence. Time after time, characters whom we have not expected to see again pop up once more in circumstances at once surprising and ironically fitting. The absurd obsession of Colonel Grace-Groundling-Marchpole, an Intelligence Officer who fits every piece of information that comes through his hands into one vast global conspiracy, parodies the author's own controlling vision. Waugh's mature style, more measured and subdued than that of the early comedies, more disciplined and self-denying than that of *Brideshead Revisited*, is a flexible medium which allows him to move effortlessly between the comic and the serious.

Sword of Honour has gradually won recognition as the most distinguished British novel to come out of World War II: no other work has approached its grasp of the multiple ironies—some absurd, some tragic and terrible—of that war. It thus made a fitting climax to Waugh's literary career, in assessing which we are probably driven back upon the "placing" of Mr. Pinfold. Measured against the very great novelists, whether of the nineteenth century or the twentieth, Waugh falls a little short of the first rank. But almost everything he wrote displayed

the integrity of a master craftsman, and much of it was touched
with comic genius. His best novels will bear infinite rereading,
and still retain their power to reduce the solitary reader to tears
of helpless laughter. That is a rare and elusive gift.

GROVER SMITH

Ford Madox Ford

"For factual exactitudes I have never had much use," wrote Ford Madox Ford in the epistle prefatory to *Portraits from Life* (1937). That must have been one of the last of his many asseverations to the same effect. The book is subtitled *Memories and Criticisms;* it concerns eleven of Ford's literary contemporaries, five of whom (James, Conrad, Hardy, D. H. Lawrence, and Turgenev) were very great indeed. It is an interesting, even illuminating book, though composed in an unpleasant style of fits and starts and revisionary inspirations, according to the "time-shift"; and within limits it is a critically true book in the sense that it "renders" Ford's impressions of these men as artists and thinkers: there is no conscious cant in it. Ford (born in 1873) does not even pretend that he had long conversations with Turgenev (who died in 1883)! But the impressions stand out as defiantly subjective, because for Ford subjectivity was truth. Graham Greene, calling attention to Ford's boast that the accuracies he dealt in were the accuracies of his impressions, has pinpointed the procedures of Ford not only in fiction but in criticism and autobiography. Ford even treated of things that were done, and of the people who did them, exactly in the ways he invented incidents and imagined characters in his novels. He set down what ought to have been, and this then represented the reality. *Portraits from Life* does not purport to be factual. As its title warns the reader, it is a work of art, a record of views. And between facts and views lies the vast distance which brings us to what we call meaning. At the end of the Conrad essay there, Ford quoted, as he had done in his book on Conrad, the (sinister) declaration of Rumpelstiltskin: "Something human is dearer to me than all the wealth of the Indies." This, Ford said, was what the writer who wanted to be great had to inscribe on his work. He might have amended the sentence to end, "dearer to me than a respect for fact." For in passing from fact to meaning, so his convictions held, the writer passed from the dead to the living, from the merely material to the human. Facts did not count for anything until converted into life.

Now, only an excessively narrow belief in art as imitation would exclude the right, indeed the necessity, of the novelist to subject real-life materials to a process of transformation. Even most notions of imitation allow that in some sense this is what he does. Without it there can be no fiction, whether the transformation is of one set of particulars into another for the sake of a "universal," or of diverse and scattered particulars into a new whole. And what of the historian? Must not he transform facts into meaning? And isn't this an analogous undertaking? And does it make any difference if, like Ford writing about Henry James or H. G. Wells, the historian is chronicling what he himself has witnessed and not what is buried in the past? Perhaps it does make a difference; but some people would argue that the difference is one only of degree. The historian must find out what the facts were; then he must find out, or conjecture, how they affected later events near their own time; and finally he must define their significance in the perspective of his own day. (There is a school of historians who argue that he should ignore anything in the past which is not "relevant" now, and that he should continually revise history to conform to modern ideology. In the same manner Soviet encyclopedias are periodically expurgated; in George Orwell's *Nineteen Eighty-four* old newspapers are withdrawn from library files and replaced with new editons brought up to date for orthodoxy.) The chronicler's task is generally not more than the final third of the historian's, mainly being just a reporting of what seems important—something subjective in part and in part regulated by custom. Both the historian and the chronicler (like Ford in writing memoirs) deal in impressions not by choice but by necessity. They are therefore doing what the novelist does in fictions which confess to be such. And yet—surely—things are not quite this simple. Is the truth of "reality" no different from that of "imagination"? Granted that all vivid impressions have a truth for the mind which conceives them, is this where we will agree that truth shall be lodged and established—in the mind only? The answer, of course, is that the question is an epistemological one, answered in one way by Realists, who distinguish between subjective and objective truth, and in another way by Idealists, who (more or less) do not. For the mass of mankind, there is, in theory if not in practice, a distinction which leads to calling the violator of it—a liar.

Certainly there are different sorts of liars, something that may redeem Ford from the baser charge. A careless critic once observed that Ford was, after all, only the second biggest (nonpolitical) liar of his time, the biggest being Frank Harris. That was absurd. Harris was an unprincipled liar; Ford the opposite, a liar on principle. Ford's intention was to get at the truth *au fond*, the meaning hidden under appearances. He professed nothing

else, though his habit of indulging in "impressionism" even
while in the act of explaining a detected "inaccuracy" fortified
the stiff-necked suspicions of the enemy. James had written a
story called "The Liar" (published in 1888—too early, alas, for
it to be about Ford himself, whom James was to portray as
Densher in *The Wings of the Dove*) whose title character is a dig-
nified and respected person with but one flaw, his irresistible
compulsion to tell tall tales. A painter, from a petty revenge motive, determines to expose this man by doing his portrait in a
style that will show his sins on his very features. James seems to
imply that true art is innocent: the so-called liar, whose lies
deceive no one but rather are enjoyed, is the eternal amateur, an
artist in spirit; his enemy, who tries to humiliate him, is no le-
gitimate artist but an exploiter of art. In *The Nature of a Crime*
(first published in 1909), a novelette on which Ford collaborated
with Conrad, we read: "A lie is a figurative truth—and it is the
poet who is the master of these illusions." James's rather broken-
backed *miles gloriosus* is not a poet; but Ford was. Richard Aldington, who for a short time was Ford's secretary (it was while
The Good Soldier was being written, 1913), recorded later a fantastic performance by Ford in which he displayed a poetic virtu-
osity rivaling that described by James. All he did was to retell
for an ingenuous auditor—Aldington's father, who was unac-
quainted with his ways—some of the tallish tales he had already
published in his first memoir, *Ancient Lights* (1911), about Ruskin and the Rossettis and about how he had met Liszt and had
been kissed by the Princess of Wales, and so on; but to these he
added some remarks on his meeting with Byron. Aldington
shrewdly compared Ford to Falstaff because both were funny
and lovable—and also mendacious—the point being well taken
because Falstaff's lies, too, were meant to be seen through. But
Ford was not precisely the endearing, self-depreciating clown;

he was too serious for that. He was rather the prophet speaking
in parables. He was born almost fifty years after Byron died;
and yet, *anagogically*, Ford or at least his childhood Pre-
Raphaelite aunts and uncles were Byron's apostolic successors;
he *had* met Byron by a laying on, which through a very natural
process developed into a laying *it* on.

There is a story in *Ancient Lights* which is more famous and
also better, because it is about someone other than Ford.

Dimly, but with vivid patches [he wrote], I remember being taken for a
walk by my father along what appeared to me to be a grey stone quay.
I presume it was the Chelsea Embankment. There we met a very old,
long-bearded man. He frightened me quite as much as any of the other
great Victorian figures who, to the eye of a child, appeared monumental, loud-voiced and distressing. This particular gentleman, at the instance of my grandfather [*sic*], related to me how he had once been at
Weimar. In a garden restaurant beneath a may-tree in bloom he had
seen Schiller and Goethe drinking coffee together. He had given a
waiter a thaler to be allowed to put on a white apron and to wait upon
these two world-shaking men, who, in court dress with wigs and
swords, sat at a damask-covered table. He had waited upon them.
Later, I remember that whilst I was standing with my father beside the
doorstep in Tite Street of the house that he was entering, I fell down
and he bent over to assist me to rise. His name was Thomas Carlyle.

In his epistle at the head of *Ancient Lights*, Ford explained that
the anecdote, for which he had already been taken to task, "was
intended to show the state of mind of a child of seven brought
into contact with a Victorian great figure," and that of course
the details of the Weimar story could not have happened. Indeed the tale is a parable. Whether it shows the state of mind of
a child of seven or not, it represents (*a*) Carlyle's relation to German culture as viewed by an Englishman and (*b*) the adult
Ford's opinion of Carlyle's servility to that. Therefore, in the
same anagogical sense, it is true.

These equivocations were full of comic intent as well. Ford's whole life was a web of paradoxes. He had to be ironic to be wholly serious. His childhood upbringing had established the necessity of seriousness: the irony was his own addition, or palliative, a mode of defense. Later he was to be attracted to the problem of psychological identity in dealing with the various fictional characters through whose embroilments with fate he inwardly refined his own. But to start with, almost in infancy, he learned to be obsessed with scruple and sin. From this grew his habit of weighing the conscience; of depicting it racked with the temptations of fraud and with the social penalties of virtue (the children of darkness being wiser in their generation than the children of light); and of honoring the lie courteous, the lie merciful, and as well the lie *penetrant* by which the world's hypocrisy is breached. Thus he came to irony. The truth never swimming on the surface of life, he was obliged to fish for it with ironic misrepresentations. These in turn became exaggerative (as in the Byron story), that is to say comic, by way of drawing attention to the irony and in a sense apologizing for it, or perhaps legitimizing it by recognition.

Had Ford been the only artist of his time who dealt in *duplicities* (if the word may be employed in a laundered sense), it would seem uncannily coincidental that he should have been both Hueffer and Ford—and then, being Ford, be Ford *doubly*. But it was an age of double vision—and double speech. Ford's change of name, which was his own business (to escape one or both of the women who thought they should call themselves Mrs. Ford Madox Hueffer), was not even unique; but it was unusual. Moreover, after all, it was of his making. To hunt it into symbol country would be ridiculous—and yet . . . he *was* fascinated with doubled characters, *doppelgänger*, the lot. It is a subject which wisdom bids one shun. It will be returned to.

Ford was the son of Francis Hueffer, the music critic of the
Times, who was of German birth, and of Catherine, daughter of
the English painter Ford Madox Brown, whose elder daughter,
Lucy, was the wife of William Michael Rossetti. Thus in childhood Ford knew the Rossettis *en famille,* including the more
famous Dante Gabriel and Christina. He was brought up in a
house in Fitzroy Square which figures as the home of the New-
somes in Thackeray's novel. From Francis Hueffer he seems to
have inherited a tendency toward obesity and early heart disease. The father died of a heart attack at forty-three; Ford's
younger brother, Oliver, who was also a novelist ("Jane Wardle"
was *his* other name), died of a heart attack in his fifties; and Ford
himself suffered from cardiac weakness for years. From the
Hueffers he had his conviviality; from the Browns his deport-
ment, his conscientiousness, and his emotional bondage to the
arts. Both families were artistic, and Ford grew up both with a
conviction of the supreme importance of being "clever" and, we
may credit, with an acute sense of his own inadequacy to the
standard. There are signs both of priggishness and of conceit in
young Ford; but despite his father's premature death he, at fifteen, was not permitted to drift. His mother was very much on
the scene, though it was his grandfather Brown who took charge
of the family and saw to it that Ford's education continued—formally at University College School, casually in reading and
travel. At eighteen, during a visit to Hueffer relations in Paris,
Ford became a Roman Catholic. The Hueffers had always been
Catholic, and the remarkable thing about this step was his later
and truthful explanation of it, that he had hoped thereby to
become eligible for a Hueffer bequest. Two further reasons
suggest themselves: that he wished to pay honor to a family
tradition which implied a break, however symbolic merely, with
the Browns and the Rossettis and the art world; and that he had

experienced religious emotions, perhaps even convictions. There is no need to assume that he retained any such convictions in primitive form; but there is much evidence, in his prose and in his verse, that he had a christened heart. Brown, doubtless hoping that this unpromising young man might still do something artistic, had indulged him by arranging the publication, as a book, of a children's story he wrote at about this time, *The Brown Owl* (1891), even supplying illustrations for it. Brown in name and decoration, it sold; and so did two more fairy stories over the next three years.

What drove Ford to literature, in the issue, was curiosity about life. He was not yet nineteen when his first novel was published. *The Shifting of the Fire* (1892) is a tale of passion and morality with, as might be expected, a sensational plot: from the beginning, romance was his strong point, with a theme of deception, fraud, and often violence predominating, which only occasionally, in his best work, is elevated into one of self-delusion, that is, a psychological theme. In this novel, already, the romance is designed to demonstrate the split between activity and values, it being Ford's lifetime obsession that what people do often falsifies their ideals, and that ideals can be asserted only by reinterpreting acts. As Paul L. Wiley has noted, there is much here that portends *The Good Soldier* (1915). The basic situation, moreover—of a fraud perpetrated for the sake of secret and illicit passion—is common to various Ford novels including *The Nature of a Crime*, on which he collaborated with Conrad.

In the spring of 1894, Ford was married to Elsie Martindale, the seventeen-year-old daughter of a medical man. Balking her father's opposition, the couple had eloped. They moved into a cottage in Kent and there lived quietly for a time, doing a little gardening and writing, Ford mainly of verse. There seems to have been no want of money. Later they bought a farmhouse

near Stanford; it was here at the Pent farm, after another removal (to Surrey), that Ford in 1898 became Joseph Conrad's
landlord and collaborator. He had meanwhile written a book on
his grandfather Brown, who had died. Of greater importance
was his slowly labored book *The Cinque Ports: A Historical and Descriptive Record* (1900), which has not only antiquarian but technical interest; for it uses devices of narrative refraction by which
Ford, in his historical romances, was to round an image of the
past through the medium of contemporary ideas and ways of
thinking. In this regard it bears comparison best with *The "Half
Moon": A Romance of the Old World and the New* (1909), a novel set
in the commercial life of the Jacobean Cinque Ports. Before *The
Cinque Ports* was published, Ford was already working with
Conrad, against whose techniques of impressionism his own
were to be sharpened. The two men had met through Stephen
Crane. It was arranged that Conrad should lease the Pent farm,
and he moved there with his family late in 1898. Ford and his
wife and daughter occupied a cottage within easy reach. Work
began in a desultory fashion. Ford had started a novel, *Seraphina*, finally published as *Romance;* for a time he and Conrad
talked about that and learned each other's peculiarities. Meanwhile Ford got to work on *The Inheritors* and Conrad resumed
work on *Lord Jim*. When Conrad read Ford's first drafts, he suggested that they make *The Inheritors* a joint effort. Within a
year's time, early in 1900, they completed this novel; later the
same year they took up the manuscript of *Romance* and kept
working together until this was finished as well. *The Inheritors*
was published in 1901, *Romance* in 1903. Ford and Conrad were
later to join forces occasionally, as on *The Nature of a Crime;* but
the two long novels made up the bulk of their collaborative writings.

Ford was to comment expansively on his ventures as Conrad's

collaborator, but he failed to clarify them quite. The undertaking seems rather paradoxical, since in the first instance it was Conrad who required guidance and help: he wanted to become more skillful and productive, for he needed more money than he had been earning. But as things turned out it was Ford's books that got written, all three of the novels being of his own conception. Conrad's gains were, in a pristine sense of the word, educational. *The Inheritors* and *The Nature of a Crime* appear more truly Fordian than *Romance*. John A. Meixner, whose critical work on Ford is among the best, considers that the novel *Romance* is Conradian as a tale of vicissitudes, its rough-and-tumble situations being suited to Conrad's talents, as psychological explorations were to Ford's. It may also be to the point to suggest the Conradian strain in the narrative strategy here. The use of a central intelligence at two levels of time coincides with the same device in Conrad's own fiction: Marlow, as narrator of his past adventures, was just then being created in *Youth* and *Heart of Darkness*, both conceived in 1898 and the former written entirely in the summer of that year. John Kemp, the fugitive adventurer in *Romance*, has the same type of role but is not an ironist. (Neither, for that matter, is Marlow—at least not primarily—in *Lord Jim*, written between 1898 and 1900.) *Romance*, that is, Ford's *Seraphina*, was unavailable to Conrad before the end of 1898. Yet, very curiously, unless Ford's memory was short-circuited or improved on in his 1924 essay about the writing of *Romance*, the thematic similarities between this novel and *Youth* were wholly coincidental. Ford said:

Originally conceived, in the attempt to convey realistically a real story of adventure recorded in a State Trial, as the thin tale of a very old man—and this before the question of collaboration arose—the book contains of its first version only the two opening sentences—and the single other sentence: "And, looking back, we see Romance!"

This final sentence is the one beginning the last paragraph of the novel. It sums up generally what both *Youth* and *Romance* are about, a fact which would be unremarkable if Conrad and Ford had gone into partnership a year earlier, at the end of 1897, or if *Romance* had acquired its narrator only after Ford read *Lord Jim*. The evidently Fordian aspect of *Romance* consists in the topicality of the Caribbean setting and of the national rivalries depicted; the latter, in a Conrad sea novel of the period, would be kept in the background.

The Inheritors is Fordian even to being a fantasy, though it is Ford's first one; it bears his stamp in almost every particular except, at many points, in the rhetoric of its dialogue, where Conrad is highly audible. The plot involves Fourth Dimensional beings who insinuate themselves into human society and take it over; symbolically this Wellsian proceeding refers to the takeover of political power by the "new gang" of *fin de siècle* British industrialists, yellow journalists, and colonial imperialists (some of whom are but thinly disguised in its cast of characters) and looks forward unconsciously to the social satire of Wells's *Tono-Bungay*. Ultimately, it looks forward to Ford's Tietjens novels. It is striking that the displaced *civilisés* who succumb to the artistic and political machinations represent, in one way or another, the Jamesian sensibility mode. All this is far from Conradian.

The charges that *The Nature of a Crime* is fragmentary, that it neglects characterization, that it ends with a *deus ex machina* are partly justified, as is the verdict that, after all, Conrad was not gifted for psychological web-spinning. But as a work of Ford, this queer pseudo-novel, constructed in the form of a confession by an embezzling trustee writing to a married woman with whom he is hopelessly in love, and to whom he publishes his suicide plans, is fascinating because it relates to so much on its periphery. For example, it presents in uncomplicated form the theme of passion as the "mainspring" of action, and of action as but a manifestation of the passional drive. The protagonist foreshadows Dowell of *The Good Soldier*, but unlike him has translated his passion not into the colored-up doings of others but into action of his own. He sees his own fatal involvement in love and in madly retributive crime as having arisen from a cause as overwhelming as the love-philter in *Tristan und Isolde*. His disappointed passion has goaded him to embezzle: he has, so to speak, as an offended deity presumed to visit his frustration upon his ward, Edward Burden, who thus becomes his double in misfortune. The resolution of the tale, in which all this is undone by chance (except of course the passionate attachment first mentioned), brings down the whole house of cards; but transitorily the situation has evoked the typical later Fordian devices of refraction—that is, of views through distorted views, the author's through the narrator's, the narrator's through his crystal of symbolic self-identification, for example, the Wagnerian love ethic. This refraction always needs, for a main character and center of focus, someone who looks inwards and backwards.

The spirit of the Conrad-Ford collaboration was retailed by Ford in *Joseph Conrad: A Personal Remembrance* (1924). Whether that spirit was its real essence is exceedingly doubtful: Ford always filtered everything and reflavored it. Some of his sayings remain so good that, true or not, they deserve the honor of belief. Thus his profiles of Conrad at work, cursing the English language, begging for an equivalent to the epithet he had already found in French (and of course getting from Ford an English phrase far richer than the prototype), for all that their robustness angered Mrs. Conrad, exalt Ford's impressions into truths. Besides Jacob Epstein, only Ford has ever had the genius to resolve the contradiction between the elfin, the mercurial, intellect and the monumental stolidity of Conrad.

Of literary realism the book says: "We saw that Life did not narrate, but made impressions on our brains. We in turn, if we wished to produce on you an effect of life, must not narrate but render . . . impressions." Of style it says: "The first . . . second . . . third . . . fourth business of Style is to make work interesting." Of development it says: "In writing a novel we agree that every word set on paper . . . must carry the story forward and, that as the story progressed, the story must be carried forward faster and faster and with more and more intensity. That is called *progression d'effet*, words for which there is no English equivalent." Of chronology it says: "You meet an English gentleman at your golf club. He is beefy, full of health, the moral of the boy from an English Public School of the finest type. You discover, gradually, that he is hopelessly neurasthenic, dishonest in matters of small change, but unexpectedly self-sacrificing, a dreadful liar but a most painfully careful student of lepidoptera and, finally, from the public prints, a bigamist who was once, under another name, hammered on the Stock Exchange. . . . Still, there he is, the beefy, full-fed fellow, moral of an English Public School product. To get such a man in fiction you could not begin at his beginning and work his life chronologically to the end. You must first get him in with a strong impression, and then work backwards and forwards over his past. . . . That theory at least we gradually evolved"

These critical memorabilia, the last containing an "impression" of its author, apply hardly to the products of the collaboration. They apply to Ford's early and middle-period fiction either not at all or not very much. They apply to Conrad's major novels exactly and punctiliously. At his finest, Ford was to illustrate all of them, but that was at a long remove from his association with Conrad. Impressionism, however, belonged as much to the one writer as to the other: Conrad's is strongest when it is perceptual, descriptive of things; Ford's when it is conceptual, revelatory of states of feeling and understanding. What we may feel the want of, in Ford's recollections of that time, is any sharp definition of what sort of consciousness manages, presides over, a novel—who, in other words, the narrator ought to be. In *Thus to Revisit: Some Reminiscences* (1921), published in Conrad's lifetime, Ford said: "We set out . . . to search for a New Form for the Novel, and, possibly, a formula for the Mot Juste." The first was Conrad's interest, Ford said; the latter, his own. This is credible, though in due course Ford was to go further than Conrad in manipulating form, namely by projecting it through a narrator of strange model—Dowell in *The Good Soldier*—and by apparently borrowing from James the, surely, monstrous invention of the all-containing untrustworthy narrator. (*The Sacred Fount* was a turgid source of the pollution.) Conrad, for his part, was to make form subservient enough to an array of divided narrators, including several mere "reflectors," in *Lord Jim* to be entitled to claim first hit. His wilderness of mirrors reflected the diversity of men (*quot homines tot sententiae*); Ford's was to reflect the confusions and interior cross-glare of a single observer. Impressions again—with Conrad as always the more objectively, Ford the more subjectively, oriented. Ford spoke of Marlow in *Thus to Revisit*, mainly with reference to James's dislike of that character (that, however, had to do with *Chance*, not *Lord Jim*). More usefully he pointed out that Marlow's time-shift method of narration "dallied" from later to earlier to still later to earlier again, and he remarked: "It is in that way that life really presents itself to us." Literally this remark is not at all true; it ought to be referring to the way we *think about* life. What remains odd is that Ford seems not to have felt the attraction of the method in the years when he was close to Conrad and

Conrad was perfecting it. It was a very proper way of writing the book *Joseph Conrad*.

The collaborators remained friends but saw each other seldom after Ford's estrangement from Elsie in 1909; Mrs. Conrad disapproved of his conduct. In 1904 Ford went alone to Germany and there had a nervous collapse. He failed to get better until, as his biographer Frank MacShane suggests, his need for a literary success was appeased: in 1905 the first of his studies of English life, *The Soul of London*, was favorably received and he was stimulated to work again. The same year his novel *The Benefactor* came out. This, which has been admirably discussed by Meixner in its Jamesian aspect, was Ford's best book to date. Typically Fordian it is, in projecting Ford's own character as Moffat, the patron whose artistic protégés repay him with ingratitude. Ford felt, and was to feel throughout his life, that his help to struggling writers was undervalued by them. When he wrote *The Benefactor*, he had just finished his collaboration with Conrad; in this connection his choice of a theme displays that tactlessness which he seemed never able to check, even when it went beyond good taste. This was a main flaw of Ford's; at times it is uncomfortably close to vulgarity.

Between 1905 and the end of 1908, when he founded the *English Review*, Ford came out of obscurity both as a novelist and as a "literary personality." *The Soul of London* and its two successors, *The Heart of the Country* (1906) and *The Spirit of the People* (1907), reached a wide audience; his novels, chiefly the *Fifth Queen* trilogy (*The Fifth Queen*, 1906; *Privy Seal*, 1907; and *The Fifth Queen Crowned*, 1908) and in a more modest way *An English Girl* (1907) and the fantasy *Mr. Apollo* (1908), all crowded into a short span, made his reputation solid. All of these books were authentic and durable Ford; and that was well, for his life was now half over. When he and Conrad finished *Romance*, Ford was not yet twenty-nine; by the time he was thirty-five he had become a known man of letters. Then, in 1909, his life broke in half socially when he became infatuated with Violet Hunt.

In 1906 he and Elsie Hueffer went to the United States, he to lecture and to come to an understanding with an American publisher. It was hoped that the American reading public might declare themselves admirers of Ford; this failed to happen, but he became an admirer of America, though a rather uncertain observer of it. In Philadelphia and elsewhere he picked up enough local information to furnish Dowell, later, in *The Good Soldier*, with what has seemed to many readers a credible background. Ford's conception of Americans and American life, however, was a shade dimmer than Galsworthy's, if that be possible. Ford returned to England and acquired a flat in London, where over the next two years he manifested a new zest for literary comradeship, amounting to clubbability. More important, he began to write literary criticism. The mystery is how he found time to do so many different things.

In 1908 he and H. G. Wells entered into discussions about starting a new literary review which should be devoted to writings of the highest quality. Also it was understood that the review should serialize *Tono-Bungay*. Wells later had second thoughts, and Ford quarreled with him; but the enterprise began well in December of that year when the *English Review*, Number 1, appeared with contributions by all the first-raters possible. There was Hardy's poem "A Sunday Morning Tragedy," previously rejected everywhere—a fact which was supposed to have inspired Ford with the resolution to start a magazine in which that sort of thing could find space; there was James's brilliant story "The Jolly Corner"; there were stories, chapters, articles, or reviews by W. H. Davies, Wells, Conrad,

W. H. Hudson, and others including Cunninghame Graham, the Stuart legitimist king of England. Later contributors in the year of Ford's editorship were P. Wyndham Lewis, Ezra Pound, Norman Douglas, and, most important, D. H. Lawrence. Ford financed the undertaking with the help of Arthur Marwood, and it went well enough until their money ran out; but it failed to sell, even at two and six, mainly because it was too highfalutin, and it provoked hostility because it was the organ of a coterie and was dominated by Ford with his exalted literary standards and blundering manner. He quarreled over it not only with Wells but with Arnold Bennett and Conrad. It continued as a magazine under other auspices but ceased to matter to the avant-garde.

What finally mattered to Ford about his editorship was the, at first, incidental wedge it gave Violet Hunt, who as a prospective contributor crowded into his life until, like the camel in the fable, she left little room for him. At length Ford had to make a new life independently of her as well as the life she had caused him to abandon. In one sense she was a blessing to him: she stirred up, through the adversity she created, as, initially, through the love he felt for her, a depth of imaginative power out of which he was to draw some of his best writing. But the cost was enormous: estrangement from relations and friends, from James, in part from Conrad; public scandal, lawsuits, bankruptcy; separation from his two daughters. He was not long in finding out that the mistress of South Lodge was possessive and bad-tempered, but it took him almost a decade to break with her. Thanks to what had seemed Elsie's criminal refusal to allow him a divorce in 1910, and to the unfavorable outcome of his attempt to get divorced in Germany in 1911, he was, at least, never able to marry his dragon. All he had to do, in 1919, to be free of her, was to stop being "Hueffer." She used to go

round spying on him and Stella Bowen during the early days of
their cottage life; but outside of England she gradually left him
in peace. From start to finish, it was the greatest educational experience of his life, simultaneously the most creative and the
most destructive. Quite literally it enabled him to live a second
life and to make a second career in succession to the first (the life
with Violet Hunt being, as things turned out, a kind of appen-
dage to the first, with the other still to come). What it destroyed
professionally was what Ford could least cheerfully sacrifice: his
pose on the literary pyramid, which as editor of the *English
Review* he momentarily felt he had scaled to the very top, and
which might have allowed him some hold for another twenty
years. He was not to have another chance quite like that; there
were to be the *Transatlantic Review* and the brief cataract of publishers' royalties in America, but neither in the American
quarter of Paris nor in New York was there really a literary pyramid at all, something that stood and could be counted on. And
then there was the matter of his age; in his second life he was no
longer young, he was "Old Fordie," dispenser of advice and
dropper of celebrated names, most of these no longer to be con-
jured with. What malicious wit thought up the conceit that,
whereas Ford Madox Hueffer was the "last Pre-Raphaelite,"
Ford Madox Ford, alas, was only the "Last Post-Raphaelite"?
The insight was better than the pun.

Apart from the millennialistic yet Wellsian fantasy *Mr. Apollo*
(1908) and the Jamesian psychological experiment *A Call* (1910),
the backbone of Ford's work between 1905 and the appearance
of *The Good Soldier* ten years later was historical fiction. Some
critics look down on his romances, the Conrad-James association
being more congenial academically; but, along with *The Good Soldier* and of course the Tietjens novels, those maintain in surest
balance the elements of good art and good *Fordian* art. At the

same time a very clear exception must be admitted for *The Bene-factor*. *A Call* has been extravagantly praised; but to some tastes it may seem too much like parody. Besides the *Fifth Queen* trilogy, the novels *The "Half Moon"* (1909), *The Portrait* (1910), *Ladies Whose Bright Eyes* (1911), and *The Young Lovell* (1913) all belong to the historical class; and all except *The Portrait* have distinct merit. Ford's theory of historical fiction included the postulate that it might be *romance;* in other words, that it was consistent with the presentation of invented along with actual personages and events, as in Scott. This is normal enough. Ford had no objection to the characters' being legendary to the point of the mythological, and the machinery might comprise paranormal or miraculous happenings. At the same time it is necessary to keep in mind certain gradations. The *Fifth Queen* trilogy is most properly historical in the sense of Shakespeare's history plays; the main characters are historical, though all the fine detail is supplied. *The "Half Moon"* has an invented hero whose destiny, though ruled by witchcraft, is bound up with a historical voyage, and so the structure is reminiscent of the plot-levels in Restoration heroical drama; the main character is on the romance level. *Ladies Whose Bright Eyes* is a *déjà-vu* fantasy with a historical setting; that is, its protagonist relives the actions of a fourteenth-century counterpart who, like himself, is unhistorical. *The Young Lovell* is a romance set at the end of the fifteenth century—so far analogus to *The "Half Moon"*—but the tale involves a psycho-supernatural element, something either less than or more than necromancy, and this parallels the Tannhäuser form of the *belle dame sans merci* legend; the story ends with the hero split into two people, though not quite like Sorrell in *Ladies Whose Bright Eyes*. (Sorrell is one man in two places; young Lovell is two *beings*, at least, in two places.) Clearly the *Fifth Queen* trilogy belongs to the genre of the historical novel; *The "Half*

Moon" and, much later, *A Little Less Than Gods* (1928), Ford's Napoleonic tale, are romances. The others may be called romances, too; but they are more or less fantasies, with *Ladies Whose Bright Eyes* vastly the stronger in circumstantial realism. All have indeed the stamp of past time. But verisimilitude is a perishable commodity: suit one generation and you are derided by another. Nowhere is this fact more true than in historical fiction, where the apparent past has to be built up detail by detail out of the notions and values of the author's contemporaries; it need not be, and preferably should not be, dealt with in the idiom familiar to these, but it must be dealt with in an ideologically translatable idiom. And that is something which all of Ford's historical tales do manage.

T. S. Eliot, in his Introduction to Charlotte Eliot's historical drama *Savonarola* (1926), talked about *Ladies Whose Bright Eyes* as a romance which filtered the fourteenth century through Ford's own time, and revealed the latter. Although one must always suspect feline intention in the Cat That Walked by Himself, his point was interesting; it was a point dear to Eliot as essential to his theory of tradition. He said that "the past is in perpetual flux," because every age reviews and revises it. In our own time we can usefully "supplement our direct knowledge of a period, by contrasting its view of a third, more remote period with our own views of this third period." His primary idea was an offshoot of the Idealistic argument of his old teacher Josiah Royce that reality is a *community of interpretation*. The supplementary refinement, about making a contrast, seems to have been his own. But it was inappropriate of him to suggest that a romance by Ford would have much evidential value for the purpose indicated. *Ladies Whose Bright Eyes* embodies neither a popular view of the fourteenth century nor a scientific view originating with a scholar historian. On the contrary, it does not embody a "view" of the fourteenth century at all. Ford, quite as much as Eliot, could *see through* history. He understood that seeing is now, that the impressionist's "past" is bathed in the time of his viewing. *Ladies Whose Bright Eyes* is essentially about the world of 1911. Any value it might have according to the scheme described by Eliot dissolves in the fact that, though a romance, it is more contemporary than historical. It has already, as it were, absorbed the scheme.

Ford's 1935 version of the novel, in which after a quarter of a century the 1911 scene is brought up to date, shows where the emphasis should fall. Ford was concerned with modern life. His chief character, Sorrell, "sees" the fourteenth century, but only as a refraction of his own time. The changes between the two versions are almost all for the sake of clarifying the modern, though some have the connected function of stressing the purely dreamlike character of the fourteenth-century world—the world of comparative health for the man who, in the twentieth century, is undergoing surgery for hurts with a twentieth-century cause. It may be argued that *Ladies Whose Bright Eyes* is not the *Fifth Queen* trilogy, and that this, a more sedate and a tragic work, clearly not a fantasy, obeys a different law from a dream vision, an allegory; it may be argued that the *Fifth Queen* trilogy really attempts to reveal a historical epoch, that of Henry VIII, by analyzing the modes of thought and feeling which governed the lives of Queen Katharine Howard and the King. But such an argument will not stand up. Not only is the proceeding impossible, it is profoundly un-Fordian. Ford as an artist knew one way to deal with facts, and that was to substitute meaning for them; as an impressionist he knew one way to fabricate meaning, and that was to mold it out of interpretations. "Historical" or "contemporary"—the words designate fancy dress and thees and thous and yea forsooths and evanescent slang; they have nothing to do with how Ford made fictions out of the timeless urges and checks of desire, memory, ought and ought not. Even witchcraft as he instances it is a psychological fancy dress. It is true that fancy dress and archaic speech, along with the profusion of circumstantial antiquities crowding Ford's historical romances, were all chosen according to the needs of the time setting; but they do not in themselves compose a historical period or, indeed, serve for more than ornament. It is character that makes a novel; if the ornamental details do their best work, they serve character. In Ford's romances they often do precisely this, by having psychological value; and so the romances in effect are metamorphosed back into novels truly. This is the same, exactly, as to say that in Ford the "past" always zeroes in on the present. Modernity of motive and sensibility populates his historical fiction with human characters belonging recognizably to his century. The "time-travel" device in *Ladies Whose Bright Eyes* forces us to notice the modern cast of values there; but the psychology (again, not just the fancy dress of the mind, consisting of science and superstition, but the laws of behavior itself) is equally slanted toward the modern in the other romances, where time is not shown as a double layer.

It is always important in reading Ford to keep in mind the implied authorial presence, which hovers offstage, beaming value judgments by stylistic telepathy. Part of its message in such a context amounts to a help in translation, as if to say: "This character has done such and such, and you can understand why, because I am here to remind you. He is one of us, though in his speech and system of beliefs the meaning of his acts must assume a different form; all you need do is reflect a moment, and you will see in him the same human machinery as in yourself." Ford in *The Young Lovell* seems to hint at a classic sort of mental aberration, perhaps schizophrenia, when he represents his goddess-infatuated hero as carried in spirit to the paradise of Venus while his body lives in a hermit's bricked-up cell. And what happens in the fifteenth-century world of young Lovell is an index to the operations of human passion in the time world we know.

Ford's own either-or description of what the historical novelist can do is too general and rough, but it provides Ford with an allegiance and explains his *donnée*. He said:

The business of all novelists is to trick you into believing you have taken part in the scenes that they render. But the historical novelist is on the horns of a dilemma: he must either present you with the superficial view of history given by the serious and scientific Historian than whom no one is more misleading, or diving deeper he must present you with the mendacities in which mankind perforce indulges when treating of contemporary events or its immediate fellows. For who are we to know the truth?

This comes from the epistle prefatory to *A Little Less Than Gods*, his last historical romance. He concluded that "the worst historical novelist is better for giving you a vicarious sense of existence than the most industrious of compilers of scientific evidence. And the novelist is there to give you a sense of vicarious experience."

The techniques, in his case, were always those which Ford was currently using in his other novels. The *Fifth Queen* trilogy uses a dense texture of snapshot impressions, exterior and interior from multiple points of view, and profuse dialogue often illustrating the principle, which he was later to describe, that people converse along parallel or diverging or criss-crossing lines, but not along the same line. The effect of this style is what Graham Greene calls "the sense of saturation." It is equally characteristic of the whole period from *Romance* to *The Young Lovell* and of Ford's modern as well as historical fiction.

But the techniques evolve, so that in successive novels the saturation changes its composition. Throughout the trilogy the impressions have immediacy and depend on concreteness. As Meixner observes, Ford's early impressionism is of an objective type. It involves things and experiences of them. The linear order of the details is different from the free-ranging order possible when, later, Ford used time-shift. The details are different, too, at least in feeling, from those which the stream-of-consciousness writer would convey. They do not seem, as details, to be altered by passage through the mind: they are not blurred, commingled, or confused. Stream-of-consciousness and free-association effects (the latter in Proust, for example) emerge in a *damaged* condition; the mind has done violence to the things which have passed through it from outside, and to time by melting and blending it. The temporal reality shown by Ford is revealed as quantum impulses, not waves of energy. His reality resembles a shooting gallery, not an aquarium: the senses are not soaked but bombarded. No Bergsonian flux here, no *durée*, no Heraclitus. The Proustian dissolving views and magic-lantern projections were still to be made known when *The Fifth Queen* was written; they never held much interest for Ford. When he came to use the time-shift, he still avoided aimless subjectivities. Really, *congestion* is a better word for his effect than *saturation:* he leaves space between the units.

Of course the congestion can be subjective in composition; the details can crowd in from memory and yet be impressionistically rendered. As Ford's work went on, external details tended more and more to be mixed with internal reflections. In the second and third chapters of *The Young Lovell*, which depict the company at table in Lord Lovell's castle, Ford uses as a matter of course the method of exposition by reminiscence (third person), telling, with impressionistic effects, what each of several charac-

ters thinks about present matters in light of experience. In particular the section concerned with the Bishop Palatine makes a
curious blend of omniscient narration and third-person interior
monologue—though not of a free-association sort: it hangs
together logically, and time is kept under rule, with pluperfect
verb tenses abounding. The general effect is not unlike the time-
shift technique; those two chapters move about in time in a
manner new to Ford's novels. *The Young Lovell*, preceding *The
Good Soldier* by two years, marked the emergence of the "Marlow" type of unchronological narration in Ford's work.

Dowell, the first-person narrator of *The Good Soldier: A Tale of
Passion* (originally called *The Saddest Story*), functions on several
levels. Only two of these are public: first the level on which he
confesses that he is no perceiver, that he has understood nothing
about his wife Florence, his friend Edward Ashburnham, Edward's wife Leonora, the ingénue Nancy Rufford, or himself;
and secondly the level on which he actually sets up as a commen-
tator on the wretched imbroglio, in effect as an artist, and reports what "must have been" the truth of it all. Such indeed is
his nature: duped by his wife, his friend, and his friend's wife,
he takes a ca' canny view when interpreting what has happened
behind his back; but half-enlightened by his wife's and his
friend's suicide, he assumes that he can now know all that is important—his various disclaimers notwithstanding. The dupe
Dowell is untrustworthy because his impressions have so been;
the mystagogue (the term is hardly too strong) is untrustworthy
because, like the "liar" in James's story, though nothing like
such a dab-hand, he has a passion for *telling*. It follows that *The
Good Soldier* incorporates three histories finally: the one which
Dowell has ignorantly lived through, the one which Dowell impressionistically constructs, and the one which really happened.
The first two are visible, not separately but as twined together,

and they are remarkably alike in feeling. For they are both rather cheap and crude. The *ignorant* Dowell's is farcical: the story of a dullard who marries a slut and is cuckolded by a cad, the cad's own wife being a middle-class prude. The *impressionistic* Dowell's is literary, in fact melodramatic: the story of a decent but cold man whose wife and best friend, the one outwardly respectable and the other a passionate idealist, become lovers but are divided when the idealist falls tenderly in love with an innocent young girl; the guilty wife kills herself when her sins find her out; the idealist, frustrated by his censorious wife's intervention, kills himself with a *penknife;* the young girl goes mad; she is tended by the compassionate, decent, but cold man.

And the hidden history—the meaning which might raise these events to a tragedy commensurate with the suffering intrinsic to them? This, alas, is not told—not by Dowell, who does not know it. Meixner points out that at the core of *The Good Soldier* is a potential tragedy of enormous intensity and broad implications, whereas the story-telling apparatus surrounding it is ironically comic. The apparatus suits the scale of Dowell's affective values, namely, from farce to sentimental melodrama. It is to the credit of Dowell's *unconscious* sensibility (if such a thing can be) that the reader picks up the vibrations of tragedy. Trying to catch the tragedy through Dowell's system of transmitting feeling is like listening to a stereophonic recording on a wind-up gramophone with a steel needle and a heavy pick-up arm. We know what kind of record it is, not much more. This is not a very good analogy, for in the case of *The Good Soldier* our human imagination is stimulated to supply something of what is obscured, as in the fancied case our ears would not be. We sense that behind Dowell a tragedy does lurk. For this vibration he deserves thanks. The heresy of Donatus—which was, and is, that the priest has to be in a state of grace if the sacrament he administers is to be efficacious—is no heresy in literature but an all too dismal truth. It is no good the voltage's being high if the wire cannot carry it. Dowell was created as an unknowing vessel, by an unshaking potter's hand which needed that kind of vessel; but it seems that the tragic perceptions such a vessel can bear are of the receiver's, the reader's, own providing.

Dowell, failing to grasp the principle that if truth is unknowable the ignorant man is wise, insists on contriving a dramatic image, a character, for himself as revealer. *What* he is, we cannot be certain; the image he chooses to employ is that of a leisure-class American from Philadelphia, which he calls "Philadelphia, Pa." Surely many readers have noticed that his account of his background does not hold up well: he calls his country the "United States of North America"; says that he carries about with him the title deeds to his ancestral farm, "which once covered several blocks between Chestnut and Walnut Streets. These title deeds are of wampum" (not anachronistic for such a purpose?); boasts that he came of a family originally English, the first Dowell having "left Farnham in Surrey in company with William Penn" (there are no Penn associations at Farnham; *Ford* once lived near Limpsfield); most astonishing, reports that he learned "Pennsylvania Duitsch" (*sic*) in childhood. In general, American probabilities are so foreign to him that, if we met him on a Cook's Tour, we might suspect him to be bogus. American politics, for example, he considers enigmatic: his "sort of second-nephew," Carter, "was what they called a sort of Vermont Democrat. . . . But I don't know what it means." This same Carter was "a good cricketer"; it is not impossible. Florence's uncle, a manufacturer in Waterbury, was "a violent Democrat" (could it have been because of the tariff on foreign clocks?) Dowell's America, in short, is essentially Ford's America; but Ford must have known much more about it—Dowell's "Pennsylvania

Duitsch" makes it certain: Ford could not have been guilty of this howler, for he of all people would have known that Pennsylvania *Deutsch* is not Holland *Dutch*. Dowell is marked as ignorant and pretentious—and, in some sense which, even so, is not quite the literal one, as an impostor. He has touched up and tinted his own photograph.

Since this is what Ford did, too, in his memoirs, and since *The Good Soldier* is a memoir of Dowell as well as a novel of Ford, there are excellent reasons why Dowell should behave like Ford. (The Philadelphia land grant is amusingly analogous to the baronial estates in Germany for which Ford hankered in the first flush of his romance with Violet Hunt.) Does it follow that Dowell, from start to finish, is simply telling a tall tale? This question can be rephrased to come better to the point: does it follow that Dowell is inside, as well as outside, the tale Ford tells through him? Inside it *twice*, that is?—for he is certainly in it once, since it is partly about himself. Clearly it does follow, if a dupe can dupe himself. (Dowell need not be *dishonest:* that is not in question.) At the same time, it does not much matter to the tale if its frame, as well as itself, is untrustworthy. But it was essential to Ford that the untrustworthiness of the frame, the narrator, should point to the untrustworthiness of the tale. For most readers Ford's clues have proved too subtle: they have rushed in and hailed the romance of Edward Ashburnham as something ideal and noble, paying Dowell the compliment, if it is not an insult to his art, of believing in his dime-novel version of life—the version which has ousted what might have been a tragic masterpiece. Whatever we conclude about all this—and probably we had better conclude nothing—one thing may be meditated on: the indication that Dowell is not merely an untrustworthy narrator but an untrustworthy impressionist.

Before *The Good Soldier*, Ford never handled first-person narration quite successfully. There may have been two handles to his prejudice against this. On the one hand, the technique seems to involve a limitation in point of view, an absolute limitation; on the other hand, it seems absolutely committed to narration—and "we . . . must not narrate but render . . . impressions." Both criticisms, in fact, concern the impressionistic method. Any narrowed point of view, even if not of the first person, substitutes something else for impressionism, or pushes something else into the foreground, namely, the nature of the single character thus favored. Ford valued the rich variety of impressionistic effects he was able to produce without point of view, and presumably saw no reason to pursue a conflicting enterprise. If point of view was to be of the first person, then narration posed a forbidding alternative to impressionism. In the event, however, the difficulties were met by inventing a narrator who could not narrate but could only "render impressions" of a life, his own, with the time-shift as a token of his ineptitude. The impressions became, as before, the tale. An untrustworthy narrator came into being as a result of the mistrust of narration. The new creation to be recognized in *The Good Soldier* is not time-shift, for Conrad's Marlow used that; it is the untrustworthy narrator as chief and clinching evidence of the essential untrustworthiness of narration.

No need, here, for the mysteriousness which, in James's *The Turn of the Screw*, leaves it to the reader to guess whether the narrator (the governess) is neurotic or clairvoyant or simply romantic; or which, in *The Sacred Fount*, invites suspicions that the narrator is mad or that the stylist, the old Master, is parodying himself. Here the untrustworthy narrator practically denounces himself. Moreover he is the norm for narrators, all of them painfully inept at sizing up life as it is; all obliged to back and fill, to contradict themselves and admit it. The truth, finally, can only be what convincingly *seems*.

The purposes of the time-shift are various. In the Tietjens tetralogy, which has no consistent first-person narrator, it works above all to advance the story thematically. Ford said in *It Was the Nightingale* (1933) that the novelist must never digress but always seem to digress, on the (rather odd) theory that the reader likes to be distracted and that his attention can be kept moving in a straight line only by being beguiled with the sensation of diversionary movement. (Presumably a line if crooked *enough* appears straight.) More important, the time-shift establishes a symbolic architecture of events. In *The Good Soldier* it also characterizes Dowell, largely by defining his distance from and attitude toward the incidents he relates. It is fundamentally a rhythmic, cinematographic device and belongs to the films. With the first-person narrator on hand, it recalls, though usually it does not much resemble, stream-of-consciousness monologue. One big difference is that Dowell's rendering, with the time-shift (how well named! it is as consciously controlled as the gearshift of a racing car, or a heavy truck), keeps him separate from his tale, his vehicle. One is aware of him *here* and of his tale *there*. And the *progression d'effet* takes place in the present he fills with past events. The past is layered, not fluid like the stream of consciousness; its contents are as if arranged in trays in a cabinet, able to be drawn out of dated slots. Or to return to a metaphor already used, events in time are bulletlike, not all mixed up together like the water in a fish tank. Stream-of-consciousness techniques are constantly violating chronology. Dowell never violates chronology: he shuffles it. So he is at a distance from his past and treats it as a series. Yet he still manages to treat it as a series of appearances rather than facts, even while he acclaims as facts the impressions his memory pulls out. Lastly, his undertaking seems far more logical than stream-of-consciousness reverie, where free association becomes a lord of misrule. Time-shift effects were to recur in Ford's novels. Ford's first novel of the war, *The Marsden Case* (1923), contains an even more complex array of them than *The Good Soldier*.

It is impossible to read *The Good Soldier* without being moved, indeed almost rocked, by the emotional force of Dowell's plea for idealism and self-sacrifice on the one hand and for the legitimacy of intense physical passion on the other. It is this intensity that has won Dowell the allegiance of so many readers, most of whom are likely to remain deaf to a criticism calling into question the way he imputes both moral idealism and passion to Ashburnham's relations with women. Yet surely he is mistaken in his estimate of Ashburnham's character: the blend of these virtues, one passive and the other active, is conceivable; but Ashburnham's tactics belie the claim Dowell makes for him. Ashburnham's relations with women are anything but morally idealistic; in the case of his supposed Dulcinea, Nancy, Ashburnham is only baffled of his prey. If the reader can believe Dowell's report of Ashburnham's flirtations and seductions, they would appear to be carried on independently of the moral virtues which make Ashburnham a good landlord—or is not this what is expected of the feudal seigneur? The conceit of Dowell that Ashburnham mirrors *him* is what explains Dowell's romantic misjudgment of the other man; in Dowell, too, a celibate ideal is yoked with a baffled and inhibited passion. Certainly this conceit accords with Dowell's habitual misjudgment of his wife Florence, whom in a sense he has encouraged in her compulsive promiscuity by his unquestioning chivalric deference to

her "bad heart," and of Leonora as well, who, cold though she is
in her marriage to Ashburnham, is not only a wronged woman
but a good one.

To Florence's nymphomania (or whatever it is), to Ashburnham's lecherousness, and to Leonora's justice Dowell is insensitive to the extent of condemning or praising without reck-
oning with them. These are mainsprings of the characters'
actions; it is not surprising that, failing to understand, he substitutes for the several inner agonies, the heartbreaks in solitude, a
romantic melodrama stage-managed by a splendid mock-up of
himself. Is uncommunicated tragedy really tragedy? The novel
is there for the reading.

The device of mirroring turns up in Ford repeatedly. Ashburnham is the kinetic to Dowell's damped potential; he fulfills
what Dowell only dreams of, even the "heroic" death for love—
the Tristan grand stroke—with a penknife. Also he is pragmatic
where Dowell is theoretical, realistic where Dowell is idealistic.
He is opposite—but so is a mirror image, or what Yeats called a
mask. Conrad used the romantic device of the double in "The
Secret Sharer" (1912) by providing a ship's captain with an alter
ego in the person of a fugitive, a murderer, who looks like him.
This double externalizes the protagonist's weakness; but in the
course of the tale he represents also the resourcefulness summoned up to cope with himself, and having been the secret self,
he imperceptibly becomes the not-self of the protagonist. The
paradoxes are confusing; perhaps Conrad was not clear about
them. In *The Good Soldier* the same contradiction occurs, but it is
a mistake of Dowell's, not a paradox: Dowell thinks Ashburnham is, but Ashburnham is not, his secret self. James in
"The Jolly Corner," which Ford published, presents not a twin
or living "other self" (in the Conrad story it is a type of Jamesian
reflector, as for that matter Marlow is for Lord Jim) but a super-

natural or hallucinatory apparition, what is called an autoscopic double, but with the specialty that it is a "might-have-been" self of the protagonist. A double of this classic type appears briefly in Kipling's "At the End of the Passage" (1890). Ford's "impersonator" double, usurping the identity of the man whom he resembles (in *Vive le Roy*, 1937) or whose name is similar to his own (*The Rash Act*, 1933, and its sequel *Henry for Hugh*, 1934), is of the twin type, as Meixner observes, and so is analogous in psychological implication to the double in Conrad. The dream-traveler or shaman type, recalling both George du Maurier's *Peter Ibbetson* (1891) and Kipling's "The Brushwood Boy" (1895), appears early, in *Ladies Whose Bright Eyes;* but the double as latent personality, whether autoscopic as Dostoevsky's tale *The Double*, or "schizoid" as in Stevenson's *Dr. Jekyll and Mr. Hyde* (1886), or guardian as in Poe's "William Wilson," is almost foreign to Ford's work, though in *When the Wicked Man* (1931) an autoscopic double appears spectrally as a symptom of neurosis and, beyond this, of moral decay. It seems hardly necessary to assume that in Ford the double is any more a morbid sign than it is in James. As James would say, it is a means of "bringing out" another character. Ford may have been unable to dispense with the double for long, but artistically he was a healthy man.

During the whole period from the collapse of Ford's marriage in 1909 to 1915, when he went into the British Army, he was occupied with literary pursuits, including journalism, writings under a pen name ("Daniel Chaucer"), poetry, novels, memoirs, criticism. He and Violet Hunt traveled and in London held court at South Lodge. Outwardly it was a good period, except financially; but Ford was perhaps never more discontented except in the closing phase of his collaboration with Conrad. There is no doubt whatever that he joined the Welch Regiment (as a subaltern, at forty-one) because of his sense of duty, which as Mac-

Shane observes was focused on his notion that he belonged to the ruling class; but an escapist motive must also be suspected. His liaison with Violet Hunt had run its course, so far as his emotional loyalty was concerned. Patriotic feelings dominated, naturally; he had written two books of anti-German and pro-French propaganda at the behest of his friend C. F. G. Masterman, who was in charge of this branch of warfare. Unlike many propagandists, he had meant what he wrote: Ford would not prostitute his art or his mind. He spent his first year in the Army doing garrison duty, largely training exercises, at Cardiff Castle and elsewhere; then he was sent to France with his battalion, performing routine duties for a time and then going through the Battle of the Somme. He had to be hospitalized for lung damage, which resulted in a permanent partial disability. Sent back to England in 1917, he was shifted to a different regiment. After various assignments compatible with his impaired health, he spent the rest of the war as a military lecturer, finally with the rank of acting brevet major.

By the middle of 1919, Ford had a new life. With Stella Bowen, a young painter, he was living in Sussex; in June he changed his name from Hueffer; the Fords lived frugally and bucolically (not having much money) and raised pigs. He wrote *No Enemy*, a feeble novel but a vigorous autobiographical impression of the war; no one would publish it until 1929. He fathered a daughter. His second memoir, *Thus to Revisit*, appeared in 1921; but of three more novels written at this time only one was published, *The Marsden Case* (1923), filled with bitterness and rage against official mentality. Though, as usual, Ford said that it had been suggested by a "case," fully accredited, the real case was his own; for it deals with an Englishman thought to have German sympathies and persecuted for them. Doubtless, during the war, Ford *had* been sneered at because he had a German name. Later, he was slightly tilted toward a paranoia of indignation, a condition from which he soon recovered outwardly except as it affected his novels. It must be remembered that the postwar letdown was almost universal, being strongest perhaps in young civilians such as Hemingway. The Fords remained headquartered in England only three years; in 1922 they moved to the south of France, and there Ford wrote the first Tietjens novel, *Some Do Not.* . . . The following year, in Paris, he became the editor of a new critical monthly, the *Transatlantic Review* (or, absurdly, *transatlantic review*), instigated by Pound and financed by Ford and the New York book-lover and rich lawyer John Quinn. The first number came out in January, 1924. Ford's tribulations during the twelve months the review continued, along with some tall tales, are told of in *It Was the Nightingale*. The *Transatlantic Review* led from weakness as the *English Review* had led from strength. The earlier project had had the backing of established talent, and it might not have failed if Ford had not been so foolish as to create a coterie where none was needed. (The resentment of writers whom Ford snubbed is attested by MacShane.) The later review was, lock, stock, and barrel, the arm of the Ezra Pound coterie, including of course some writers who, like Joyce, were never Pound's property but served themselves with Pound's good offices. This group was made up of outstanding talents, in the main, but it tended to remain static by comparison with the host of contributors to the *English Review;* the weakness consisted in the "in-group" character of the *Transatlantic's* editorial advisers. Hence the small number of new authors launched was disappointing to Ford.

The Tietjens tetralogy (the title *Parade's End*, though Ford's own, was not added before the four novels were brought together in an American edition) is a moral and psychological, social and sociological document—what Ford always insisted fiction ought to be, a *constatation*, a rendering of life. It is moral in the grounds of criticism on which it, like most of his serious novels, approaches human behavior; in this it is rooted in Victorian moral idealism, like the work of most of the Edwardians, who applied ideals to cases. It is psychological in two senses: it displays its characters as conditioned agents, and it "renders impressions" as a counterpart of the way one's world-view is put together, as a Gestalt. It is social in its panoramic view and in its application of moral criticism; the sins of the individual are the sins of his society. It is sociological in that it reveals forms of relation among human beings which, while evolving or decaying, provide the guidelines of their conduct, as a spider's web contains paths for the spider. This series of novels, which begins with *Some Do Not . . .* (1924) and continues with *No More Parades* (1925), *A Man Could Stand Up—*(1926), and finally *The Last Post* (1928), transmits (not *narrates*) a section of life centering on the brothers Mark and Christopher Tietjens, Christopher's unfaithful wife Sylvia, his mistress Valentine, his friends, fellow Army officers, children, other relations. The time-shift is common to it and to *The Good Soldier;* but instead of the first-person impressionist an impersonal author-cameraman (as it were) trains his lens where he will—into the characters' minds, their past, their range of vision, and so uses a fluid presentation as well.

The tetralogy is often laborious to read, for reasons which have been well explained by Arthur Mizener in his special Afterword published as a two-part appendix to the volumes of the Signet edition. In an oversimplified form the difficulty might be accounted for as follows: the story is not narrated straightforwardly but in oddly related time chunks; it must therefore be read with sufficient attention so that the content and, above all, the texture of each incident are felt; in this way, when the same group of characters, or an analogous situation, or even the same pattern of imagery recurs, a cross-reference will be perceived. Since almost all students of the twentieth-century novel have read (or looked into) Joyce's *Ulysses*, it may help to suggest that the "Wandering Rocks" chapter there prefigures, on a miniature scale, the cinematographic time-shifts of Ford's tetralogy. *Parade's End* is not nearly so hard to read as the "Wandering Rocks" chapter. Even so, Mizener's chronological summary at the end of the second volume of the edition mentioned is very useful indeed.

A work of so great an extent and complexity as the tetralogy cannot be analyzed or even summarized in brief compass. It has of course been made the subject of several thorough studies in books on Ford. Its hero, Christopher Tietjens, is a survival figure, an honorable and gracious man living out of his time (or, since it is doubtful whether his time ever existed, out of his milieu of decency). His world—England and the Continent in the years immediately before, during, and after World War I—is dominated by the pinchbeck and dishonest ethics which to Dr. Johnson was connoted by the mentality called *Whig*. Whatever is pettifogging, canting, self-serving, wasteful, stupid, and tyrannical—the same idiocy against which Ford aimed his satire in *The Inheritors*, where it was imputed to the power-politicians of that day, puppets of industry and Fleet Street—is antipathetic to Tietjens' nature. The war of course, in which Tietjens honorably and patriotically fights, is run by men whose lives are regulated by greed. On the level of the personal life, he is forced by circumstances to endure the emotional equivalent of this filth as his wife Sylvia's contribution to their marriage. The tetralogy has as one of its most comprehensive effects the counterpoint and interaction of sheer foulness at the national and personal levels. Tietjens wages two wars, the one for the cause of ethical

transactions among people, the other for honorable emotional—
that is, passional—values. Unlike Ashburnham in *The Good Soldier*, who is a caricature of the fusion of passion and idealism,
Tietjens lives it. Against the apparent madness of heroism in the
shadow of betrayal by the politicians and their henchmen, the
love story of Tietjens and Valentine looms as a vindication of
the private life in a world of institutionalized suicide. *Parade's
End* is the monument to the Edwardians' faith in *rational emotion*,
that complex of values for the sake of which novelists cursed
grundyism, and also to the old predemocratic English faith in
the dignity of *worth* as against numerical preponderance. It may
also be the only lasting monument to World War I. It is the
main reason for remembering Ford.

After the *Transatlantic Review* stopped publication, a victim of
financial troubles following the death of Quinn in mid-1924,
Ford spent a couple of years more or less quietly, in Paris and
Toulon, working on the second and third parts of the tetralogy.
From the end of 1926 to the end of 1927 he was in the United
States, lecturing and being lionized; this was his time of instant
prosperity, when *Some Do Not . . .* and *No More Parades* enjoyed
huge success in America and he was feted by New York critics
who revered the fame they had concocted. By 1930 he had frit-
tered away everything these novels had earned. The indifference
of the British public to the Tietjens books seems more normal,
somehow, than the artificial acclaim and bridge-table admiration
of the Americans; it seems questionable whether anything like
so many people read, as bought, the four novels. Upon his return to France from the United States, Ford decided to separate
from Stella. He remained in France except for forlorn visits to
England in the early 1930s; gradually, toward the middle of the
decade, he turned more and more to America again, where he
had more friends than anywhere else and where money could be

earned. He was in the United States for an extended visit in 1934–35, and for a large part of 1937 and 1938 was engaged in traveling and lecturing and taught several terms at Olivet College, in Michigan. During his last winter, 1938–39, he lived in New York and tried his hand at several editorial schemes for publishers. His health plagued him, and on borrowed money he returned to France on the *Normandie* in May, 1939, and in June died of uremia at Deauville.

Ford wrote prolifically in his final decade. Of his four published novels, three can be rated as serious though they are too crudely melodramatic to strike most critics as "good" after Tietjens. *When the Wicked Man* (1931), which is about wickedness in the publishing business, is a parable of personal corruption through corrupt institutions. *The Rash Act* (1933) and *Henry for Hugh* (1934) are fanciful tales of an impersonation (of an Englishman named Hugh Monkton Allard Smith, who commits suicide, by an American named Henry Martin Aluin Smith, who only meditates it). The latter two novels are, at the same time, allegories of a kind, depicting two cultural traditions, the one self-destroyed by the war, the other narrowly saved but now burdened with the responsibilities of the first as well as its own. They thus rework the Tietjens theme in part, but with an American hero. Ford's most entertaining and impressionistic memoirs, *Reminiscences, 1894–1914: Return to Yesterday* (1931) and *It Was the Nightingale* (1933), were contemporary with the novels but much better—a fact which suggests that the whole trouble with the later Ford novels may have stemmed from his mistake in resuming fantasy, when ever since the war his interest had increasingly been directed toward himself. Altogether his most significant work in these years is to be found in *Provence* (1935) and *Great Trade Route* (1937), which between them set forth his appreciation of the civilized life, defined as artistic to champion

the love of beauty against mass-produced ugliness; as Mediterranean to reject the neuroses of schismatic and puritan; and as
agrarian to counter the suicidal onrush of industrialism toward
war. On the whole his thesis anticipates, in terms of feeling, that
of Sir Kenneth Clark in his book *Civilisation* of more than three
decades later. It is descriptive and speculative, in fact poetical.

Ford was a poet all his life—in prose—and for much of it in
verse. If, as here, we come to his verse only after considering
some of his novels and "nonfictional" impressions, this does no
harm. Chronology was never his strong point, and so it will not
matter if the verse of a lifetime is glanced at selectively all in one
place. It is typical that his *Collected Poems* (1936) arranges his
verse, with a few exceptions for emphasis, in "reversed chronological order." It follows that, including the exceptions, the
poems ought to be read from front to back of the volume—if
only in compliment. The proceeding has moreover some symbolic use: it imitates, as Ford may have intended, a backward,
inward plunging of the mind toward its first distant visions. The
exception with which the book begins is highly important. It is
entitled "On Heaven" and is a completely Fordian, impressionistic adaptation of D. G. Rossetti's "The Blessed Damozel"
to Ford's autobiographical purposes. (The lady, when she dies,
comes in a red car to a small town in the south of France, which
is Heaven, where her lover has been awaiting her for nine years,
drinking wine and playing dominoes in a street café, and there
they are united forever.) This sentimental exercise, the charm of
which is considerable, presents the fable anecdotally, in the context of a real, not a fabulous, love. It was written for Violet
Hunt in Ford's "good soldier" period; it is conversational in
idiom and cadence, with time-shift; it is in free verse based on
blank verse; it is an intensely *dramatic* dramatic monologue with
Browningesque touches. It is pure Ford in his German *schmalz*

vein and is (to mix the metaphor) a touchstone for all the rest of his mature poetry. Beside it, a better poem, namely "Antwerp," is set as if to have its own strong personal emotion at a contemporary outrage sympathetically revibrated by the personal emotion which has no public cause.

Ford's method in his poetry, after an early period in which William Morris, among others, more or less faintly called the tune, emerged about 1910 as something very much his own. Were it necessary to surmise what poet then writing may have influenced Ford, besides Hardy occasionally perhaps, the guess would have to light on D. H. Lawrence. Ford read some of Lawrence's early poetry in 1909 and printed it in the *English Review*. The two have in common an intense, subjective relation between poet and poem, *in* the poem, and also an "imagistic" technique allied to Ford's prose impressionism. It would be no compliment to either Lawrence or Ford to "justify" them by associating them with the Imagiste school, though they did not object to the association at the time. They, too, wrote vers libre. But Lawrence and Ford were serious poets, which the Imagistes were hampered in being—fatally, as a rule—because the most treasured rules of their craft, those having to do with *compression* and *image-making*, deterred them from saying anything much with language as vocal music or argument. In a "good" sense Ford was indeed an imagist, as so was Lawrence. Both knew how to weave the vivid image into a vocally dramatic movement which passed from emotion to emotion. Ford's use of free verse went back to the nineties, being found in poems published in 1897, on which he commented in *Thus to Revisit*. He liked free verse with rhyme in it; and because he—again like Lawrence—was in the tradition of oral poetry, his poems seem fairly remote from the productions of Imagisme.

He was, of course, a war poet, perhaps as good as any. Not

being young he was not much tempted to write on inspirational abstractions to be fitted into a wartime context; rather he wrote about what he saw and felt, and usually the poetry came out public, as all poetry should do. It is, as all of Ford's, profoundly moving, yet often terrifying for not clear enough reasons; and this fact makes much of it seem timeless. "To All the Dead," a prewar poem not about war, has a hallucination worthy of young Lovell (Ford's own hallucinatory experiences were common knowledge among his friends); but the war-service poems create instead a hallucinatory effect through ironic juxtaposition of details. In " 'One Day's List' " the gradual accretion of death images, interspersed with flickering mind's-eye time-shift recollections of the most pathetic character, culminates in the image—fantastic yet acceptable—of the dead happily resting "on silvery twilight pillows." It is one of the most haunted poems in a haunted book.

Ford, who was a good poet sometimes, was once or twice for a protracted time a great novelist. Yet he has been refused his fame, and it is no accident at all; some of his bad luck was accidental, but his failure to catch on was not. To be blunt, he was the victim of his character, which made him "second-guess" everything; the fact that his artistic motives were superbly decent and his judgments of literature, men, and nations angelically pure was insufficient to gain him pardon from a world whose opinions, and indeed very way of seeing and reflecting, he obstinately flouted. The decency and purity themselves became an outrage. Not that Ford puffed himself morally—but he did so critically. His erotic energy, of course, and his indiscreet exercise of it damaged both his moral and his critical reputation. And then there were the lies. He insisted on making life work like art, on transforming chronicle into parable. But he simulated: he did not dissemble. Ford reminds one of Giordano

Bruno in his confidence that truth is found in its antithesis. While only a superior form of irony, such discernment is unsettling to the multitudes.

MacShane cites Lieutenant Colonel G. R. Powell, commanding officer of the Third Battalion, Welch Regiment, as having recorded in Ford's "Soldier's Small Book" the following testimonial to Ford's soldierly skills:

Has shown marked aptitude for grasping any intricate subject and possesses great powers of organization. A lecturer of the first water on several military subjects. Conducted the duties of messing officer to the unit (average strength 2,800) with great ability.

In *It Was the Nightingale*, Ford set down a version of this improved by himself, naturally without hinting that he had revised it. Among other touch-ups the final sentence had been altered to read: "Has managed with great ability the musketry training of this unit." Precisely.

ROBERT S. RYF

Joseph Conrad

Joseph Conrad raised more questions about the nature of human experience than he or anyone else could answer, but they were the right questions. To what extent is man a free agent, and to what extent is he a victim of forces beyond his control? Does life inevitably find us out by placing us in that very situation which most severely tests our values? When society's restraints are removed and we are thrust back upon our own emotional and spiritual resources, do we frequently prove to be "hollow at the core?" What is the nature of human motive: is selflessness merely a façade for egocentricity? Can isolated man experience and serve human solidarity? Is there anything in which to believe?

E. M. Forster once wrote that Conrad didn't believe in anything, and the picture of the novelist groping without certainty through jungle labyrinths and the swirl of the sea, both somehow analogous to Forster's own Marabar Caves, is partially convincing, but the matter is not so simple. The categorization of Conrad as a nihilist, frequently advanced, is a more simplistic view of him than in fact his own complex vision of experience warrants.

In the world Conrad perceives, it is difficult, as he points out in the Preface to A *Personal Record* (1912), to be "wholly joyous or wholly sad"; the two moods mingle and merge. He carries his distrust of absolutes further when he tells us that he has never been able "to love what was not lovable or hate what was not hateful out of deference for some general principle." In a yet more crucial passage, he indeed approaches a nihilistic position when he comments that "the ethical view of the universe involves us at last in so many cruel and absurd contradictions, where the last vestiges of faith, hope, charity, and even of reason itself, seem ready to perish, that I have come to suspect that the aim of creation can not be ethical at all. I would fondly believe that its object is purely spectacular."

But Conrad does not let the matter rest there. "Spectacular" suggests both spectacle and excitement; his world is a world in which, as he tells us, there is room for every emotion but despair, which he regards as "inverted piety," a kind of spiritual arrogance. It is a world, as we shall see in his central fiction, in which man has a definite role.

The word "role" is used advisedly; Conrad's vision of human experience is not only existentialist but dramatic. If man plays his part well and faithfully, he may win those finite and fleeting victories which are all he is vouchsafed in and by a spectacular universe; he may hold back, for a moment, the darkness. If this sounds like a most limited achievement, it is no mean one for man frequently in conflict with himself in a world he but dimly understands.

Whether Conrad himself sensed his vision as dramatic is open to question. He once wrote, in a letter to Stephen Crane, that he had no dramatic gift. This richly ambiguous and provocative statement, at once true and untrue, is all the more intriguing in that Conrad himself apparently only half believed it. Indeed, his attitudes toward drama are so ambivalent as to suggest a deep-seated emotional conflict which persisted throughout most of his writing career. His aspirations to write plays were enduring; the results, by and large, were dismal. His only success was vicarious: the stage version of *Victory* was adapted by a professional playwright. Conrad's own knowledge of stagecraft was limited; he rather obstinately refused to learn. And yet, the crowning irony may be that his failure as a stage dramatist might well be attributed to the fact that his imagination was already heavily invested in another mode of drama. Certainly his central novels— *The Nigger of the Narcissus, Heart of Darkness, Lord Jim,* and *Nostromo* will serve as examples—abound in drama, and reveal not only a dramatic sense of situation but a highly skilled dramatic technique of presentation.

The dramatic sense is an implicitly vital part of Conrad's aesthetic theory. In that frequently quoted passage from the Preface to *The Nigger of the Narcissus,* he tells us that the overarching task of the artist is to make us "see." Undoubtedly he means the word in two related ways: to make us comprehend, and to make us visualize, and the two meanings are inextricably bound up in his fiction. It is a fiction of dramatic embodiment, as we shall see, and the fundamental issues with which he is dealing in his best novels are contained in the scenes as visually presented, so that, as Virginia Woolf once put it, "the beauty of surface," or vision, "has always a fibre of morality within."

This is not to say that Conrad's dramatic sense was limited to his powers of visualization; there are other dramatic elements present. I mean not only dramatic conflict but the involvement and participation of the audience in the attempt to sort out what happens, to answer questions about the nature of a character, or the truth of a situation, and, by extension, about the nature of reality. The dramatist does not tell us about his characters, he shows us the characters and stages the action which reveals them.

It is a commonplace to observe that much fiction of the twentieth century has moved toward this dramatic mode of presentation and away from extended expository analysis of character and event. Katherine Mansfield, Hemingway, Faulkner, and Joyce, particularly in his use of "epiphanies," come quickly to mind from a long list. Conrad's dramatic imagination brought him naturally to this method; he anticipated many later writers in this respect. I have suggested that the method was indigenous to him. One may immediately raise the question of the possible influence of the scenic method of Henry James, whom Conrad called his dear master. Although he stood in awe of the older writer, near whom he lived for several years, there is little indication that he had read much if any of James before he revealed his own interest in drama. Moreover, there are certain differences in focus between the two. James seems the more centripetal, interested primarily in states of consciousness and awareness. Conrad is the more centrifugal, concerned with the relationship, at times the conflict, between the interior and the exterior. Conrad's technique of dramatic embodiment is substantially different from James's scenic method.

Ford Madox Ford must also be taken into account; not only did he and Conrad collaborate on two novels, they theorized extensively around the turn of the century on the art of fiction, during the period when the Conrads were tenants of Ford's in Kent. Aware that in real life our understanding of character and events proceeds, not in serial order, but by indirection, they thought fiction should reflect this indirection. They called the method literary impressionism. Yet Ford's influence, which he and others have thought to be considerable, should not be overestimated. Although Conrad embraced the theory of indirection, his best fiction involves the reader in a considerably more active role than that of receiving impressions. His reader becomes directly involved, is drawn into the game, either by the exercise of his own filtering consciousness, as is the case in *Nostromo*, or by the presence of a dramatic narrator such as Marlow, who is himself a central character.

Marlow, a virtuoso of indirection, is at once a literary device and far more than that, as he tells and retells his stories and inextricably intertwines himself and us with them. Suitably, he is an ambiguous figure, a loner, surrounded not only by the inscrutable universe but by a welter of scholarly pronouncements as well. Some consider him English, to others he is a Pole. He may have been based on a friend of Conrad's, but the prevalent view is that he came into being in response to the internal demands of Conrad's art, which posed the necessity of finding the proper vehicle for dealing with the increasing complexity he found himself confronted with as he came of age artistically.

To some he is merely Conrad's mouthpiece, projection, or alter ego. So close is this identification that Conrad has been taken to task for Marlow's extensive use of blur-words such as "inscrutable," "mysterious," and "incomprehensible," which have been held to indicate Conrad's own difficulties of understanding. Yet to others he has more autonomy as mediator and midwife, as possessor of that consciousness within which the central action unfolds.

He himself is a vital element in each story he tells. His involvement and ambivalences become centrally interesting and important to us. The real separation between Marlow and Conrad is nowhere more in evidence than in Marlow's incomplete perceptivity. His partial perceptions serve as foil for our own; from the resulting dialectic, additional meaning radiates. And it is of course Conrad who arranges the synthesis.

This account of Conrad's literary theory thus far has centered on the dramatic element, or, as Conrad himself put it, on his "single-minded attempt to render the highest kind of justice to the visible universe." But there is more to the matter than this, for the novelist works with words. Thus, the aesthetic function of language itself must be taken into account, and it is upon this aspect of literary creation that Conrad also centers his attention in the Preface to *The Nigger of the Narcissus.*

He had perhaps even more reason than most novelists to take language specifically into account, for the language in which he wrote was not only an acquired tongue, but was in fact his third language. Born a Pole, he learned French as a child, and then taught himself English in late adolescence, after he had gone to sea, and with the help of the English Bible, Shakespeare, and the London *Times.* If this partially explains why his style tends toward formality, it may also explain the seriousness with which he took the language he adopted. To him, indeed, it was the other way around; he once commented that English had adopted him, and that if he hadn't written in English he never would have written at all.

His keen appreciation of the literary potential of English naturally led him to a sense of the function of words which is not far removed from that of the French Symbolists. It is his basic creative attempt, as it is theirs, to find and arrest from the flux of experience its essence, what endures, what "endows passing events with their true meaning," through "an impression conveyed by the senses." The writer's language "must strenuously aspire to the plasticity of sculpture, to the colour of painting, and to the magic suggestiveness of music—which is the art of arts."

More specifically, with regard to language, "it is only through complete, unswerving devotion to the perfect blending of form and substance; it is only through an unremitting never-discouraged care for the shape and ring of sentences that an approach can be made to plasticity, to colour, and that the light of magic suggestiveness may be brought to play for an evanescent instant over the commonplace surface of words; of the old, old words, worn thin, defaced by ages of careless usage." What is involved here, as in the poetry of his French literary forebears, is evocation, and transformation by the creative imagination and the alchemy of the word.

Even so, and granted that "art is long and life is short," Conrad does not go the whole way toward the concept of art for art's sake held by the Symbolists and by the late nineteenth-century English aesthetes. What holds him back, he tells us in *A Personal Record*, is that to "hold the magic wand giving that command over laughter and tears" which is held to be "the highest achievement of imaginative literature" means, to Conrad, that the magician must surrender himself to "occult and irresponsible powers." In short, he must surrender himself fully to his art. But Conrad refuses to do so, feeling "a positive horror of losing even for one moving moment that full possession of myself which is the first condition of good service." The idea of "good service," he adds, derives from his life at sea: "I, who have never sought in the written word anything else but a form of the Beautiful—I have carried over that article of creed from the deck of ships to the more circumscribed space of my desk, and by that act, I suppose, I have become permanently imperfect in the eyes of the ineffable company of pure esthetes."

What we seem to have here is a basic conflict or tension between aesthetic and activist impulses. The demands of art and duty contend, and the resulting tension is highly creative. It may

account for the achievement of rich complexity in his writing up
through *Chance* (1913), and the gradual subsidence of this tension thereafter, as the purely aesthetic impulse lost ground, may
form a partial basis for the prevalent view that his later novels
declined in quality, with the notable exception of *The Shadow
Line*, to my mind an extremely significant and generally under-
rated novel.

The kind of tension I have referred to above is one of many in
Conrad; indeed, conflicting impulses may be an important key
to our understanding of his basic themes and their derivation
from the circumstances and dynamics of his life. His almost
obsessive concentration on certain motifs can clearly be traced
to central events and traumas in his own life.

Born in 1857 in the Ukraine as Josef Teodor Konrad Nalecz
Korzeniowski, he was orphaned at the age of ten. His father,
Apollo, a poet and member of the underground Polish national-
ist movement, was arrested by the Russians when Conrad was
three and was exiled to the north of Russia with wife and child.
Five years later, Conrad's mother's health failed in exile, and she
died, to be followed to the grave in 1867 by Apollo, who had
been paroled but whose stamina had been undermined by his
ordeal. Brought up by his dutiful and hortatory uncle, Conrad
left Poland and went off to sea at seventeen.

From even such brief biographical data, it is easy to see how
the theme of isolation, so prominent in his writings, had ante-
cedents in his early life and constituted a major portion of his
twenty years at sea. His early romantic adventures as a seaman,
including his involvement in a Carlist gunrunning plot and his
infatuation with a mysterious woman who was probably the an-
tecedent of Rita in *The Arrow of Gold*, and who may even have
been the mistress of Don Carlos, came to a jarring if temporary
halt with Conrad's attempted suicide in Marseilles at the age of

twenty-one. His uncle thought it was Conrad's depression over squandering his money that caused him to make the attempt on his life; more probably it was his feeling for and possible rejection by "Rita" which was responsible. In any case, the episode marked the very kind of bruising collision between illusion and reality which was to form another of his basic themes. Certainly the frequently grim realities of his life at sea, and the trauma of his ordeal in the Congo which was the genesis of *Heart of Darkness*, must have emphasized in his mind, and later in his fiction, the constantly recurring pattern of shattered illusion.

Similarly, it cannot be coincidence that he postulated the power of the irrational in many of his writings. Surrounded for many years by unmistakable evidence of the cruel fury of the sea, and aware of the complex vagaries of his own impulses, he could not but recognize the irrational, sometimes in the form of primitive impulses, as basic to the given of human experience.

To mention but one more aspect of his fiction, it has been frequently noted that motifs of guilt and betrayal are persistently evident. It is understandable that Conrad, orphaned at an early age, would have felt somehow betrayed by the loss of his parents. It has also been suggested that Conrad may have experienced pervasive guilt at having left Poland, having, so to speak, turned his back on the cause for which his father had given his life. If Conrad later expressed great skepticism with regard to causes, the death of his parents may have formed a part of his reaction, but his stance may have been in part defensive. Certainly his later feelings about Poland were ambivalent, as was Polish opinion of him up until the time he had reached the peak of his career and revisited his native land.

And yet, it is not adequate simply to identify such overt themes as isolation, irrationality, illusion, and betrayal and let it go at that, for the matter is not so simple. Each must be qualified, for Conrad perceives its counter or antithesis inextricably bound up with it in his complex vision of human experience, so that his distrust of univerals has affirmative as well as negative implications. For example, over and against isolation he perceives a basic underlying human solidarity. Although man is in part a victim of dark forces beyond his control, including the power of the irrational, he is also to some extent a free agent, determining, or at least shaping, a portion of his destiny in those "flickers of light" which represent his value-centered choices. True, illusion is part of the given, yet some illusions are "saving," without which life would be "too dark altogether."

Finally, we come to the theme of betrayal, and here again there is a counter deriving from the very complexity of human motive. That counter is fidelity, which is one of those "simple ideas" on which Conrad's view of reality rests.

In 1890 Conrad was commissioned to take a river boat up the Congo to bring out an ivory trader named Klein. The experience debilitated Conrad both physically and emotionally, and although it gave rise to *Heart of Darkness* some ten years later, it left him in poor health and apathetic about continuing his career at sea. In the period of lassitude that ensued, he began, "in a moment of idleness," his first novel, *Almayer's Folly*, based upon a Dutch trader he had known in Borneo. The novel was completed in 1894.

In this novel, Almayer, who had come to Borneo to "conquer the world," is married to a now aging and no longer attractive native woman. His life has come to center on his beautiful half-caste daughter Nina, whom he plans to take back to Europe with him on the strength of wealth not yet acquired but dreamed of. The fantasy of their projected life together governs him completely. Her beauty and his money would be both accepted and respected. But the dream is his folly or illusion.

Nina's native heritage comes to dominate her. She falls in love with a Malay warrior. Almayer's illusion is shattered. He is destroyed.

Almayer's isolation, his illusion, and the presence of powerful irrational or primitive forces which will draw him to his doom and his daughter to her Malay heritage are all visually prefigured and embodied in the opening scene, in which Almayer contemplates the river which flows past his trading post. He sees a drifting tree "raising upwards a long, denuded branch, like a hand lifted in mute appeal to heaven against the river's brutal and unnecessary violence." Clearing a point in the river, its course now free toward the sea, the log becomes a symbol of his own desire to escape, his own projected flight to freedom with his daughter. But dramatic irony is at work: the tree in the river serves as symbol not only of his aspiration but of his destiny, as he in the end is borne irresistibly downstream to his fate, like his daughter. The river itself serves as symbol of the unpredictable forces beyond man's control, a forerunner of the sea in later novels.

In his second novel, *An Outcast of the Islands* (1895), Conrad returns to the setting of *Almayer's Folly* but as of an earlier time. The central action concerns the deterioration and ultimate death of a young opportunist, Willems, who betrays his patron, Lingard, to gain wealth and the beautiful native girl Aissa, with whom he is infatuated. Again we see the now familiar themes. Willems is isolated both by his moral defection, his irrationality, and his egocentric illusion, and, near the end of the novel, literally by Lingard, who maroons him on an island with Aissa, whom he no longer loves. Again Conrad reaches toward visual embodiment at the very beginning of the novel, this time intertwining visual and moral elements. Willems, we learn, is determined to make of his dishonesty but a short episode, and to

resume the paths of morality as soon as his nefarious excursion
has produced its profits. "He imagined," we are told, "that he
could go on afterwards looking at the sunshine, enjoying the
shade, breathing in the perfume of flowers in the small garden
before his house. He fancied that nothing would be changed
. . . and he was unable to conceive that the moral significance
of any act of his could interfere with the very nature of things,
could dim the light of the sun." This connection between inner
and outer landscapes will prove even more significant in ensuing
novels, as will the relationship between character and destiny,
which implies that man is at least partially a free agent.

As has often been noted, it was with *The Nigger of the Narcissus*
that Conrad came of age artistically. Based upon an actual incident, and using the real and unexpectedly felicitous name of
the ship involved, the novel concerns an ill-fated cruise with a
crew which includes a black man, James Wait, who may be a
malingerer, may really be ill, or may, obscurely, be both. We
are never quite certain whether his illness is illusory or real, or
whether, in some strange way, his initial illusion is somehow ac-
tualized. All we know is that his illness is finally real, and fatal.

This may be a novel without a hero; indeed, Wait may be
regarded as one of the first antiheroes of the modern novel. Old
Singleton, the single-minded seagoing patriarch, almost the ar-
chetype of the old wise man, might qualify in part, except that
his role seems more peripheral than central, his unswerving
devotion to duty robs him of human dimension, and he seems
curiously detached and remote from the central action and resolution of the novel. The best guess is that the ship and its crew
combine into a collective hero, enduring the ordeal of a terrible
storm which almost capsizes and destroys the ship, and an ensuing calm which renders it equally helpless. We see a pattern of

near-death and rebirth, the latter, in the form of freshening breezes, coinciding significantly with the death of Wait.

The feelings of the crew toward Wait are ambivalent. He appears to be a catalyst of their own progressive demoralization. He is perceived partially as jinx, partially as talisman. Initially resentful of his refusal to stand watch, they somehow come to connect their survival with his, and scramble frantically to rescue him from entrapment in his cabin during the storm. When the captain decides to take Wait's professed illness seriously, and bans him from duty, the crew almost mutinies, and the captain's action may well have helped actualize Wait's illusion and in effect may have condemned him to death.

Wait's presence speaks significantly to each member of the crew. "He overshadowed the ship. Invulnerable in his promise of speedy corruption he trampled on our self-respect, he demonstrated to us daily our want of moral courage; he tainted our lives." The name of the ship enters here. Wait serves as a dark mirror in which various members of the crew see a distorted but recognizable image of themselves. To the religious cook, he is a sinner, to be redeemed and saved. To Donkin, he is a fellow malingerer, out to beat the system, to be joined initially, but later to be robbed as he lies dying. To Singleton, the dark vision is to be rejected: he ignores and thus endures Wait. To the rest of the crew he is inscrutable, perhaps a threatening reminder of their own unexamined lives. When the ship finally reaches port, the crew have achieved a fleeting solidarity in the face of cosmic indifference or hostility. They have survived their ordeal together. But the sense of union does not endure. They are paid off, drift apart, and never see each other again.

Conrad's technical skill in this novel represents a marked advance over previous work. He has achieved, in *The Nigger of the*

Narcissus, a firm grasp of the use of such nondiscursive and visual
structural elements as light and darkness, which will prove to be
the central substance of *Heart of Darkness*, to provide power and
resonance, and to convey total meaning, of which narrative
elements form only a part.

In this connection, the opening scene of the novel is instructive. The ship is in port at night, ready for sea. The chief mate
steps out of his lighted cabin into the darkness of the deck. We
are at once plunged into the visual milieu which, as we increasingly realize, sets the mood and frame for the novel: a small
amount of light in an encircling darkness. Forms are blurred and
flat; voices are indistinct. An atmosphere of disorder, mystery,
and unreality hovers over the scene, effectively setting the mood
for the spectral cruise to come. If the novel is, in part, an allegory of the state and pilgrimage of man's soul, the opening scene
reveals the darknesses to be plumbed.

The crew is mustered; one man is missing. Suddenly he
strides into the lighted circle; it is Wait. Himself black, he turns
out to be, during the course of the story, the paradoxical agent
of illumination, for light comes only after and as a result of insight into darkness; in the case of the crew of the *Narcissus*, the
darkness is that of their souls' estate.

Similarly, at the end of the novel, light and darkness are skillfully blended to suggest the ambiguity of the final outcome. The
ship has reached port; the crew have been paid off. The vision is
sunlit, suggesting solidarity and grace. They decide to have a
drink together at a nearby pub before they part, which may represent a final communion or celebration of the solidarity they
have achieved. They are momentarily illuminated by a "flood of
sunshine," which falls from heaven "like a gift of grace." But the
light is fleeting; the "dark knot" of seamen drifts out of sight.

Conrad had now left the sea for good, and was married in

JOSEPH CONRAD 145

1896. He had written some half-dozen short stories, the most important of which, in terms of his next major work, is "An Outpost of Progress," for the setting is the same as that of *Heart of Darkness*, the Congo, and the story traces, in a minor way, the same triumph of darkness over light that becomes a major theme of the novel.

Shortly after his marriage, Conrad met Ford Madox Ford and rented Ford's farmhouse in Kent. He and Ford collaborated on two novels during the period of their association, and theorized extensively about literature, but it is in Conrad's own writing that we are centrally interested, and his next significant venture took shape when he laid aside a short story, "Jim," on which he was at work, and undertook *Heart of Darkness*, which he completed in six weeks, early in 1899.

Although the plot of *Heart of Darkness* is absorbing, it hardly accounts for the total impact of the novel, which in the short space of slightly more than one hundred pages profoundly probes the darkness not only of the Congo but of the psyche. Marlow's journey up the river to find and bring back the mysterious ivory trader Kurtz is also Marlow's journey into himself, is also man's archetypal quest for enlightenment.

Marlow, squatting Buddha-like on deck as he tells his "inconclusive" story to his fellow yachtsmen in the Thames estuary, cannot convey its full significance to them, possibly because he but dimly grasps it himself, and probably because each man is isolated in his attempt to make sense of his life. "We live, as we dream—alone," he says. His story would have to be inconclusive, for, we are told, he sees significance flickering here and there on the surface of experience, rather than discerning any single kernel of truth within. In other words, Marlow is a symbolist.

He is also a seeker, drawn irresistibly into the quest. Hypno-

tized by the Congo, coiled like a snake on the map, he applies
for the job at a shipping office in Brussels, before which sit old
women knitting, suggesting the Fates. The jungle whispers
"Come and find out" to Marlow, and that is exactly why he is
there. His ostensible mission is to rescue Kurtz; his actual quest
is to visit an oracle in order to find out about himself. What he
seeks is knowledge of himself. What he finds is, grimly, that and
something more. The shrunken heads on poles outside Kurtz's
stockade are grim harbingers of the dark reality of Kurtz's estate. The man who came to Africa to win his fortune and civi-
lize the natives is also the man who, removed from society's restraints, has "kicked himself loose from heaven and earth," and
who wills himself either to exterminate all the brutes," or be
their god.

Marlow, a lesser Kurtz, is privileged, he tells us, to stand at
the edge of the abyss and look at the fallen man below, who
"lacked restraint," who was "hollow at the core," whom the
jungle had found out, a man claimed by the "powers of
darkness."

But apparently not completely. His properly ambiguous
dying ejaculation, "The horror, the horror!" sets us wondering.
Is this the frustration of a man who must own all, but cannot? Is
it rather the final self-judgment of a man who was not quite
hollow at the core after all? Marlow seems to think so; perhaps
he must. Because he thinks so, he lies, at the end of the novel, to
Kurtz's fiancée. He must maintain her "saving illusion" with his
own; otherwise, it would have been "too dark altogether."

There may be some evidence on the side of Marlow's interpretation of Kurtz's final words. Shortly before Kurtz dies,
he attempts to escape from the river boat to the native camp.
Marlow, almost gleefully intent on recapturing him, is oblivious
to his own safety, and follows Kurtz dangerously close to the

natives. All Kurtz needs to do is raise his voice; his natives will rescue him and take Marlow captive. Instead, he calls Marlow's attention to his danger, urges him to lower his voice, and returns with him to the boat. This concern for another person causes us, and perhaps Marlow, to wonder which is the real Kurtz.

Marlow does not know, and lies to perpetuate the Kurtz in whom the fiancée believes. Ironically, his lie becomes a moral act, and demonstrates that underlying solidarity Conrad sees as inescapable and redemptive. Marlow, at the beginning of the novel, tells us that he "hates and detests" a lie, because it has a strong "flavor of mortality" about it. So that in lying at the end, Marlow is revealing his own mortality, is joining the human race.

Two aspects of Conrad's technique are particularly noteworthy in *Heart of Darkness:* his use of the visual, and his use of indirection. The entire novel is a chiaroscuro. Light and dark are the principal elements, and, of course, the darkness dominates the light, except in momentary flickers. Thus the novel as a whole comments on human existence, or at least Conrad's perception of it. The "impenetrable darkness" ascribed to Kurtz by Marlow yields but for a moment, "as though a veil had been rent," as Kurtz passes final judgment on himself, if that is indeed what he does when he gasps, "The horror!"

The insight is all the light Marlow can stand at the moment. He blows out the candle and leaves the man who may have in that instant partially alleviated the darkness to slip into the ultimate total blackness of death.

In a sense, the novel represents Marlow's initiation into the complex pattern of darkness and light which is representative of the human situation. Aware of the darkness in himself and his fellow man, he recognizes the power of the irrational and the presence of the ineffable. He sees at firsthand man's potential for reversion into total darkness, but he sees as well the flicker of light which is the moral vision and which, if only briefly, can arrest the darkness.

Marlow's involvement with the complex of light and darkness does not end with the death of Kurtz, whose spirit seems able, afterward, to lay hands on Marlow out of the final darkness. Acting from a mixture of motives not entirely clear to him, he assumes the role of unofficial administrator of Kurtz's estate, and visits Kurtz's "Intended," thinking possibly to free himself from "this shadow darker than the shadow of the night," whose grip upon him is "regular and muffled like the beating of a heart—the heart of a conquering darkness."

What finally forces Marlow to lie to the woman who loved Kurtz is the vision of her: "With every word spoken the room was growing darker, and only her forehead, smooth and white, remained illumined by the unextinguishable light of belief and love." It is this light in the midst of darkness which Marlow suddenly realizes he must help preserve even if by a lie. He bows before her faith, "that great and saving illusion that shone with an unearthly glow in the darkness," and he lies to conceal the horror of Kurtz, as he tells her that the man's last word was her name. Otherwise, it would have been "too dark altogether." In this novel, the visual and the moral dimensions merge.

If Marlow turns out to be an agent of light, he is also, however, an agent of indirection. His meandering tale, presenting bits and pieces of information about Kurtz before we ever see him, mirrors Marlow's own fumbling search for significance, indeed, for reality. The method Conrad uses here for the first time is the method he and Ford discussed at length. Described generally as literary impressionism, it seeks to duplicate the actual process by which we come to understand character and event, a process in which information accretes not in order of serial time but in order of psychological or dramatic significance. This is indeed the case in *Heart of Darkness* with regard to Marlow's attempt to understand Kurtz. The preliminary and conflicting swirl of impressions or versions of him is at once focused and displaced by the sight of the shrunken heads, then modified still further by what seems to be his final self-judgment. But the real significance of the method does not finally dawn upon us until the end of the novel, when we find ourselves left with the abiding and unanswered question, What was Kurtz really like? Was his "Intended" right about him after all? Her faith was so strong that it shifted Marlow's own perceptions, or at least undermined his previous convictions and judgments. The one thing we know is that we will never know for sure.

Conrad's method of indirection, then, raises specific questions not only about Kurtz but, by extension, about the nature of motive, of human nature, and of reality itself. This method, brought into play for the first time in *Heart of Darkness*, achieves its fullest expression in Conrad's next novel, *Lord Jim* (1900), in which it becomes in fact the central substance of the book.

Our uncertainty with regard to Jim is so marked that it is possible to tell his story in two markedly different versions. Version A is that of a worthy young man who wants to prove himself a hero, to be generally esteemed and trusted. In a weak and confused moment, however, he is more or less pressured into abandoning ship by his disreputable fellow officers, leaving the passengers to their fate, which, as the ship remains afloat, is not consequential. The other officers flee the court of inquiry, but Jim remains to face the music, and loses his license. His pride forces him from one menial job to the next, as the story of his defection hounds him from port to port. Through Marlow's overtures to Stein, Jim goes to Patusan, where he achieves his destiny as hero and leader of the people, until a brigand named Brown and his cutthroat crew appear, intent on plunder.

Jim, a gentleman himself, mistakenly gives Brown the benefit of the doubt and offers him and his crew safe-conduct in return for their promise to leave the area at once, without harm to the natives. Brown violates his promise, and Jim's friend, the chief's son, is killed. Assuming full responsibility, Jim presents himself as a sacrifice to the chief, who shoots him. Jim dies finally redeemed, and the story is thus one of guilt and expiation.

Version B is rather substantially different. This Jim is a young egocentric, who must see himself a hero at all times and at all costs. The word "see" is intended literally; Jim's image of himself unfolds visually to him as a kind of interior cinema. He is so heavily involved in his fantasy, that of living beforehand "in his mind the sea-life of light literature," that he suffers from paralysis of the will, and cannot respond to the exigencies of external reality, either with regard to the rescue attempt he misses out on as a cadet, or the crisis leading him to abandon ship, an action he never could finally confront and accept. ("I had jumped—it seemed.") Another way of putting his problem is to say that he is so heavily invested in becoming that he has little psychic energy left for being.

He cannot tolerate any threat to his absurdly unrealistic self-concept. That is why he must stand trial, and also why he must move from port to port to evade the threatening accounts of his defection. It is in Patusan that his self-concept comes closest to actualization, until Brown turns up. Facing each other across a very narrow stream, they suggest by their proximity that not much separates them, unless it be, ironically, Brown's moral superiority at that moment. He insists that his men be provided for in any agreement reached; after all, he avows, he will not jump out of the boat and abandon them. This unwitting reference to Jim's own past is a direct threat to his self-concept: Brown must be gotten out of there in a hurry. Rashly accepting his word, Jim is of course undone by Brown's treachery. There is only one way for him to preserve his heroic image of himself. He takes that way and dies, in every way but literally a suicide. An egocentric until the end, he leaves the people of Patusan without a leader, victims, like himself, of his own illusion.

The truth about Jim, we suspect, is not quite so simple as either of these versions; it probably lies somewhere between them. At any rate, Marlow seems to think so. Drawn once again into the search for meaning by motives only in part rational or humanitarian, he involves himself in Jim's life, as he did with Kurtz, for reasons he but dimly understands. Mingling sympathy and judgment, he tells us on the one hand that Jim is "one of us," and, on the other, condemns him for "leaving a living woman to embrace a shadowy ideal of conduct," which leads to his death.

Marlow is not the only one who has mixed feelings about Jim. Brierly, to whom Jim's defection was so odious that he offered a bribe for Jim to clear out, must have been not only threatened but undermined as he sensed that Jim spoke to his own potential soft spot. Brierly, too, jumped off his own ship, taking his own life.

To Stein, the oracle in the jungle whom Marlow consults about Jim, the matter is much simpler, or so it seems initially. Jim is a romantic. Like all of us, he has "fallen into a dream," as one would fall into the sea. The prescription: to immerse in the "destructive element," and, by moving hands and feet, to be kept afloat by the sea itself. We are unclear as to whether the destructive element is illusion, or life, or both. What is most extraordinary about this extraordinary metaphor is the matter-of-fact manner with which Marlow accepts it. Is he content to take

it at face value, and ignore the complexities of meaning and the
ambiguities which attend it? Do they escape his attention entirely? Or does Marlow, himself a metaphorist, read Stein correctly as simply advocating, in figurative language, that we all
do our best?

Whatever Stein's meaning, Conrad has staged the scene in a
manner calculated to raise considerable questions about the in-
fallibility of the oracle. As he speaks, Stein moves back and
forth from lightness to darkness in the room. Initially, he
gathers conviction in the dark; when he advances into the light
he falters, loses conviction. Clearly, his abstractions do not fully
stand the test of existential reality. And yet, we feel that he is
close to the truth about Jim, that he knows as much about him
as does Marlow, or as do we. For Jim *is* one of us, and our final
sense is that we know as much or as little about him as we do
about ourselves, which of course is one of Conrad's central
points. In this story of a romantic illusionist, isolated by his betrayal of solidarity, Conrad by theme and technique raises again
the questions, What is the nature of man? of reality?

These same questions find voice in Linda's despairing cry to
her dead lover at the end of *Nostromo* (1904), thought generally
to be Conrad's most considerable novel, and at least agreed by
all to be his largest canvas. As we shall see, the nature of Nostromo himself, although never completely and finally clear, is
the crux of his novel, and the indirect presentation of his character in the novel carries forward the technique by which Kurtz
and Jim were earlier conveyed to us.

The genesis of the concept of the novel should be given
proper note. In his preface, written years later, Conrad tells us
that he had heard a fragmentary story of a man who had single-
handedly stolen a boatload of silver during the course of a South
American revolution. Although, as he tells us, the original ac-

count evoked visions of "bits of strange coasts under the stars, shadows of hills in the sunshine, men's passions in the dusk, gossip half-forgotten, faces grown dim," it was not until he realized that the thief need not be the "unmitigated rascal" of actuality, but rather could be an imaginatively conceived man of character caught in the swirl of revolution, that the full potentiality of the vision presented itself. "It was only then that I had the first vision of a twilight country which was to become the province of Sulaco, with its high shadowy Sierra and its misty Campo for mute witnesses of events flowing from the passions of men short-sighted in good and evil."

In other words, character and visual setting intermeshed in Conrad's mind, and his extraordinary novel was the result. Extraordinary in many respects, not the least of which is the fabrication of an entire country, with its people, its history, and its political intrigues. Of all his novels, *Nostromo* represents the setting least familiar to Conrad from firsthand experience, and consequently the most concentrated feat of imagination. Costaguana, then, bears comparison with Faulkner's Yoknapatawpha County as an imaginative creation, except that Faulkner's own origins put him in closer touch with his fictional world than was the case with Conrad, whose creation becomes all the more formidable for that difference.

Nostromo is a novel about many things. It is the story of a South American revolution, complete with violence, betrayals, disillusionment, and cynicism. It is a penetrating study of human motive and illusion. It is a devastating critique of the idea of progress as it is connected with materialism. Above all, it is the story of a silver mine and a man. The San Tomé mine and Nostromo himself stand together at the very center of the novel. Nostromo, the "incorruptible" servant of the forces of law and order, who, feeling betrayed by them, betrays them in turn by

stealing a boatload of silver—and the silver itself, incorruptible
yet corrupting all who touch it—the man and the metal form an
amalgam which is the core of the novel.

Conrad visually connects Nostromo and the silver from the
outset. Nostromo rides a silver-gray mare; his gray sombrero is
adorned by a silver cord and tassels; silver buttons, silver spurs,
and silver plates on his saddle complete the picture. He summons his cargo-workers with a silver whistle. He comments that
"silver is an incorruptible metal that can be trusted to keep its
value forever." "As some men are said to be," retorts the skeptic
Decoud, and we begin to realize that the reference may be to
Nostromo himself. To this point we have had to rely on various
flattering perceptions of him, but as he moves into our direct
view we experience a sudden jarring realization about him that
is not completely dissimilar to our abrupt focus on Kurtz's
shrunken heads.

Nostromo, charged with preventing a load of silver from falling into the hands of revolutionaries, stands suddenly alone in
the swirl of events, cut off from his former life, aware he cannot
reclaim his position or count upon the adulation his vanity demands. A victim of circumstances, he is suddenly aware that he
has been somehow "betrayed" by his employers—exploited and
demeaned by being given this difficult charge. It is only one step
more to his decision. He will gain his revenge and recapture his
vision of self by hiding the silver on an island, announce that it
sank with the lighter in the bay, then gradually and stealthily
grow rich.

As time passes, however, Nostromo begins to realize that he
does not own the silver; it owns him. He is tainted and cor-
rupted by his act; his vision of self suffers. He is ashamed of the
greedy animal who makes furtive nocturnal expeditions to carry
away an ingot or two. Occasionally he stares "fixedly at his

fingers, as if surprised they had left no stain on his skin." The
net of his own complicated intrigues tightens round him. Star-
tled to learn that a lighthouse is planned for the island, and fear-
ful that it will lead to the discovery of his cache, he uses his influence to place his aged friend Giorgio as the keeper of the
light. Arranging his betrothal to one of Giorgio's daughters gives
him a pretext for regular visits to the island. Secretly, however,
he is courting the younger daughter. The desperation of their
love is matched by that of his vision of self. He has become, essentially, a creature of darkness, and the beam from the lighthouse stares at him remorselessly.

The ending is ironic. Mistaken for an unwelcome suitor of the
younger daughter, Nostromo is shot and killed by her father.
The silver has claimed its victim, and the mourning cry of his
faithful betrothed, Linda, echoes over the empty gulf its assurance of undying love which brings, for the moment, surcease
from darkness, and again provides the life-sustaining flicker.

With regard to visual techniques, *Nostromo* constitutes a kind
of watershed in Conrad's work. Up to that point, each novel
marks an advance; beyond that point, Conrad consolidates his
gains. His next novel, *The Secret Agent* (1907), offers a marked
change from impressionistic to realistic method, but the visual
component is still much in evidence. The story took shape, as
was the case with *Nostromo*, with a vision, this time one of an
enormous town, with "room enough there for any kind of
story." In perhaps none of his novels does he succeed more
nearly in merging character with scene. His initial description of
Verloc's shop in the "grimy brick house" vividly sets the opening mood of squalor and mystery in this tale of a rumpled and
slightly comic secret agent whose ineptness culminates in the
farcically tragic attempt to blow up the Greenwich observatory,
and in the death of his wife's dimwitted brother. As Conrad tells

us about Verloc, "He had an air of having wallowed, fully dressed, all day on an unmade bed."

Conrad also employs such familiar devices as the pattern of light and dark, the darkness here representing the forces of irrational anarchy. But visual techniques are not the central achievement of the novel, although everywhere present, and occasionally extremely explicit, as in the scene where Verloc's agonized and vengeful wife, Winnie, stabs him to death, which reads exactly like a screenplay. The central aspect of the novel is that of dramatic irony. Conrad tells us, in his introduction, that his "artistic purpose" is that of "applying an ironic method" or treatment, in the belief that this method alone would make it possible for him to say what he had to "in scorn as well as in pity." Having formulated his objective, he felt that he did manage "to carry it right through to the end."

Most readers would agree. Surely the deliberately distanced, frequently droll, and always dispassionate tone with which the horrors of the plot are recounted manages to produce its effect, as Conrad himself discovered, much to his discomfiture, when some years later he tried to adapt his story for the stage, and was horrified to discover, when he stripped away tone and style and got down to the bare bones of the plot, what a grisly and macabre story it really was.

The irony in *The Secret Agent* takes several forms. There is, of course, the incongruity of Verloc himself as a secret agent, to say nothing of his choice of his feeble-minded brother-in-law, Stevie, as the purveyor of the bomb which is to blow up the observatory, but which actually blows up Stevie, as the plot collapses into grisly fiasco and the absurdity of the entire enterprise reverberates with the explosion. More important, however, is the dramatic irony arising from the erroneous perceptions of reality by the characters. Winnie's avenging murder of Verloc is a case in point. Failing entirely to comprehend the depth of her feeling for her dead brother, Verloc attempts to console her with heavy-handed banalities. In final incongruity, it is by asserting his own crumpled male ego that he precipitates his death. He mistakes her quietly murderous resolve for passive acceptance, and summons her to his couch. She goes to him at once, intent, however, not on venery but vengeance, bearing, as he discovers too late, not her wifely affection but a knife. The sequel to his death is even more a sinister farce. Winnie runs out of the house and into Verloc's fellow terrorist, Comrade Ossipon, who promptly concludes that she is leaving Verloc and is therefore fair game. Realization of what is what is followed by his desertion of her. Her subsequent suicide fastens a burden of guilt on him that constitutes the final irony: her death cements their incongruous relationship.

In this, the second of three overtly political novels, Conrad engages, or rather confronts, extremist political philosophies. In *Nostromo* he had expressed his skepticism of both revolution and the reform supposedly accompanying it, and implied strongly that the new order was little better than the old, that there was in fact little to choose between the greed of the revolutionaries and the "material interests" advocated and defended by Charles Gould, manager of the silver mine. In *The Secret Agent*, Conrad's target is the more extreme philosophy of anarchism, with its accompanying terrorist tactics. The plot to blow up the observatory is, symbolically, an attempt to eradicate serial time, and, by implication, order and rationality.

Characteristically, however, Conrad's most telling comments on senseless violence are embodied and implicit rather than discursive. It is the vision of the Professor, the human bomb, silently walking the streets of London unnoticed at the end of *The Secret Agent*, which most eloquently suggests the unseen presence of violence and terror in our midst. "He walked, frail, insignificant, shabby, miserable—and terrible in the simplicity of his idea calling madness and despair to the regeneration of the world. Nobody looked at him. He passed on unsuspected and deadly, like a pest in the street full of men."

Conrad continues his critique of political philosophies in *Under Western Eyes* (1911), although with a somewhat different and broader focus, equating in viciousness and repression both extremes. He condemns both the "ferocity and imbecility" of an autocracy which rejects legality and bases itself upon what is in reality "moral anarchism," and the inevitable reaction provoked by it, the "no less imbecile and atrocious answer of a purely Utopian revolutionism encompassing destruction by the first means to hand, in the strange conviction that a fundamental change of heart must follow the downfall of any given human institutions." To Conrad, all that is effected is a change of names.

The story itself concerns an ambitious but poor student, Rasumov, who is approached for aid by Haldin, a fugitive who has assassinated the prime minister. Rasumov, terrified lest his future be jeopardized, agrees to assist Haldin escape, then informs on him. Haldin is executed, but this is a police state, and we realize that Rasumov will always be under surveillance. He goes to Geneva as a police spy and falls in love with Nathalie, sister of Haldin and member of the ring of revolutionaries on whom Rasumov is spying. The burden of guilt and fear becomes too heavy: he confesses his role, has his eardrums smashed, walks unwittingly into the path of a streetcar, and, hopelessly crippled, is cared for by a streetwalker.

If in this markedly Dostoevskian novel, Conrad's judgments of political philosophies seem somewhat extreme and simplistic, we must remember that the early loss of his father to a revolutionary cause, together with his own possible guilt at disengaging himself from his culture and its thrust toward freedom, may well have produced the powerful feelings which are evident in his attacks on causes and movements, together with their underlying philosophies. However this may be, with *Under Western Eyes* we see the last of his concentrated attention to politics, for it was shortly after the completion of this novel that he wrote what is probably his most effective short story, "The Secret Sharer," in which the focus and perspective are not collective but individual.

Although Conrad's short fiction cannot receive adequate attention in this essay, this particular story needs mention as an example of Conrad at the peak of his powers. Like Rasumov, the captain in this story is asked by a fugitive for aid and sanctuary. Unlike Rasumov, however, the captain harbors the fugitive, Leggatt, possibly because he recognizes in the man some suppressed semblance of himself. Conrad skillfully links the two men visually, to the point where we see Leggatt at once as a separate identity and as an aspect of that of the captain. In the end, the captain helps the fugitive make good his escape and is somehow himself liberated by the experience. The familiar theme of betrayal is here given a new twist: the captain betrays the conventions of society rather than an individual, and thereby perhaps is spared the betrayal of self. The tale is taut and masterfully unfolded, in contrast with the turgidity and fatigue which were now beginning to creep into Conrad's novels.

Chance (1913) is a case in point. Ironically, although not his greatest artistic success by any means, it was the novel which first brought him considerable public acclaim and commensurate financial return, possibly because of the cumulative impact of his growing reputation. The novel marks Marlow's final appearance, and although he is, as usual, involved in sorting out reality

from a meandering swirl of event and character, one senses a
diminished involvement on his part, more aesthetic than active.
It is he who gathers together the diverse strands of the narrative
and, his consciousness the loom, weaves them into the intricate
pattern of the novel, which must for the most part be seen,
then, as an elaboration of previously established themes and
techniques.

Perhaps the most interesting thing about *Victory* (1915) is the
philosophical disengagement of the principal character, Axel
Heyst, an isolate living alone on an island, a man whose father
had told him to "look on, make no sound." His affair with Lena,
a stranded music-hall entertainer, is characteristically passive,
almost vegetable. The inevitable evil of external reality, in the
person of Jones, like Brown in *Lord Jim* an intruder into the
idyllic existence, forces Heyst out of his passivity, but he
"learned too late to put his trust in life," and in the ensuing tragedy Lena's life and his are lost. Conrad thought well of the
book, feeling he had "grasped at more life stuff" than in his earlier efforts. Critics have been less impressed, however, and one
senses a growing lassitude which even the melodrama, more apparent in the stage version than in the novel, fails to conceal.

Conrad's next novel, *The Shadow Line* (1917), generally undervalued, is one of his best-realized efforts, and may mark a final
fleeting return of full creative power. For setting, he abruptly
returns to life at sea, for technique, to the symbolist mode of *The
Nigger of the Narcissus* and *Heart of Darkness*. A young first mate
suddenly quits his snug berth on a comfortable ship, owing to
boredom, restlessness, a vague emotional or spiritual malaise.
He learns that a command has become available in Bangkok,
because of the death of the captain. He assumes command and
the rest of the novel recounts his ordeal: the entire crew falls ill,

the malevolence of the dead captain hangs over the ship, a deadly calm almost does the whole cruise in. But he perseveres, and finally brings the ship into port.

In this classic story of initiation, the hero loses his innocence and illusion as he encounters evil in the form of malice or hostility. He must also confront his own irrationality, in his sudden decision to quit his former berth. The pattern of guilt and absolution becomes overt: he assumes responsibility for the crew and brings them safely through. Unlike Jim, he acts. He engages his world, and although almost overwhelmed by evil, guilt, and fear, he emerges and crosses the shadow line that separates youth and maturity.

If *The Shadow Line* represents a successful return, in setting and technique, to a period of greater robustness for Conrad, his next three novels suggest more regression than return. *The Arrow of Gold* (1919) seems to be a romanticized and self-censored version of some of the events which may have led the young Conrad to attempt suicide. Young Monsieur George's involvement with the glamorous Rita in a gunrunning plot and in an affair with her may indicate his assumption of adulthood, but certainly in a shallower fashion than that of *The Shadow Line*.

In *The Rescue* (1920), we finally see the result of Conrad's efforts, extending over twenty years, to bring that novel to completion, and must question whether the achievement was commensurate with the effort. Captain Lingard, of *Almayer's Folly* and *An Outcast of the Islands*, is the central character. The conflict of loyalties he experiences between Malay and white, in the hands of the more vigorous Conrad who started the tale, might have emerged as a powerful story of a man caught and agonized between love and duty. Instead, what we sense is a general air of lassitude; Lingard's love for Edith Travers is even more passive than that of Heyst for Lena; his paralysis seems more attributable to a kind of psychic impotence than to the destructive equilibrium of two powerful opposing impulses.

This air of enervation is even more noticeable in *The Rover*, Conrad's last completed novel. Certainly it is understandable. The weariness of old Peyrol, returning home after forty years at sea, may be Conrad's own weariness as, in increasingly poor health, he nears the end of his career. Peyrol's self-sacrifice to ensure the future of the young lovers, Lt. Real and Arlette, has some robust moments, but the generally blurred quality of the novel may derive not only from Conrad's possible identification with the old man but from his decreasing ability to deal effectively with visual equivalents.

It is apparent, and generally agreed, that the quality of Conrad's novels ascends during the earlier part of his writing career and, by and large, declines during the later part. What needs possibly more attention is the correlation between quality and visual sense. In Conrad's best work, we find not only visual presentation and individually expressive images but several functional patterns of connected visual imagery. One of these is the leap or fall by which several of his characters sever the bond of solidarity. The first of these characters is Kurtz, who had "kicked himself loose of the earth." As a result, he had, in Marlow's mind, fallen into an impenetrably dark abyss. Jim's leap is of course the crux of the matter in *Lord Jim*, but we must remember that he was not the only one who jumped. Brierly, unable to accept Jim as "one of us," unable to tolerate the possibility of the taint within himself, had "kicked himself loose" from his ship and had taken his own life at sea.

Another central visual pattern concerns the intrusion of reality and/or evil into the walled circle or tight little island of egocentric and/or untested illusion. In *The Nigger of the Narcissus*

Wait steps into the small, pseudo-secure circle of light. In *Heart of Darkness* Marlow intrudes as moral reality into Kurtz's savage kingdom and precipitates Kurtz's downfall. In *Lord Jim* the repeated attempts of reality to breach the walled circle of Jim's self-image direct his actions, and Brown's final intrusion into the "tight little island" of Patusan brings with it the final tragedy. Significantly enough, it is also an island on which Nostromo has hidden the stolen silver he desperately hopes will maintain his own self-concept, an island "invaded" both by the searching beam from the lighthouse and by Nostromo's own final moral judgment upon himself.

The ship in *The Shadow Line* is also a small walled circle, but the difference from *The Nigger of the Narcissus* is that the "invasion" of reality-evil represented by the dead captain's malevolence in the later novel is in part external, in that he is no longer on board, and in part internal, in that he had been the captain and had, by destroying the ship's medical supplies, rendered it incapable of defense against fever. Fittingly, it is with a combination of inner and outer resources that the young captain combats evil successfully. His acceptance of responsibility helps him break through the walled circle of self.

In short, visual elements are a central aspect of Conrad's writing. The more he was able to embody his material visually, the stronger and more effective his fiction. The more he himself "saw," the more he could make his reader "see," and the more powerful his work.

One of the principal things one "sees" in Conrad's fiction is the relationship between man and his environment. Put visually, this is the linkage, by image and symbol, between inner and outer landscapes. External landscape is itself, in most cases, symbolic. Whether river or sea, jungle or sprawling city, it

serves as representation of the inscrutable and labyrinthine complexity of human experience and the power of the irrational in
Conrad's universe. This is not to say it is malevolent, but it is
also not to say it is neutral. More precisely, it is not passive. It
presses in on man, it probes him; if he has a weak spot, it
surely, inevitably, finds it. This is perhaps the most significant
aspect of Conrad's cosmos: whether by chance, choice, through
forces beyond his control, or by some cryptic combination of
these, man finds himself, sooner or later, in that very environment which seems peculiarly able to reveal him, to test him,
and, in some instances, to assist if not to preside at his destruction. Conrad raises but never finally answers the question as to
what extent man is the master of his destiny and to what extent
he is the victim of forces beyond his control; the only thing that
is clear is that the answer cannot be.

Conrad's sense of the probing and testing environment is
present in his fiction from the beginning. *Almayer's Folly* is set in
exactly those somnolent and apathetic surroundings which offer
both occasion and need for daydreams, which coalesce into Almayer's ultimately disastrous illusion. In *An Outcast of the Islands*
Willems's contempt for his environment seduces him into believing himself sufficiently above this subhuman culture to be a law
unto himself. He is undone by this very feeling of superiority,
and claimed by the forces he had thought he could ignore or
spurn.

Sea and sky dramatize the isolation of the ship and her crew
in *The Nigger of the Narcissus*, throwing the men back upon one
another and upon themselves, probing and revealing the central
moral issue of the novel. Life at sea revolves around the standing
of watches by each member of the crew. The safety of all is en-
trusted, by turns, to each. Duty at sea, then, signifies the acceptance of responsibility, and the demonstration of fidelity and sol-

idarity. To refuse or avoid standing watch is thus to defect from the human race. And this is precisely what James Wait does. Whether malingering or actually ill, Wait shirks the fundamental obligation pressed by the sea on all men.

This is why he demonstrates to the crew daily their "want of moral courage," why he taints their lives. If he has defected, it reveals to each the possibility of his own defection. It seems fair to say, then, that the sea, in this novel, probes and exposes the disease of the spirit that is central to the story, and serves not only as a fitting stage on which the moral drama unfolds but, in a sense, as director of the drama.

The press and probe of the environment are nowhere given more effective treatment than in *Heart of Darkness*. If the sea in *The Nigger of the Narcissus* bears in on man at the very point of his weakness, so does the jungle on Kurtz in the later novel. As Marlow observes, it has found Kurtz out. And we sense that it has whispered to him with Mephistophelean insinuation, promising him absolute power in return for his soul. Alone and seduced by his environment, lacking either society's restraints or his own, Kurtz joins the forces of darkness and claims his jungle universe.

In *Lord Jim*, environmental press may be somewhat more complex, yet it is not dissimilar to what we have already seen. The book, as has been frequently noted, breaks rather sharply into two sections: that centering on the *Patna* and that centering on Patusan. Each setting, however, proves to be one in which responsibility for not only the well-being but the actions of others becomes crucial, and it is exactly this problem which Jim never solves. In the first instance, by jumping from the *Patna* he abdicates his responsibility to the helpless passengers and to the code of his calling, an action he is only able to perceive as an opportunity missed. But for him the "opportunity" comes again, this time in Patusan, the environment designed once more to meet him head on at the point of his greatest need and his greatest weakness. And once again Jim is tried and found wanting. Again Conrad has used setting to lay his man bare.

In *Nostromo*, setting and situation combine and intertwine to corrupt Nostromo by the sudden availability of great wealth. This is an imprecise way of putting it, of course, for it might be more accurate to say that Nostromo corrupts himself. In any event, the environment is particularly propitious for the seduction. The swirling lawless confusion of the revolution, the sudden entrustment of the silver to Nostromo's care, and the opportunity to disguise the theft catalyze Nostromo's underlying discontent with his lot. In his own mind the aggrieved plaintiff deserving justice denied him, he seizes that which he believes will assure the material well-being which is of a piece with his sense of personal worth and reputation. It is a temptation he cannot resist, a temptation which presents itself because of the peculiar confluence of the external and the internal, of moment and motive, of setting and defect.

Possibly a single additional example will suffice. The central character of *The Shadow Line* finds himself in exactly that situation which will precipitate his ordeal. Suffering initially from a kind of spiritual apathy or paralysis, he finds himself in command of a ship which is paralyzed. Still in bondage to his own past in that he has not yet crossed the shadow line from youth to maturity, he finds himself on a ship in the clutches of its own past, as symbolized by the malignant aura of the dead captain. Unlike some of Conrad's other heroes, the young man triumphs, but his ordeal nonetheless results from the interaction of self and surroundings.

In much of Conrad's best work, then, setting assumes major significance and becomes a kind of precipitant of the crucial action. Are we saying, in short, that this universe is one which plays dirty tricks, one in which man after man finds himself, naked and alone, inevitably in the one situation with which he cannot cope, in which his values are in most cases revealed as inadequate? I think not. To Conrad, the crucial issue is not so much the inevitable encounter between man and the cosmos as it is the outcome of that encounter. True, the universe finds man out, reveals his defects, but what happens then is up to man, not the universe. In other words, the final focus must be, in Conrad's mind, on the values which motivate man's actions, and the final question for him is essentially the same one Camus raises later: How ought one to live?

I have said that Conrad's vision of human experience is essentially dramatic. I suggest now, that, far from being a nihilist who believed in nothing, Conrad had a rather clearly defined sense of the role man could and should play in an enigmatic universe, and that this role is adumbrated in the closing pages of *The Nigger of the Narcissus,* as the narrator recognizes his bond with the crew, and salutes them: "Haven't we, together and upon the immortal sea, wrung out a meaning from our sinful lives? Good-bye, brothers! You were a good crowd. As good a crowd as ever fisted with wild cries the beating canvas of a heavy foresail; or tossing aloft, invisible in the night, gave back yell for yell to a westerly gale."

This is perhaps as close as Conrad ever comes in his fiction to articulating explicitly man's dual role in a spectacular universe: to "wring" meaning out of his experience, and to give back "yell for yell" to the forces which press in on him. Life does not guarantee meaningfulness or yield meaning simply to passive endurance. Man must, in the best sense of the world, fabricate meaning, forge it, wrest it from event. He must invest the process with value. And the meaning he captures is somehow bound up

with a dealing of blow for blow which constitutes, if not defiance of an unrelenting universe, at least courageous and indom-
itable engagement with it.

It is clear, however, that activism for its own sake is not
enough. Many of Conrad's central characters who might well be
characterized as activists go down to defeat in one way or another. Almost without exception, these characters are egocen-
trics. We may begin with Almayer, involved in his own visions
of greed and luxury, indifferent to all else and all others, except
for his fixation on his daughter. We may follow with Willems,
similarly centered on and obsessed with self-aggrandizement.
But to see the first instance on a grand scale we turn to James
Wait, the complete egocentric whose horizon is himself. Kurtz
looms even larger as an egocentric. He has achieved the ultimate: to be worshiped. He has yielded, as Marlow tells us, to
the darkness, and we see that it is the darkness of complete absorption in self.

That the central character of *Lord Jim* is an egocentric needs
no further documentation. Jim is Conrad's most effective and
disturbing portrait—disturbing because he is "one of us"—of a
man completely oriented toward, and governed by, his ego-ideal.
What is particularly significant is Conrad's growing conviction
that egocentricity necessarily entails a disengagement from the
common stream of humanity. Kurtz has kicked himself loose
from earth; Stein refines and extends the metaphor in *Lord Jim*
by contrasting one of his precious butterflies with man. The
butterfly, he observes, "finds a little heap of dirt and sits still in
it; but man he will never on his heap of mud keep still." How to
be, in the face of all this, is the question, as he points out.

Stein's "destructive element" has been dealt with earlier; what
should be pointed out here is that Stein himself is a rather
disengaged spectator, and that Conrad displays considerable vir-

tuosity in showing us this character, who on first view seems so imposing and wise, but who on closer inspection is revealed as an imperfect sage. What may throw his doctrine into doubt for Marlow and us is his failure to discriminate among dreams. One should follow his dream whatever it is, should attempt to actualize his illusions whatever form they take. Clearly that is not enough for Conrad. All men have illusions, but the nature of these illusions is crucial, and we see that Conrad evaluates them, discriminates between those which are ego-involved, privatistic, and ultimately doomed to defeat, and those which are "saving illusions" because they lead beyond and away from egocentricity.

Nostromo brings us not only another egoist primarily dedicated to his own self-concept but also the overtly disengaged and uncommitted Decoud, a dilettante dedicated to nothing, who can find nothing to sustain him when he is removed from that society which had served as a foil for his skepticism. Thrust back upon himself, unable to endure his isolation, he crumbles and destroys himself.

It is in *Victory*, however, that Conrad comes to closest grips with the philosophical and moral question of disengagement in the person of Axel Heyst, the fulcrum of the novel. To understand Heyst it is first necessary to understand his father. The elder Heyst, apparently a kind of Faust, had for more than sixty years coveted and striven to capture "all the joys, those of the sages." His quest ending in disillusionment, he sets down in writing what he has learned, and its impact on his young and impressionable son is formative and crucial. "Look on, make no sound," is the sum and substance of it. As the uncommitted spectator, the younger Heyst is a passivist. He observes but he does not act, and what he observes are facts. "There's nothing worth knowing but facts," he says. He wants no traffic with feelings, attitudes. Among the main things he has renounced, then, is action, for "all action is harmful."

This is not to say that he is unaware of the conflict symbolized and triggered by his act of bringing Lena to the island. Inevitably, he makes love to her. But as he goes to her his is the feeling of an animal about to be trapped, "by life itself—that commonest of all snares." After the act, his reaction is that of a transgressor. He has sinned against his creed of disengagement, and he is disgusted by what he regards as his "abominable calumny." Regressing to his father's books, he finds the appropriate golden text: "Of the stratagems of life the most cruel is the consolation of love—the most subtle, too; for the desire is the bed of dreams." Lena's is a relatively simple mind, but with unerring intuitiveness she diagnoses Heyst's disease and prescribes the sovereign remedy. "You should try to love me," she tells him. This is not, as it might well appear, the imperious vanity of a woman demanding adulation, but rather the straightforward summons from the cell of egocentricity to the life of relationship and commitment.

Heyst can only be perplexed at the summons, and it is at this point that external reality, in the persons of Jones, Ricardo, and Pedro, intrudes. Events now move with accelerated pace toward the tragic climax. Lena, firm in her desperate conviction that she alone can save Heyst from the designs of the sinister trio, sacrifices herself in the attempt, a victim of Jones's bullet. Heyst, even in her final extremity, cannot overcome his psychic impotence. He bends over her, "cursing his fastidious soul, which even at that moment kept the true cry of love from his lips in its infernal mistrust of all life." She dies, out of his arms.

Heyst, in the end, passes judgment on himself, and writes his own epitaph in his final words to Davidson: "Woe to the man whose heart has not learned while young to hope, to love—and to put his trust in life." Like Decoud in *Nostromo*, he cannot tolerate the life of disengagement any longer. He sets fire to his island bungalow and remains inside, to join the dead Lena in her funeral pyre. Clearly, Conrad is showing us in this novel that the way of commitment is the way of life, the way of disengagement the way of death, and that to withhold one's trust in life is to abdicate one's humanity and secede from the human race.

The models discussed thus far have been essentially negative: the Waits, Kurtzes, Jims, Nostromos, Decouds, and Heysts of the world fail because they do not successfully confront and engage life on its own terms with viable values which enable them to win even the limited victories Conrad seems to feel are all we may hope for. But Conrad offers at least two counters to these negative models: the captains in "The Secret Sharer" and *The Shadow Line*. In harboring Leggatt, the captain in the short story breaks out of the prison of self to involve himself, at his own risk, in the welfare of another. If in the end Leggatt is a free soul, the captain has also been liberated from his isolation.

The young captain in *The Shadow Line* serves as a more considerable example. When he discovers the perfidy of the dead captain, who has substituted useless white powder for urgently needed quinine, he himself accepts full responsibility for the calamity. This is the crucial point of the story, the moment at which he makes his full commitment. Regardless of the past, it is now his ship, his crew, and the safety and welfare of both are in his hands and his alone. He engages his ordeal, and he weathers it.

It is in this context of total engagement that Conrad's vision of man's role coalesces. "Those who read me," he writes in the Preface to *A Personal Record*, "know my conviction that the world, the temporal world, rests on a few very simple ideas; so simple that they must be as old as the hills. It rests notably,

among others, on the idea of Fidelity." Within the boundaries of
this felicitous term aesthetic and activist impulses merge. For
Conrad, the writer must render, with extreme and painstaking
fidelity, the truth of human experience, and, in the other sense
of the word, in Conrad's universe it is the man who fully
engages life, commits himself, and discharges his obligation who
expresses fidelity, who keeps the faith. A central and familiar
theme in his fiction we know to be the betrayal-fidelity polarity.
As we have seen, it is the egocentric or the victim of the "dark
forces" of self who betrays not only his fellow man but himself,
while it is the hero, in the affirmative sense of the word, who
demonstrates fidelity to a cause other and greater than self,
which becomes an expression of solidarity. This is the end toward which fidelity leads us. Both implicitly and explicitly,
Conrad posits solidarity as that value which, perhaps more than
any other, infuses life with dignity, informs human experience
with worth, represents man at his highest, and constitutes his
only enduring defense against the corrosive of isolation.

And all of this, of course, in the face of the ultimate possibility that none of it may be true. It may well be, in Conrad's universe, that fidelity, solidarity, human dignity, and human worth
are but illusions. For illusion is a part of the given, an inescapable concomitant of the human situation. We are much mistaken
if we believe that Conrad's novels are simply attempts to condemn illusion and extol reality. True, his fiction is full of colli-
sions between specific illusions and specific realities, but he
knows full well that it is not a question of whether or not man
should have illusions; all men do. Like fingerprints, they dif-
ferentiate one man from another, and no man is without his own
set. What matters, then, is the sort of illusion to which each
man is committed. We have already seen examples of what
Conrad regards as the destructive sort of illusion. It customarily

consists of the immersion in self and the progressive loss of touch with external reality. On the other hand, Conrad refers occasionally to the "saving" or "sustaining" illusion. He is, I think, speaking of faith, belief in the worth of someone or something outside oneself, the conviction that belief and faith themselves must not be allowed to die out, that life without them would be "too dark altogether," that fidelity, service, and solidarity give meaning and value to human experience, and make man, man.

How may Conrad's views of man's role best be summarized? Shall we say that he sees egocentricity as original sin, and "saving illusion" as redemptive? Isolation as original sin, and solidarity as redemptive? However we put it, we touch the same chord over and over: man cannot live for himself alone. If he does he will destroy himself.

To be sure, even if he does not live for himself alone, victory is by no means certain, nor can we know the outcome. It is not of first importance that we do. "The earth is a stage," Conrad observes in *Last Essays*, "and though it may be an advantage, even to the right comprehension of the play, to know its exact configuration, it is the drama of human endeavour that will be the thing, with a ruling passion expressed by outward action marching perhaps blindly to success or failure, which themselves are often undistinguishable from each other at first." Whether or not good is distinguishable from evil at all times, whether or not the final outcome can ever be known, whether or not victory or defeat will be the ultimate outcome, man is here to play out his role with courage and dignity. For all he knows, he may be destined for defeat, but he must deny it to the very end. Only thus can he give back yell for yell to the universe. Only thus can he wring meaning out of his life. Without knowing whether life has purpose and meaning, he must act as if it has. And in that commitment to value and meaning *lie* value and meaning.

Conrad, it is clear, gives us no easy answers, no pat assurances. His affirmations may be sounded in muted tones, yet they are affirmations none the less, affirmations of courage, fidelity, and the invincibility of the human spirit in the face of the unknown. I think he would have agreed with Yeats, who observed that man can embody truth but he cannot know it. In the embodiment lies the drama, and what Conrad is telling us through his fiction is that we are all of us on the stage.

CARL WOODRING

Virginia Woolf

Virginia Woolf can delight those who delight in language or metaphor. She can bring cheer to any who love wry humor, clean pattern, or private traps set by a writer to catch life. Her subjects are sometimes thought to be epitomized in the first sentence of her second novel: ". . . In common with many other young ladies of her class, Katharine Hilbery was pouring out tea." But the second sentence answers detractors: "Perhaps a fifth part of her mind was thus occupied . . ." To say the worst, her characters pour out steeped emotion and sensibility, not tea. In the power of making images, she told her diary, she was to Shakespeare as the housekeeper was to her. She did not wish to waste a keen mind in making rational statements that any educated fool could make.

The physical beauty of Adeline Virginia Stephen, as a girl and long after her marriage to Leonard Woolf in 1912, came from the delicate but continuous line of her profile. She lived among persons who acknowledged their own intellectual superiority and helped to direct the national mind. Sir Leslie Stephen, her father, entertained the major living writers later included in the *Dictionary of National Biography*, of which he was the first editor. It meant something to him that in 1882 Arnold published *Irish Essays*, Darwin died, and Virginia was born. An agnostic and a liberal, he opened his library to his daughters. After his death in 1904, Virginia, her sister Vanessa (an accomplished painter who married the critic Clive Bell) and their two brothers moved to the house in Gordon Square where the Bloomsbury set began its well-advertised exclusiveness. For Virginia the escape from Victorians meant a change in human nature. Morality began in the kind of question the men had learned at Cambridge from G. E. Moore: Are you sure? Their set included persons of such varied success as the deflationist biographer Lytton Strachey and the economist John Maynard Keynes. Virginia Woolf's Preface to *Orlando* acknowledges aid from fifty distinguished friends. Most of them were wittier than her father, and much readier to learn from Marx and Shaw. Much in her novels is built on affection for these friends, but she was herself less brittle than the Bloomsbury envisioned by outsiders who quote D. H. Lawrence. Her novels handle discreetly the sexual errancy of some in the group.

She began to write professionally as an anonymous reviewer for the *Times Literary Supplement*. Like Hazlitt, Sainte-Beuve, and Shaw, she attempted general truths in the rush of journalism. In weekly papers she disciplined her style and clarified her standards for fiction. As a reviewer and leadwriter she chose to concentrate on memoirs and biography, new editions of canonized novelists, and writers whose styles deserved appraisal.

In reviews shaped into essays she applauds economy and proportion. She cries for Life, more Life. She stresses the interrelationships and solidarity, not of fictional characters, but of people reported on in novels. A novel, she says, whether by Proust or Defoe, deals with impingements upon the individual consciousness. Novelists manipulate words to make life on the page vital and real. Her emphasis on fuller life has been ignored as consistently as the similar emphasis by Henry James, from whom in part she learned it. In a step beyond James, she says over and over that the history of the novel carries forward no external rules. She read the new experimenters, but she was learning from Scott and the Brontës; as a novelist, she was first freed by Sterne. She translated powerful bits from the Russians. As a critic, she is very unlike Bloomsbury as well as its chief opponents in her ability to give a reason for admiring most of the canonized English novelists. Nearly half of the essays so far reprinted appreciate recognized authors. Although she had a special skill at revivifying writers who had long since become inert cells in standard literary histories, she was no enemy to Olympians who had long pleased and awed the many. Arranged chronologically, her papers would make a history of English fiction better than most, although her comprehension of the past was tempered by concern with the current situation and the possibilities of further development or intelligent change.

Some of her most famous papers, like "Mr. Bennett and Mrs. Brown" and "Modern Fiction," survey deficiencies in Galsworthy, Bennett, and Wells as a way of defining her own problems as a novelist. Despising mere facts, she tried to say that a character's half-conscious memories are more real than his income. She did not admit that a novelist who imagines memories is reporting facts no less than a novelist who imagines bank accounts. But her argument went beyond Bennett to undercut most of the earlier novelists also. Both in her critical essays and in her major novels she was less concerned to deny fact than to protest against conventional arrangements of fact. From self-observation, from a Bergsonian sense of the past enduring in the present, from David Hume (quoted by her father as declaring reason "nothing but a wonderful and unintelligible instinct in our souls"), and from the new psychology, she concluded that character, as presented in plotted novels, does not exist in life. Nobody is of good or bad character, for character is a literary convention, like a soliloquy or the heroic couplet. Character is a convention designed to make a drama or novel march toward a predictable end. Each of us has a sharp sense of living, of acute pain and sudden joy, but a very blurred sense of continuous progression in time. Life is not a series of gig lamps, she said, but a luminous halo.

Although her critical papers did not stress her distrust, she distrusted ratiocination: This happened because that happened. She would avoid attempts to prove. She would say instead: This one perceived while that one felt. She could have found the purloined letter and the gold bug's treasure by instinct.

Time and space, declared in her heyday to be psychologically as well as mathematically relative, had been put to conventional order by reason and further codified for storytelling. In Mrs. Woolf's novels, as Joan Bennett admits, critics can notice "that her flowers bloom at impossible times and in impossible places; that her champagne bottles can be opened with corkscrews, that Claridges stands where no Londoner has ever found it." She distrusted the mind of a novelist who studies maps too closely. When she comments on the work of a friend, we see even more clearly what elements she is struggling to exclude from her own fiction. In a review of E. M. Forster now available in *The Death of the Moth*, she finds it notable, and a little curious, that Forster should show the effects of fashion on his characters, that he takes sides "in the human conflict," that he has messages for us, and that he makes Mrs. Moore too realistically a nice old lady for the reader to accept equally her symbolic function as sibyl.

He ought to show more delight in "the beauty or the interest of things as they are."

The seventh selection from her literary journalism to be published, *Contemporary Writers*, enables her to tell posterity why certain Edwardian and Georgian novelists have not survived. Before writing *Jacob's Room* she explained why the "realism" in Dorothy Richardson's handling of human consciousness had to be dislodged by a flow of impressions that would be more selective, more clearly graded as to moral value, and more smartly paced.

She went from reviewing to fiction by way of the essay. Between the two wars she trembled for sick Europe, but she retained faith in the personal essay, where contrived personality half finds and half devises an individual style. Most people who trembled for Europe gave up the essay for dead. Holding no college degree, Mrs. Woolf offered long essays under the mask of an amateur in *Orlando* (1928), *A Room of One's Own* (1929), *Flush* (1933), and *Three Guineas* (1938), along with shorter essays. These, if any, are her "Bloomsbury" books. Each of these recreations helped her recuperate from the novel preceding it. The first two also gave her time to mull over *The Waves*, which she then thought of as The Moths.

Orlando: A Biography traces the chief transmutations in English literature and manners from about 1588 to 1928. It anticipates *Between the Acts*. Orlando is a long-lived writer of a noble line— recognizable as the Sackville family. He lived so long that in youth he wrote a five-act tragedy as rough as *Gorboduc*, became a duke and an ambassador under Charles II, changed sex in Turkey, and thereafter became more modest of her brain and more vain of her person. Of course she sought euphony in the company of Addison and Pope, but she found Defoe's kind of peo-

ple even more congenial. She survived the brain-soaking damp
of the nineteenth century with so much reserve strength that she
observed at last with the quickness and sharpness of Victoria
Sackville-West. Mrs. Hilbery in *Night and Day* is the grand-
daughter of a composite Romantic poet; Orlando, a composite of
all English authors, is also a battleground of the sexes, a treaty
between the sexes, a caricature of his/her creator, and a study
in heritage. Orlando carries ancestral genes through many
changes in the nation's manners and accordant changes in literary style. The book is a fantasia on several of Mrs. Woolf's favorite themes, such as "the sixty or seventy different times
which beat simultaneously in every normal human system."
Combining the effects of Bergson's duration or flux with Jung's
racial memory, Orlando is a contemporary conscious of the androgynous past that lives inside as she/he perceives and writes
on any given day.

A Room of One's Own urges young women to gain financial in-
dependence. Its argument was already obsolete, but no reader of
its descriptive passages will doubt that college men savored par-
tridges while college women gulped prunes. Its prose is the kind
of partridge that college freshmen should be led to savor instead
of naked lunches. The force of mind that organized its simplici-
ties hits with a sharp whack.

Flush, with the same subtitle as *Orlando*, parodies popular biography. Through the nose of a spaniel known to readers of
Victorian letters, the book sniffs briefly at Flush's first mistress,
Mary Russell Mitford, and then shows what it would do to a
dog to be loved by Elizabeth Barrett before and after her elope-
ment with Robert Browning. Affection imbues even the factual
notes. Besides photographs, the first London edition includes
four drawings by Vanessa Bell, who also designed the informa-

tive dust jackets for her sister's novels. Never buy a Woolf novel without its dust jacket.

Some reviewers lamented the whimsy of *Flush*. In *Three Guineas* some detected bad temper. It answers a question that had been put to the author: What can women do to prevent war? The answer appears in 220 icy pages, 124 notes and references, and five devastating photographs of men attired as archbishop, judge, don, herald, and general. Since neither the dullest nor the brightest girl in England ever enriched the playing fields of Eton, how could women acquire the disciplines that purport to explain men's motives? As her strongest contribution the author offered the second of her three guineas to help the daughters of uneducated men enter the professions. The insistence on uneducated fathers, as a way of giving civilization a fresh start, is as shrewd as the financial manipulations of Keynes. The cruel aptness of the photographs combines two strands—a fine sense of that art, as represented in *Victorian Photographs of Famous Men and Fair Women* (1926), edited by Mrs. Woolf and Roger Fry, and the pleasure in hoaxing that had made Virginia Stephen one of six who boarded a flagship at Weymouth in the guise of an Abyssinian prince with his retinue. All of her longer essays skirt parody and hoax as deflationary and disdainful forms of social criticism.

Having proved herself the loyal daughter of a knighted biographer by frequent commentary on the problems of biography, she was asked to write the official life of a close friend. The embarrassed result, *Roger Fry* (1940), is a kind of anti-essay in its chronological march and its astringency of style. Selective in its facts, it touches Fry's mind only in the quotations, which are richer than her commentary dares to be. Fearing her own possible indiscretions, she tried to make Fry reveal more of himself, as an autobiographer collaborating with her, than the material permits. As Fry denied that aesthetic emotion is ever moral, and is so quoted in the book, we probably have Mrs. Woolf's sense of her own work when she chooses a less distinctive side of Fry's essays on art, where "morality and conduct," she says, "even if they are called by other names, are present; eating and drinking and love-making hum and murmur on the other side of the page." Something like the "significant form" named by Clive Bell and independently described by Fry had replaced conventional plot in *Jacob's Room*. Fry's and Bell's advocacy of the post-impressionist painters, like the group's devotion to Wagner's Ring cycle and Keynes's introduction of the ballerina Lopokova as his bride, brought the techniques of other arts into Virginia Woolf's novels, but her life of Fry is one of several kinds of evidence that she raided other arts less to borrow techniques than to give analogous feeling. Form gave feeling.

Her attention to memoirs, strengthened by her interest in levels of consciousness, had a better issue in a work of her own choosing, her diary. In the selections so far published, a writer speaks to herself as honestly as she possibly can. Such honesty gives pain to most readers. If she feels that a novel in progress somehow hedges the "truth" in order to create a "whole vision," she may continue to hedge in the novel, but she says so in the diary. Its pages record the torment of caring what every friend, friendly rival, and enemy thinks of novels that can be allowed only the one shape that her inmost being creates and approves. She liked being liked because she wouldn't change if she could.

While the diary explored in secret and her second novel worried itself with fictional convention, she published spurts of promising experiment. She wrote and hand-printed two stories with her husband in 1917. From the same Hogarth Press they issued pieces by Forster, Eliot, Graves, Read, and Katherine

Mansfield, among others. As the press grew, their list included translations from the depth psychologists of Vienna.

A wag has said that the short story advanced beyond Chekhov when sophisticated editors began destroying the first and last pages of stories before publication. Mrs. Woolf did not wait for the editors. She chose quiet episodes as seen by impressible observers. She went inside sensitive minds and slackened the brake of the superego. Yet in nearly all her stories sensibility is outrun by humor. In "An Unwritten Novel," the *I* who emits the words is a novelist less troubled by her (or his) misjudgment and misrepresentation of the central character than by the inappropriateness of rhododendrons needed for a "fling of red and white" in a crucial scene. We get three levels: Minnie's story, her story as a novelist distorts it, and the process of turning distortion into unique balance. This piece, along with five others from *Monday or Tuesday* (1921), was reprinted by Leonard Woolf in *A Haunted House and Other Short Stories* (1944), which includes also similar pieces from later years, when her humor of image and phrase had been communicated to Elizabeth Bowen, Katherine Anne Porter, and Eudora Welty, to name three who heard. Their work, by what it changes, can make us notice what seemed essential in her influence and what did not. All of them exploit and dramatize character more than she does.

Above all, the stories helped establish a new set of conventions for fiction. In her novels after 1919, plot gives up the Aristotelian rungs of suspense for a subdued nexus of questions answered only by implication as the psychological circumstances unfold. As action is seldom resolved, the reader learns not to ask questions stimulated by his familiarity with Fielding, Dickens, and Conrad. He begins to ask instead about the "gigantic old nail" that appears to the registering mind of the story "The Mark on the Wall." The submerged author, who tries or pre-

tends not to interfere, guides by manipulation rather than asser-
tion. Briefly, about 1920, Mrs. Woolf must have thought she
had learned not to interfere. For many novelists between World
Wars I and II, effacement of the author led to ambiguity as a
tactic to hide moral indecision. Mrs. Woolf, although she did
not avoid this weakness, is saved from the worst dilemma of ef-
faced narration by the value she places on tolerance. Until you
can bear uncertainty, her work says, you have an insufficient
tolerance for our human condition. Without deliberately avoid-
ing moral judgment, she is trying to put the reader in the novelist's chair. The initial principle behind her method was fidelity
to the uncertainties of judgment in life, at least for judges decently tolerant. Even the character prejudicially named Miss
Kilman enjoys the advantage of our uncertainty that Mrs. Dalloway is right to hate her.

Although the first two novels belong to Mrs. Woolf's apprenticeship, *The Voyage Out* (1915) is the novel of a beginner already
sturdy. It handles indistinctly the major elements of plot and
theme, but it shows attention to degrees of awareness, appreciation of selected detail, care with metaphor, and skill at aphorism
and glancing satire. The new novelist had an almost Dickensian
ear for stray talk. "I look strong," says a Mrs. Elliot, "because of
my colour; but I'm not; the youngest of eleven never is." The
scenes are buxom. Conversations last up to 3,000 words—long
enough for *Middlemarch*. The opposition of Ridley Ambrose,
scholar, and Willoughby Vinrace, shipowner, leads to other
contrasts. Richard Dalloway, who embodies statecraft, is
overactive in pursuit of Rachel. His wife makes calculatedly silly
remarks: "Some dogs are awful bores, poor dears." At the end of
the voyage on a cargo ship to a South American island, a party
goes upriver to observe primitive life. These two voyages, like
two novelettes by Conrad put end to end, provide the setting for

the life voyage of Rachel Vinrace, who defies convention by enjoying her first kiss. She battles in her virginal way against the
decorous and intellectual society that lets her out only by death.
She dies in the heart of the dim emotional light she has followed. It is not clear that social aridity killed her, but the com-
menting author has limited our regard for the intellectuals and
public servants who will return to the port of origin.

In style, method, size, and shape, *Jacob's Room* would be the
first distinctly Woolfian novel, but *The Voyage Out* asks right off
her characteristic questions about the relation of the upper middle classes to life itself, their own lives as well as all others. Like
Mrs. Dalloway and *Between the Acts*, it ponders the relationship of
civilized consciousness to the prehistoric past that our consciousness sits trembling on. And it pleads with suffering and love to
explain themselves.

Night and Day (1919) comes from a craftsman looking before
and after. It updates Jane Austen's heroines, gives them George
Eliot's topics of conversation, and hurries them through London
streets. The intermittent satire against such types as humorless
suffragettes and crumb-headed men trying to guide suffragettes
must have seemed at least keener than Gissing's. Nothing in
Gissing, and nothing in *The Voyage Out*, called for so many fresh
metaphors and surprising adjectives as the thoughts and dreams
of the new young people occupied night and day in London.
Katharine Hilbery ponders reality as an image-making Kant.
Not systems—there is no Hegel in her—just reality. The creator
who put her on paper was trying to find a way to show in fiction
what life feels like. To show, not tell. From Dostoevsky come il-
logical conduct and contradictions of personality, such as the
mingling of love and hate that will deepen from *Mrs. Dalloway*
on. Symbols to be central in later novels, the lighthouse and the
breaking wave, enter surreptitiously. The novelist had yet to

remove the large scaffolding of external fact erected by the earliest novelists and maintained by the Edwardians. Her second
novel, like her first, was longer than any she would write in the
next twenty years. The characters confess to each other as often
as Dostoevsky's. They spend more time than Galsworthy's rid-
ing omnibuses and looking for cabs.

The later novels tempt us to be flippant about the kind of
novel *Night and Day* represents. The plot, moving to a happy
ending through bumps of suspense and near melodrama, is a
love-go-round. Mary Datchet loves Ralph who loves Katharine
who is engaged to William who loves Cassandra. The cycle ends
when Cassandra, in Chapter 29, takes William. At the end, only
Mary is left to work at social causes. There is some talk of
cohabitation without marriage, but propriety wins. Such conventions of subject and technique do not prevent subtlety. In a
perfectly timed chapter, when Mary tells Katharine who it is
that Ralph loves, the artistic point of the scene transcends convention: Katharine sees for the first time, in Mary, what being
in love is like. When she has comprehended love, and found that
she has it, she is still wary of conventional marriage. If obedient
girls marry in 1919 just because heroines written into novels by
their parents always tie down a mate and end the story with a
proper knot, then she had rather be marked down as a sulker.
She sulks until a romantic instinct inside tells her that Ralph is
ready for a conventional ending. Sensitive, fumbling Katharine
seems to be the heroine, and seems to engage a large part of the
author, but it is possible to see all the people finally destined to
happiness as indeed finally cleared away in order to let lonely
Mary stay at her feminist post with us.

That Mrs. Woolf admired the dedication of feminists but
stood back from their typewriter-and-placard absurdities comes
out partly in the analysis of Katharine and partly in the blurred

allegiance that allows Mary to suffer more than the heroine. Although she gave up trying to make readers sympathize with dedicated typists, she continued through all her later novels to say how employers looked from inside the heads of charwomen. She almost got away with it in *The Years*, where she could give several different servants a page or two at a time, but her determination to sympathize with those who kneel in prayer is not half so touching as the persistence of her puzzled sympathy with those who kneel to work.

Her first two novels are not uninteresting of their kind. Weaker novels of the same kind are still being written. But their author had looked into her heart and had collaborated with the past. Hereafter she would look into a secret part of her head and collaborate with the future.

Jacob's Room (1922) has interested literary historians because it makes new departures, particularly in the design of a rhythmic shorthand to expose streams of consciousness. Memories, thoughts, and sub-thoughts blend with impressions of external objects. With this novel the devices of narrative become at once more concentrated and more indirect. In the first two novels we watch Rachel Vinrace and Katharine Hilbery grow into persons. The third is a *Bildungsroman* of a different kind. Jacob Flanders is the learner, but we seem to see him mostly through the women—and one or two young men—who have known and revered him. In one focus the book is an elegy for Virginia Stephen's brother Thoby who died in 1906 and for young men of similar grace (like Rupert Brooke) who died in the war of 1914–18. After showing the effect of the paragon Jacob on others, the novel closes on an empty room. From another focus, we see the experiences and episodes that make up Jacob's being. Submergence of the narrator leads to stress on what the characters think of each other and how one responds to the acts or remarks of the next. A shuddering effect resulted when Mrs. Woolf submerged at once the narrator and the consciousness of the central character. Yet this device, germinal to the denser method of *The Waves*, leaves Jacob with a charm that would have worn off if he had meditated in our faces from childhood to grave. In short, Jacob's author is infinitely wiser than Dorothy Richardson and other streamers-of-consciousness.

Of the fourteen sections, the first two seem preliminary. They depict Jacob's widowed mother living among attentive neighbors in the seaside town of Scarborough, without any heavy hints that the boy Jacob has a mind worth looking into. They begin discreetly the picture of a community that is continued indiscreetly, with the same rhythms of speech, in *Under Milk Wood*. When Mrs. Woolf herself took up this unfinished business of the provincial community in her last novel, her outlook and inlook converged in a style of quicker strokes and firmer line. From Jacob's reaction to a crab and a skull, we imagine how he saw the adults around him, but we use other eyes than his to see them as persons in their own right. There was life before Jacob mattered.

Jacob's Room, denoting a succession of rooms, covers a lot of ground. When the book came out, critical praise of a single Jamesian mind registering impressions, praise that reached its apotheosis in *The Craft of Fiction* by Percy Lubbock, encouraged novelists to be intense rather than omniscient. Even here, where Mrs. Woolf begins to emulate the linguistic concentration of poetry, she resists the temptation to be timidly intense. She retains the Victorian virtue of scope. She enters the minds of most of the named characters, in this experimental novel as well as in those before and after it. If she thinks she understands a character well enough to include him, she sympathizes enough to report his thoughts and feelings. Of the dozens of minds entered, whether or not their owners are made personally acquainted, most are sharing or exchanging impressions. In consequence, the mind entered is usually either a general mind or a representative local mind.

All the mental activity occurs within a firmly drawn external world. The method of drawing is impressionistic, sometimes expressionistic when the author sympathizes fully with her observers, but topography controls the impressions. Except for *Virginia Woolf's London*, by Dorothy Brewster, critics have studied time in her novels at the expense of space. The past lives in the minds of the characters, but London lives too. After Jacob went up to Cambridge in October, 1906, we get in turn a palpitating old woman in a train, scenes in undergraduate rooms, vacation on a sailboat in the Scilly Isles, streets and spires in London, and the great wheel of desks and eccentrics in the reading room of the British Museum, where Mrs. Woolf herself often worked. When Jacob climbs the Acropolis, description brings the reader along. In keeping with the new morality that followed the war, Mrs. Woolf takes us with Jacob to visit whores and whorehouses, but without blunt language that repelled her in Joyce and Lawrence.

Night and Day had coddled and celebrated the sentiment of romantic love. Having an unromantic man as protagonist brought a greater stringency and made Mrs. Woolf face as an author the sword between the sexes. The isolation of individuals, a wakeful theme in the first two novels, is worsened when the conventional goal of marriage drops away. Not individuals but fragments of an ideal whole, "split apart into trousers or moulded into a single thickness," become isolated by gender as Jacob leaves behind various kinds and conditions of women in his attempt to build a room against the world.

In *Jacob's Room* problems of technique remained. For one, the revolution was not severe enough. In Chapter 7, for example, there are a few too many bits of conversation. Not every careful detail in other chapters has become a symbol reverberating beyond an individual mind. In some of its physical manifestations, "Jacob's room" does not expand to mean the form he gave to his life. Even though a point is being repeated from *The Voyage Out*, that life flows before and after an individual joins it, the reader's attention is misdirected at Scarborough toward an actual ocean that provides work for adults. Several analogies— the march along a tremendous argument, a blind woman singing a wild sinful song beside the wall of a bank (introducing in *Jacob's Room* a passage on the segregation of social classes)—will become compact, manifold, and multiform in later novels. Meanwhile, this author did not choose to give up any aspect of reality.

In addition to troublesome vestiges, experiment introduced problems of its own. In the new economy, to take a small but nagging problem, alliteration sometimes makes sentences too rich. Overrichness will linger to burden *The Waves*. But there were larger hazards. As creator of the show, after the Thackerayan manner abhorrent to Henry James and others who believe in airtight illusion, the narrative voice inserts little jokes about the novel. The author does not pretend to nonexistence as the creating artist, but only to nonexistence as judge. More than halfway through the book, in the middle of a sentence, the guiding voice cries, "oh, here is Jacob's room." The cry arises at least partly out of a stubborn belief in the interpolated essay that is being interrupted in mid-sentence. Symbols bind the characters in *Jacob's Room*, but the author does not trust them to remind the reader how hard life is to understand. She inserts essays that are readable enough, but are too many, and too many of them worry over life. The insertions both renovate the practice of

Fielding and innovate in their own context, but they do not please those pleased by her later intensity of symbol. Despite a novelty of method beyond anything attempted by Forster, Jacob's room had not answered the objections she raised against her friend's work. She, too, had failed to achieve Ibsen's perfect fusion of actual and symbolic. Even so, *Jacob's Room* should survive through the force of its creative energy and the charm of its hero, its vignettes, and its topography.

Suddenly in *Mrs. Dalloway* (1925) the central character has no circumference. For the next four novels some of the characters perceived by the central consciousness are enclosed by a bounding line, but the author seems to look at some one character from the core inside. Beginners often produce a similar effect, but Mrs. Woolf was seeking a center for the thin-blown glass balloon of complete vision. She had a greater and greater hunger to convey her sense of life's essence, which could put any one mind at the center as well as the next. Even Proust, she believed, had not gone as far as a novelist might in awaking readers to the quality of life itself. Hoping to share with poets this power of awakening, she wished also to prove fiction generally capable of conveying essence along with appearance. As she wrote enviously of Jane Austen in "How It Strikes a Contemporary," in *The Common Reader*, "To believe that your impressions hold good for others is to be released from the cramp and confinement of personality." Not only Mrs. Dalloway but several of the minor characters overflow the boundaries of observed conduct and presumed motive to take part in a larger awareness. Scenes in flashback would have been too rigid and too divisive. The past is sometimes mixed, sometimes fused, in the luminous halo of the present. We follow mental images from one person to another, either physically near at the moment or emotionally near in the past. Events of the past repeated as metaphors for the present can take the breath: "The sheet was stretched and the bed narrow. She had gone up into the tower alone and left them blackberrying in the sun." If *Jacob's Room* shows cinematic cutting and fading, *Mrs. Dalloway* borrows from montage and superimposed frames.

The intense immediacy of the method has its counterfoil in ironic distance. Through contrasts of awareness, we find Mrs. Dalloway an unreliable register who gives off increasingly wrong clues. The method is valid. We learn of her coldness when she herself remembers her moment of love for Sally Seton. In *Jacob's Room* the author did not mean flatly that "every woman is nicer than any man," but she intended her words to convey as much of the point as she could get away with. In *Mrs. Dalloway* only the various characters mean something by the words attributed to their lips or minds. The reader cannot know the past precisely, but he can know it better, because four minds remember the same past differently.

As evidence of a guiding hand, the external world changes little from one observer to another. Several characters see the same car of state, with similar implications for each (but not identical) built into what is seen. The most fluid of the eight novels, *Mrs. Dalloway* retains much grit of the senses.

In a preface to the Modern Library edition, the author denied that this novel was written by any method to work out any scheme of ideas. Although she mentioned no names, she meant that she was not explicating or illustrating Bergson's *élan vital*, Freud's death-wish, or anybody's theory of relativity. But one conviction, fairly constant in her work, inevitably underlies a novel with the form this novel achieved: all of us are parts of one fluid life and therefore of one another. You can try to know other consciousnesses by examining your own. Readers had come to expect novelists to tell what it was like to walk past a given corner on a certain day at half past five. Mrs. Woolf asks what it *means* to say that Mrs. D. was alive on that corner. To the question "What is life?" she was seeking an answer not previously given through a novelist's art. Yet she sought a novelist's answer, not a philosopher's or a psychologist's. It is not that she ignored Bergson, Freud, or other writers who similarly influenced the thought of her time, but that she transformed and exploited without propagating doctrines or studying details.

As in *Ulysses*, which she admired but disliked, the action of *Mrs. Dalloway* occurs within a single day in carefully designated locales of a loved city. In all minds the past imbues today. Clarissa Dalloway, whom readers had encountered in *The Voyage Out* and in detached episodes such as "The New Dress," makes preparations for the party she will give at the end of the day. She is now fifty-two. Her husband Richard, going about the chilly business of Parliament, thinks from time to time of returning home to tell his wife he loves her. Their daughter Elizabeth spends part of the day in the clutches of a sanctimonious predator, Doris Kilman. Shaking free, Elizabeth rides a bus beyond the boundaries of ordinary life in the West End. As the exemplar of youth in the novel, she offers some hope of spiritual adventure to match in time her physical excursion.

By memory and reflection, the principal characters in her mother's circle bring into this important day the past they shared with vital Sally Seton, who otherwise appears only at the party. Peter Walsh, who loved Clarissa, recollects his subsequent pursuit of women even as he pursues one casually today. Near Regent's Park he watched an old spring welling up from aeons before London rose above the sea, an antediluvian life force still surging through an old woman who sings lustily a coarse song of love. (New meanings have accrued since her appearance in *Jacob's Room*.) Peter envisions nature as the eternal feminine coming to devour him. Clarissa, meanwhile, identifies femininity with intuition. Masculinity appears in the novel as mechanical time, the precise clocks of the physicians in Harley Street subdividing and shredding the June day. The psychiatrist Sir William Bradshaw, by dissecting a deranged mind, murders it. In opposition to narrow rationality and dissection, the leaden circles of Big Ben dissolve as they encircle the psychological awareness of living time. Septimus Warren Smith, a shell-shocked veteran who leaps to his death, has already defeated time and reality by his derangement. Smith was introduced during the composition of the novel, we are told in the Preface, to fulfill the theme of suicide originally assigned to Clarissa. At the end, her party survives the echo of his death. In the novel as completed, Smith does not die vicariously for her; rather, shallow though she is, she dies vicariously with him. Mention of his death by a guest at her party strikes her as uncivil, but even a born hostess is capable of feeling death-in-life. The novel reaches beyond its several symbols of death, such as the black car of state and a drawn shade, to affirm the puzzling richness of moments in life. If "death-in-life" is a term too theological for Mrs. Woolf's meaning, "death-wish" has a denotation too technical for the psychospiritual state she portrays.

Despite her care to avoid "the twilight world of theory," certain liberal doctrines show through. The commercial skywriting is witnessed by dull commoners for whom the Dalloways, Whitbreads, and Bradshaws have made themselves officially responsible. Bradshaw, who is far worse than Peter Walsh in the evil of trying to possess others, is decidedly second to Miss Kilman. Voluble against wealth, she is a version of the unctuous middlebrow who disrupts the natural allegiance of the highbrow and the working masses. Sensitivity means sensitivity to what others feel. Unlike Elizabeth's captor, the Smiths are deputized to speak for all victims of the system. Lucrezia Smith, lonely and silenced, an alien in the city and dependent on a madman, performs her function in the pattern without losing her identity. How could we ever have thought either that Virginia Woolf lacked interest in character or that she could not portray it?

The author of *Mrs. Dalloway* had felt her way to a pattern acceptable to such reason as she would wish to find responsive. The methods of her success, although they include the frequently named "poetic prose" and "preciosity," include also deft characterization, sensitive impressionism, severe selection, juxtaposition, careful evocation, and symbols large and small. The leaden circles, Peter's vision, and even the car of state tell of life. Peter's habit of opening and shutting a pocketknife remains a mere trick of excited nerves, but the intimidating car aids us in evaluating Clarissa's self-congratulation that the Prime Minister chats among her guests. The characters all share the physical London of the day, the skywriting above them, the gurgling origins of Peter's vision, and a kinship deeper than the social and intellectual diversity that sunders them. More triumphantly than *The Voyage Out*, the fourth novel puts death in its place.

Although serious writing had always strained her nerves far beyond their median state of violin tautness, the novels got harder and harder to write. She chose not to impose form intellectually. She wrote, revised, rewrote, and revised again, in the expectation that a shape would emerge acceptable to her feeling for form. Mind was to recognize form, but not to determine it.

The thronging symbols of *Mrs. Dalloway* reveal in the finished form something of the intuitive method. Life is put to order more squarely by the firm central image of *To the Lighthouse* (1927). Mrs. Ramsay, at fifty, effortlessly presides over the house and grounds in western Scotland where she has come for the summer, as usual, with her academic husband, their half-dozen children, and an equal number of house guests. Mellower than the diplomatic hostess in London for whom distress underlies stress, Mrs. Ramsay is the maternal hostess in repose. The immediate objective for the children is to climb into a boat and reach the lighthouse nearby in "the Isles of Skye." Mr. Ramsay in the meantime heroically explores the road from A to his own philosophic position of Q or R, with the ideal philosophic goal of Z. Just when he chuckles selfishly over the thought of old Hume grown too fat to think, his wife grows skeptical over her own instinctive words, "We are in the hands of the Lord." Even the child Nancy gets experimental evidence that the world is will and idea as she makes minnows into sharks and cuts off the sun by a movement of her hand. The larger mysteries allow us to keep asking lesser questions. Will Minta Doyle, aged twenty-four, catch the childless widower William Bankes? Will Mrs. Ramsay finish before dark the stocking she sits knitting?

Lily Briscoe, trying to paint Mrs. Ramsay as she sees her framed in the window with her youngest child, mirrors the author's own quest. How can you know when lines and forms are balanced and taut? How can you borrow just the right amount from Leonardo and Raphael to make your madonna both unique and true in a world that has mislaid innocence? The second question implies that a copy is not art, that the isolated or found object is not art, that discoveries in art are progressive, and that the disintegration of our world is not too rapid for creative discovery to continue.

In the area of lost innocence, Mr. Ramsay tells his son James authoritatively that it will rain. It rains, which gives the atheist Charles Tansley the pleasure of repeating, "No going to the Lighthouse, James." Part I, "The Window," ends in a moment when reason is surpassed: the madonna cannot say in words that she loves her husband, but she looks it abundantly.

Each adult character has tried in his own way to make time stand still. But in Part II, "Time Passes," nature destroys. Mrs. Ramsay dies in the night. Spiders and decay precede and follow the war. Nature invades men: "The war, people said, had revived their interest in poetry." This section is a sophisticated and philosophic variation on the long views of heightened exposition in Dickens, who was never one of Mrs. Woolf's favorites.

When Mrs. Dalloway would have been sixty, Lily stands at the window and watches James sail toward the lighthouse while she herself tries to encompass both the wonder that Mrs. Ramsay was and the jolt to the nerves that her quiet way often produced. What Mrs. Ramsay was or is, not what she looked like, must be embodied in line, form, and juxtaposed color. Here in Part III, "The Lighthouse," when James finally nears the goal, he realizes that the vision from the mainland was just as much the lighthouse as the paltry thing he sees just beyond the laundry hanging outside it. By dying, Mrs. Dalloway has become somebody envisioned by Lily, who needs most of all to believe that she has painted the best she can. Ineffective personally, Lily as artist may help another Mrs. Ramsay bring guests into such harmony as life affords. Mrs. Ramsay died in a parenthesis, but she is vividly present in the final section.

Mrs. Ramsay's repose inspires Lily's balance of light and shadow, but the novel concerns nature as well as art. "Time Passes," especially, but "The Lighthouse" also is about man's place in nature. Man's love stands within cruelty, not against it. In ordinary life people do not either love or hate as they do in novels, or first love for years and then hate for years as they might in Conrad, or even feel violent love-hate as in Dostoevsky. Mrs. Dalloway should not need to hate Doris Kilman, because we feel enough hate for those we love. Mr. Ramsay's "Damn you" reminds his wife to revere him, even though he pursues truth with an "astonishing lack of consideration for other people's feelings"; but she does wish he would not make James hate him so. In the end it was Mr. Ramsay who forced them to the lighthouse, with James hating his father and urging his sister Cam to fight tyranny till death. In intellect, James has grown enough to see in his father an impersonal wheel on a great wagon rolling over one foot here and another there indiscriminately. Emotionally, he needs more than anything else the praise from his father that he finally gets. Hatred for the husband you love is no more unnatural than loving the Victorian father you hate. The sixth subdivision of the last section, quoted here in its entirety, shows our nature: "Macalister's boy took one of the fish and cut a square out of its side to bait his hook with. The mutilated body (it was alive still) was thrown back into the sea." The only answer is the artist's search for Mrs. Ramsay's calm.

Unlike Forster's Mrs. Wilcox and Mrs. Moore, similarly ripe with intuitive wisdom, Mrs. Ramsay was not to be separated into the woman and the sibyl: no putting off of the person in order to be the great essential Cybele. Genetically, she is a symbiosis combining the author's memory of her mother, with its miscellaneous detail, and the cohesive examples in fiction of the *ewige Weiblich*—except that her saintliness, as Lily saw her, refutes the earthiness of Molly Bloom. Transfer to Lily's canvas prevents the symbol from destroying the symbiosis.

The principle at work is that persons and things can emanate meanings in fiction because they do so in life. If the lighthouse is ultimately a symbol of masculine endeavor, as William York

Tindall suggests in *The Literary Symbol* and many would agree, then James's achievement of manhood is both the paltry thing he sees and a noble arrival at *Z* or *Q* in man's assault on the unknown. (Leslie Stephen, president of the Alpine Club, was the first to climb the Schreckhorn.) The feminine window competes with the masculine probe, but the artistic vision encompasses both within one novel. What the novelist gave up in denying autonomous existence to a symbolic structure she attempted to reclaim through demonstration that artists are androgynous unifiers of what life divides between the sexes. For the androgynous artist, a symbol must not be confined by reason. The successfully symbolic partakes of the multiplicity of the real. When Professor Tindall returned to the lighthouse in *Forces in Modern British Literature*, he noted its suggestions of "God, death, eternity, any absolute, and the goal of all endeavors." To such an absolute the novelist attached a clothesline.

Rationalism comes off second best, but the idealization of Mrs. Ramsay for the benefit of Lily's artistic vision is not the only view afforded. Mrs. Ramsay's daughters see her in a different way, and contrasting passages show her to the reader as inconsistent and contradictory, revering her husband within seconds of hating the inhumanity of his certitude. She is a force for life, yet like Mrs. Dalloway often drawn toward death. At the base of Mr. Ramsay stands Leslie Stephen, author of the *History of English Thought in the Eighteenth Century*, in two volumes with the paragraphs numbered viii.13, etc., as his daughters remembered him. If we come closer to 1927, however, comparison of Leonard Woolf's books of reminiscence with his wife's novels shows as clearly as books can show that the contrast of reasoning and intuition was part of their happy marriage.

The intuitive inconsistencies of Mrs. Dalloway and Mrs. Ramsay seem superior to Bradshaw's science and Ramsay's rea-

son partly because the curling sentences persuade us that fluctu-
ation of impulse is the essence of human consciousness. External
and internal impulses flow together. Description, sensation, and
meditation combine as Mrs. Ramsay serves her guests at dinner:

Here, she felt, putting the spoon down, was the still space that lies
about the heart of things, where one could move or rest; could wait
now (they were all helped) listening; could then, like a hawk which
lapses suddenly from its high station, flaunt and sink on laughter easily,
resting her whole weight upon what at the other end of the table her
husband was saying about the square root of one thousand two hundred
and fifty-three. That was the number, it seemed, on his watch.

For the sampling of consciousness, syntax is impeded. Never,
however, does Mrs. Woolf inventory consciousness. On the side
of realism, the heightened prose was licensed by the psychologists of the unconscious. Its art is indebted to Proust. The sentences fight Galsworthy and Bennett in the name of a truer realism, but more obviously in the name of art. They fight for the
continuing life of prose. The spoon is as fictional as the flaunting
hawk. Both belong to a novel that synthesizes the small dramas
of perseverance and affection instead of analyzing stagy versions
of passion. Mrs. Woolf made these novels realistic in the sense
that they illuminate the lives of their readers. She did not escape
with the naturalists, who describe events that happen to non-
readers. *To the Lighthouse* incorporates plot, not by revealing that
Miss Doyle and Mr. Bankes never married, but by showing, like
Mrs. Dalloway, that the consciousness contains every day the
greatest things that happen to the conscious: growth, friendship,
quarrel, marriage, solitude, aging, death.

    With *The Waves* (1931) Mrs. Woolf dared oblivion. Here she
drove her concrete images and phrase-making as near to abstraction as any novelist has risked driving them. She differentiates
her six central characters by the allusions, attitudes, and meta-

phors of their brief soliloquies, which follow serially throughout
the book, but she imposes a single undifferentiated style on the
consciousness of all six. Even more difficult, the first childish
content of their minds is expressed in an adult language that
conveys what each individual *must* have been like from the
beginning. These early pages press us to accept a theory of the
continuity of personality. One backs off to reconstruct the author's thought: If I, who am bold to explore, liked as a child to
"sink through the green air of the leaves," then Susan must have
liked the adventure, too; whereas Neville, who grew up to love
eighteenth-century France, must as a child have thought, "I hate
dangling things; I hate dampish things." Yet the reader is unable
to distinguish more than the six names before he is immersed in
the central theme that we are all joined in a life of uniform flux.

He does not begin by asking what each of the six experienced
in childhood. What they experienced first is childhood, and
what they experienced next is growth out of it. Friends so different as these experience the same reality. To make this point,
the characters could have lived on different continents, but the
novel comprises also the story of their friendship. This story is
itself "abstract." Their friendship differs only in chance detail
from the loose bonds of others who might seem, both as individuals and as a group, to differ greatly from these. The story of
growing up and aging is no more theirs than ours.

Readers of the earlier novels who recognize familiar episodes
and traits will suspect that the characters are the novelist and
several close friends, but seldom has autobiography been so
rigorously transformed. In *Mrs. Dalloway* physical detail and
reverie coexist; in *To the Lighthouse* they interweave; in *The Waves*
they flow together through prose that has been too close to
lullaby for all critics except those for whom the symbols suffice.

The astrophysicists Arthur Eddington and James Jeans, in

clear prose and pretty analogies, had encouraged a temptation to reconcile wave and quantum theories through parallel histories of ocean, matter, and mental impression. The descriptive interchapters of *The Waves* treat nature as both background and analogy for mind. At dawn the waves emerge. The sun rises, brightens, heats, declines. Birds carry on a life like man's; they sing, circle, swoop, gorge on worms, bloat, and sit silent. (An even smaller creature shares this life in the essay "The Death of the Moth," which belongs in spirit and idea to *The Waves*.) Waves toil forward, change with the tide, and finally break on the shore. The sun searches into a room, brings life to a potted flower there, brings out color, but never overcomes a dark shadow lumped in the far interior. In the "Time Passes" interval of *To the Lighthouse*, the rhythm of the seasons sometimes conforms to the needs of man and sometimes not. In the interchapters of *The Waves* all the analogies press inexorably forward together. Life, though its pattern is a cycle of predictable fluctuations, is made so by the energy of individual efforts. The individual streams of awareness conform to these analogies.

As the soliloquies continue, each of the friends touches the same memories but has his own aspirations. Rhoda has timid but endearing fears. Neville fears disorder. Susan wants love and children. Jinny, less realistically, wants to *give*. She wants to give what Susan wants to share. Bernard, a novelist who perceives in images, seeks to affirm in his stories as Susan to affirm in life. Louis, a cold, precise poet, sees that their soliloquies must be shared if they are to reach the pith of life. To tend toward the abstract, and toward what is called, in *A Writer's Diary*, the mystical, is to be poetic. On the novelistic side, the characters are individuals; on the poetic, where they fall into types, each positive has its negative. As they advance from childhood through youth and on to age, it gradually appears that

it is not persons who are polar opposites, but only qualities ab-
stracted from them. Rhoda, who shares imagination with Bernard, kills herself. Bernard, like Susan but imaginatively, accepts a life of measles, pantries, and nurseries. Within the
common style, speakers anticipate the discrimination of attitudes, symbols, and sensory debris in their minds by saying, I
am Rhoda, I am Louis. Nothing so unnovelistic occurs anywhere else in the Woolf canon. Yet their effort of self-assertion
wins an aesthetic response.

Of course the best training for the required discrimination is
not the stringencies of, for example, Beckett—though Beckett is
a good trainer—but Mrs. Woolf's earlier novels, beginning with
the earliest. Old themes, images, and human relationships return here. The recurring motif of an earlier novel will anticipate
a leitmotif in this one, if not specifically then in kind. Allusions
to Byron in the novels had always meant "mothlike impetuosity
dashing itself against hard glass," a meaning pointed out to Bernard by Neville. The reader who has learned to ask about the
"gigantic old nail" instead of murder and mayhem in Mrs.
Woolf's fiction is prepared to know Rhoda better as soon as she
says in childhood, "All my ships are white."

In the other novels, including those after *The Waves*, separable
elements can be admired. I would contend that scenes, devices
for characterization, perceptions, evocations, and acquiescences
should be valued for their own merits in all the novels but one.
The Waves, unorthodox or inadequate in all the elements relied
on by Scott and Balzac, either succeeds as a unified book
(whether novel or not) or it fails.

The book celebrates imaginative fulfillment within the salt
estranging sea of everyday life. It goes further, to deny that a
sea in which we are all waves can be altogether estranging. All
the waves hurry after one another toward the shore, separate

and ephemeral but joined by the common toil of loneliness and love. We live also, says Louis, in "the protective waves of the ordinary." Friends by circumstance, diverse in their adult lives, the six are both measured and enlarged by interchange within the group. Bernard is stronger for being able to say "we" have come through. All the speakers, or meditators, admired Percival, a model of action who died in India. No man of words, no receiver of sensations or speaker of dreams, he has no place among the six. If reality "is one thing," he was unaware of reality. His otherness determines his place in the other lives, and assigns him a place in the novel. He is as necessary to the contemplative as they are for him. His life suffices itself, but only the contemplative can know why.

"Now to sum up," says Bernard. "Now to explain to you the meaning of my life." As with the opening of the book he stresses at its close the solemnity of childhood. He implores old nurses to squeeze no cold sponge over a new body. But he praises also the dignity of youth, maturity, and age. He speaks to a near stranger in a restaurant where he has been meditating alone, but the relationship is that of novelist to reader. The meaning he promised is that the globe of life has walls of thinnest air. It cannot be presented whole and intact. Nevertheless, out of material that is at best no firmer than a bunch of grapes, the artist can shape a sphere to throw against the face of death. His art concentrates the random defiance of death that enables all who reflect to rise above the carrion we eat and above the monotonous bills that waiters and grocers present us with. "Against you I will fling myself, unvanquished and unyielding, O Death!" This rhetoric and this passion he throws against the rhetoric of the final interchapter: *The waves broke on the shore.*

Mrs. Woolf's diary shows that she suffered greatly in writing *The Years* (1937). As if the previous novel had drained all the poetry out of her, *The Years* illustrates too literally the distinction between the precise poet and the blurred novelist who stuffs his work with the impurities of life. A long novel containing an inventory of responses to change in general morals from 1880 to the time of writing, it defied the ordering of mental facts by intuition. Through the eyes of one generation in two families, the reader observes episodes dominated by three successive generations. Bertrand and Louis changed as waves in a changing ocean, but the years merely wash away the sand that in early life abraded Eleanor Partiger and Kitty Malone. We get rational summaries of what the characters think of each other and of the personal situation on a representative day. In the details of their reactions we hear, smell, and sometimes enjoy London as the physical setting.

Despite the historical detail, closer packed if less joyous than the detail in *Orlando*, *The Years* is of all the novels the most vulnerable to the charge of preciosity. Humor is kept on a tight leash. *The Waves*, like an encephalograph, discovered a style that reports at least one aspect of inner vibration. *The Years*, asking for comparison with other family novels about changing mores, seems to report snippets of trivia in conversation and thought. The methods of *Jacob's Room* are here mounted in a conventional frame. In a compromise between Dorothy Richardson and Samuel Richardson, the novelist has refrained from banking the natural effluvia of these minds. In consequence, one scene gives the flavor of a political meeting without any hint of the subjects argued over. *The Years* fights fascism, not by any equivalent of the pleading elsewhere for a private room where books in Greek will have replaced the sewing machine, but by the subdued hope for freedom in personal lives felt by the central character, Eleanor Partiger. Over against the continuum of symbolic impressions in the preceding novels, we get such mechanical devices as the analogical transition from one scene to another later exploited in Sartre's tetralogy *Les Chemins de la liberté*. " 'That's Eleanor,' said North"—and the reader is taken to the other end of the telephone call to see what Eleanor is like this year. The telephone call is merely a dramatized version of the author's remark, "oh, here is Jacob's room." Conceived as a way of adding further strength to a series of non-stories where everything human happens, *The Years* became a complex story in which nothing much occurs.

In theme, the novel concerns a generation oppressed by its elders but finally able to recognize in its children possibilities of freedom that it has itself fumbled for and missed. Eleanor's pleasure in freedom is vicarious. Victorian methods of smothering vitality, described indirectly in *Flush*, metaphorically in *Orlando*, and with all the powers of fiction in *To the Lighthouse*, are enacted here in small dramas. Colonel Partiger takes time off from his mistress to crush the spirits of his children. Similarly Mrs. Malone says to Kitty, "You could help your father if it bores you helping me." The generation of Kitty and Martin still cheats waiters and housemaids, but unlike the parents who left them the Great War as legacy, they feel guilt. They know that it is fear in individuals that separates nations. It is not that Eleanor, Kitty, and brisk Sara mellow; they emerge. In the final section, called "Present Day," they can sympathize with Sophocles' Antigone without risk that Victorian parents will bury them alive. Sara, the last of the vital *S*'s, is free of the childbearing that meant fulfillment for Sally and Susan in earlier novels. She gets others to tolerate those among the young who do not love members of the opposite sex. On the foundation of this tolerance, Eleanor tries to build hope for a millennium of freedom. *The Years* shares with *The Waves* the theme of effort through adversity, but disaster hangs heavy, even heavier than in the next novel, completed after Hitler had struck.

Between the Acts, left without final revision and published posthumously in 1941, deserves high rank for its diversity in both matter and method. Beyond question it combines more successfully than *The Years* the techniques of *Mrs. Dalloway* with the methods of an older realism. At Pointz Hall we meet the Olivers (whose ancestors have occupied the Hall only 120 years), scan the servants (whose ancestors came out of the primeval mud before bricks were dreamed of), and learn the names and occupations of dozens of neighbors assembled for the annual pageant. In the village just beyond our view Mrs. Sands, the cook, has a nephew Billy who is cheeky to the butcher; even the manservant Candish, a stuffed man, had a mother who was one of the Perrys. The novelist puts before us the text of the pageant as performed. Its parodies lack Joyce's transforming power, but their objective existence avoids what Mrs. Woolf called the egoism of *Ulysses.* She describes the movements, sounds, responses, and failures to respond as the author and director of the pageant, Miss La Trobe, marshals the ineptness of the county to realize her artistic intentions. After the flagging of the previous novel, vitality has returned to the method of showing the chief assembled characters from inside and also from inside the acquaintances and intimates who study them. Yet the external frame of time and place is so stable that this novel, unlike *Mrs. Dalloway,* could have been written from an outline.

From Mrs. Woolf's accustomed delicacy the style turns as if toward Gertrude Stein: "The baby had been in the cot. The cot was empty." Complacent vulgarity and "the jolly human heart" have a glorious spokesman in the vivid Mrs. Manresa. Action and symbol palpitate together when Giles Oliver bloodies his boot by stamping on a snake, attracts thereby Mrs. Manresa, and immediately shares her lust. The lyric impulse, which dilated with each novel through *The Waves*, narrows to the consciousness of Giles's wife, Isabella, except for the quotations, paraphrases, and parodies that imbue the pageant and flash through other minds. In all the novels characters quote apt poetry. Mr. Ramsay opens himself to shout from Tennyson, "Some one had blundered." But *Between the Acts* widens the range of verse called upon and multiplies the meanings for the individual consciousness, especially of popular ditties and nursery rhymes, which are rooted in the origins of the race.

The forthrightness seems to address, with indulgence but without condescension, those who had been defeated by *The Waves*. When beginning *The Waves*, Mrs. Woolf complained to her diary: "How difficult not to go on making 'reality' this and that, whereas it is one thing." Reality, which is one thing in *The Waves*, is this and that, as well as one thing, in *Between the Acts*. In this novel structure seems slack, through a skill equal to the art that made *Mrs. Dalloway* seem kaleidoscopic. When gossamer Mrs. Swithin says, "The Chinese, you know, put a dagger on the table and that's a battle," Mrs. Manresa interrupts for the common reader: "Yes, they bore one stiff." Partly, we can say, the author had developed a Shakespearean knack of disguising finesse.

More important, *Between the Acts*, is a hearty, communal, and national work. In *The Voyage Out*, Londoners make an excursion from London. All but one will return. Those who hope to reach the lighthouse leave London and the university towns for the summer. The villagers in the final novel make London their commercial, administrative, and decorative hub, but England—bird, bush, and anthem—pervades them as it pervades no Ramsay or Dalloway. In the earlier novels, London is a veiled microcosm; in the final novel such analogies are open. Only here in her fiction does the dimension of space claim equality with the dimension of time.

The pageant rises in the middle of its own subject. On a June day in 1939 villagers of suitable ages recite the early, middle, and later history of English conduct. Albert, a halfwit, "the village idiot" introduced as an emblem, speaks his lines as well as Mrs. Otter of the End House speaks hers. Some in the audience find Albert's presence distasteful, but Miss La Trobe makes the point clear: if each village has its idiot running loose, the pageant and the novel are entitled to one. In the interpolated pastiches of the pageant, rugged Tudor tragedy gives way to sentimentalized Restoration comedy, but the chorus sings on, "Digging and delving, hedging and ditching, we . . . remain forever the same. . . ." At a level above the workers, however, the refrain changes from a rowdy couplet about tumbling the girls to "The King is in his counting house / Counting out his money." In her "anonymous" summary, Miss La Trobe clarifies the implications by paraphrasing *The Way of All Flesh:* "The poor are as bad as the rich are. Perhaps worse."

The Victorians get much of the blame for 1939. After a series of prologues in which England as child and growing girl is succeeded by a Hyde Park constable and then Empire, an over-dressed couple vow simultaneously to love each other and to convert the heathen in the African desert. We allow the constable to represent suppression of desire, but the question the chorus asks is too easy: What did Victorians do "in the feathery billowy fourposter bed"? If the most obvious meaning of the title is "Between Two Wars," and the second and third are the annual event that brings villagers from their weekly routine and the stirrings of personality during the intervals of the pageant, a sixth or seventh its added by the Victorian charade. The audience of 1939 were "all caught and caged; prisoners; watching a spectacle."

Between the acts of the pageant, they reflect, exchange remarks and glances, remember that across the channel Europe bristles, and exercise lust. Recoiling from what they are shown of the Victorians, Mrs. Parker asks: "Surely, Mr. Oliver, we're more civilized?" In silent response, Giles transfers to the impotent homosexual William Dodge the contempt that might otherwise settle on his own bloody-booted intrigue. Light rain, interrupting the pageant, intensifies the talk and rumination. The Victorians onstage have been a token of continuing guilt. Bartholomew Oliver, who is ancient enough to know, summarizes: "Nothing's done for nothing in England." A flash of prosperity and progress— "witness also woman handing bricks." Then a ragtail chorus enters with fragments of reflecting glass—like Cubists or poets shouting, Waste Land!—to shiver the vision.

Cows and swallows contribute to the pageant; airplanes disturb it; external nature and human nature belong to one complexity but fall short of harmony. Oblivious of nature and of man, the Reverend G. W. Streatfield sums up the pageant: "Each is part of the whole." This summing up comes from one already marked by the audience as "a piece of traditional church furniture; a corner cupboard." He is one or two novels behind.

What the pageant interprets surrounds it. Before, between, and after the acts, the major characters interact in strong and multiple contrasts. Old Bart Oliver, with his Afghan hound, and his sister Lucy Swithin, with her *Outline of History* and her crucifix, have passed beyond the anxieties of Giles and Isa. The contrast of Bart's blunt skepticism and Lucy's innocent faith is more specifically realized in character than similar contrasts had been previously, partly because they characterize each other keenly but affectionately. Mrs. Ramsay could revere her husband and could cluck at him, but she could not encompass him in brief characterization. Visions of universal harmony, made part of the general flow of perception in the novels of 1925–31, are separable, dramatic episodes in Lucy's consciousness. Yet we allow for Bart's perception: ". . . she ignored the battle in the mud."

More than in any of the previous novels, the characters speak and ruminate in distinguishable rhythms. From Lily Briscoe and Bernard we learned something of how the imagination creates; from Miss La Trobe we hear how an artist in seclusion swears at the audience. Mrs. Manresa's earthiness is a role, an invitation, and a vicarious release for her neighbors; Miss La Trobe's earthiness, a part of the artist's comprehension, must remain beneath social gesture. Her expletives, outside art as she is herself outside society, release her from communication: "Curse! Blast! Damn 'em!"

We see every important character through at least five minds. The motif of the bloody boot, which shames Giles and embitters Isa, is modified by the motif recurring to Mrs. Manresa— "her surly hero." The caged prisoners, taken more narrowly, were Giles, Mrs. Manresa, Dodge, and Isa. The spectacle they watched was themselves. But Giles, a stockbroker, makes this list because he thinks Isa is attracted to Dodge. More seriously, we are told early and reminded often, Isa is drawn from "the father of my children" to the gentleman farmer Haines. Despite the strength of her feelings, Haines's silence and presumed inability to articulate keep him distant from the reader, just as Percival ruled himself into *The Waves* as a stimulator and out of the discourse as an insensitive.

For Isa and Giles the span of the novel is a pause in the rhythm of their lives, between the acts of love. That act requires a cycle of fight-embrace-sleep. In this novel action is unresolved only in the sense that the old conventions achieved resolution by making artificial hazards and choosing arbitrary moments to remove them. The situation involving Isa and Giles is resolved because our uncertainties are answered. Even so, the author declines to proclaim them resolved.

She did not choose to relinquish the victory that her generation of novelists had won over blatant storytellers. She had herself made a distinctive mark with each novel. At the beginning of her career she had wanted to be envied in the profession as a woman who wrote well. She wrote well in many ways and at all times. An anthologist of English prose forced to restrict the selection from her work to a few passages would feel pain at the variety to be excluded. She often outfaced the danger of smoothing the rhythm too prettily as mate to the heightened metaphor. First as reviewer for pay and then to feed her artistic conscience, she read all the books that revealed new techniques for keeping the novelist level with the spirit of thought in the age. The technicalities of thought she disdained, but the public distillation of thought kept her attentive. Her friends talked art, psychology, metaphysics, economics, and passivism.

Discerning a similarity between naturalistic representation and submission to fictional convention, she made each novel after her second find a new form to express the idea that generated it. Even *The Years*, the least distinctive of her books, was released in the cause of experimental advance. Advance depended on both intuition and reading.

Of recent novelists, she accepted the most coaching from James, Conrad, and Proust. She appraised the strengths of Dostoevsky, Tolstoy, and Hardy. Joyce was the novelist she got into the ring with. Bernard's peroration, more pointedly than Mrs. Ramsay's serene wisdom, gives the answer of the humane imagination to Molly Bloom's soliloquy. The author of *Jacob's*

Room lost all decisions against Goliath, even in the judgment of critics who sought—as critics for a while did—pure art. Fortunately her carefully contrived novels involve impurity, although their range is narrower in thought than Joyce's and their scatology is infinitesimal.

In a span so brief, the present essay has perhaps brought the reader excessively into its account of each novel. Mrs. Woolf saw her career that way. Belonging to the profession of letters, she honored her colleagues; but the art she submitted to asked her to be at all times responsible to the needs—rather than the wishes—of the reader. I confess to liking the way she saw it. With Conrad, she wants to make you see and make you feel; in a vaguer term that came to be needed, she wants to make you sense.

Theory and doctrine never clog her fiction. Statements about experience in the novels, allotted to the minds of her characters, are fingers steadying the landscape of experience so that the new perspectives can work the easiest way. She transforms to a kind of postimpressionism what she learns of dreams, totems, and duration versus time. Once granted that the novelist might be able to tell or show what life feels like, and granted that the sensitive are sensitive to the feelings of others, then the novelist has new reason to give the significance of life, by instinct and trial, to new arrangements of language. She did not see Joyce's limitation as the choice of material that could not be made beautiful, but as a failure to make it beautiful. She could see some value in the raw blood offered by Joyce for readers as anemic as T. S. Eliot. For herself and other normal-blooded people, she prefers novels of high finish. As long as language itself tells of life, she has no fear that pursuit of beauty will lead to excessive abstraction. *The Waves* may lead others to doubt her confidence.

As for critical principles, she had them. Her catholicity could

forgive much even in the stuffy Victorians, and her principles for
fiction and even more for criticism are obliquely stated, but they
are decidedly there. Even though her two series of *The Common
Reader* have been treated as minor classics, they scatter their author's power over a medley of subjects. All her critical essays
should be systematically collected, for the fuller demonstration
of her service to letters and the better understanding of the craft
of fiction as she promulgated and practiced it.

Not all her principles were literary. Clearly she felt a tension
between the responsibility to make fiction heighten life while
portraying it and the responsibility to hold and assert social
views courageously. The novels cover those views with layers of
irony. None of her novels was unmistakably sympathetic with
the proponents of woman's suffrage until *The Years*, when the
fight she had personally supported was over. It would be hard to
detect her alliance with the socialists in any novel before her
last, although a Marxist could understand better than most the
role of the economically deprived in the edges and crevices of
her books. The psychological and fictional concerns in *To the
Lighthouse* and the ontological concern in *The Waves* reduce the
social interests of those novels to their narrowest in her work.
More usually the spiritual lives of the characters unfold not only
within the masonry and foliage of a physical setting—London,
Scarborough, Rodmell, Skye—but also against an appraised social fabric. We cannot speak of "Virginia Woolf's world" as we
speak of "Dickens's world" or "Kafka's world" to mean peopled
geographies that are persuasive but not representational. Her
characters exist in two worlds: the subjective world she creates
for them (and out of them), and the physical world that she
holds too much in awe to alter for a merely fictional pattern. I
think that this duality came from her unresolved impulses toward autonomous art and toward the shaping of evidence to

support her conviction that the world she was creating was a world recognizable to all sensitive readers. Within the world that is "what life feels like," she put the stones of London.

None of the novels totally avoided the theme of resistance to Victorian damp and Victorian tyranny. With increasing insistence the books presented mystical experiences, and even basic doctrines, of escape from the senses into oneness with the all. Similar retreats from action have in recent years proved a representative ending, and possibly a fitting one, to the insistent individualism that accompanied Mrs. Woolf's early maturity.

Aside from doctrine and distinct from their art, the novels provide a testament. The sensibility most closely observed—Rachel Vinrace, Katharine Hilbery, Mrs. Dalloway and Mrs. Ramsay, Bernard, Eleanor Partiger, Lucy ("Old Flimsy") Swithin—grows gradually older. *The Voyage Out* sees no problems for the aged; *Between the Acts* has only a general concern for the young. The comic treatment afforded even to Mrs. Swithin's acceptance of age represents a long journey from a young novelist's rapt concentration on Miss Vinrace's intensity.

Virginia Woolf produced a body of work sufficient unto itself but important also to the history of extended fiction. Before the completion of her second book she became convinced that the most highly rewarded novelists of her time failed to reach deeply enough into the substance of life. Although she earned a reputation for sensitiveness and preciosity, the problem she wished to face was not how to feel and comprehend, but how to convey in novels the feeling and comprehension. She began to search for a right method. Thinking about significant form after listening to Fry and Bell led her to the conclusion, since then accepted as obvious, that the *what* is inextricable from the *how*. Comprehension grows with the form. The novelist who conveys a meaning "just on the far side of language" will produce what

Mrs. Woolf defined for the common reader as the poetic power of Æschylus: "By the bold and running use of metaphor he will amplify and give us, not the thing itself, but the reverberation and reflection which, taken into his mind, the thing has made; close enough to the original to illustrate it, remote enough to heighten, enlarge, and make splendid."

The later novels were objects of beauty. Prettiness was of course not enough. To fashion several contrivances of beauty all alike is to produce the glass beads that Ruskin had warned society against. Along with an humble search for improvement in the communication of her vision, therefore, Mrs. Woolf felt a compulsion with each new book to do something different and something new. Like other artists in her time and since, she accepted the challenge to do something that is right for the particular artist at the particular time. As James Hafley said of *Ulysses* and *Mrs. Dalloway*, "Joyce exhausted a day, Virginia Woolf destroyed a day." If a third novel could not continue the thread of refinement from *Mrs. Dalloway* beyond *To the Lighthouse*, then *The Years* would go back to recover a dropped stitch. She would want it in the summary that she had, like Antigone, scorned the laws made by the male and by the male declared natural and eternal. But her weapon through life was hard work. At the very end she rewrote and rewrote and rewrote the opening pages of a review, for the *New Statesman and Nation*, of James L. Clifford's life of Mrs. Piozzi. With as little patience as Keats for spelling but with care for every word, she fashioned her review on the back of pages rewritten and then discarded from *Between the Acts*.

In person Mrs. Woolf wore her genius as openly as Johnson, Coleridge, or Swinburne. Strangers laughed. Acquaintances sometimes trembled. Friends waited for imaginative displays as one forewarned might watch for the aurora borealis. It was after conversations within the Woolf circle that Stephen Spender saw how the imaginative power of her novels, concentrating often on small things, "nevertheless held at bay vast waters, madness, wars, destructive forces." Dame Ethel Smyth, after twenty years of international success and nearly eighty of transcendent eccentricity, listened to the novelist with awe. Dame Edith Sitwell admired in her the pursuer of "each butterfly aspect of the world," the straight talker, and the sympathetic listener. John Lehmann, as a young poet, could value the reciprocal gain from her "unique gift for encouraging one to be indiscreet." Two volumes of Lehmann's autobiography, *The Whispering Gallery* and *I Am My Brother*, both written after he purchased Mrs. Woolf's share in the Hogarth Press, tell us how thoroughly involved and how moderately practical she was, almost to the day of her death, in the selection of manuscripts for the Hogarth list. If the creator of Rachel Vinrace thought of herself as a perfecter of style and sensibility, not as a critical helmsman on the voyage of English fiction, how much less could she have imagined herself as a captain in the publishing industry! Novelist, critic, hostess, personality—even if none of her novels were major, she would live for a century or two in anecdotal history.

Virginia Woolf's mind was delicately balanced. Fatigue of body, as her husband describes the fine-spunness, made her mind speed toward imbalance. She had broken, not for the first time, after her mother's death in 1895. She had spun further in 1914 than in 1905. Each novel was an inkwell thrown like Luther's at a threatening devil. Outfacing the advance of a final breakdown during the persistent bombings of 1941, she left messages for her husband and her sister and walked into the river Ouse. Our present direction will not lead soon to another eminent novelist, mind, or person of her amused but committed refinement.

HARRY T. MOORE

E. M. Forster

Edward Morgan Forster in the ninety-one years of his life wrote six novels and parts of others, many short stories, and a series of miscellaneous books and articles, sometimes related to the fiction and sometimes independent exercises in belles-lettres. Forster's principal writings concern the failure of human beings to communicate with one another satisfactorily, their failure to smash down the walls of prejudice that have risen between them and to establish among themselves the relationships that are so richly possible.

Given a wider application, this is the history of humanity in our time. Forster, beginning his work early in this century of wars, saw from the first the schisms between people and between the separate worlds they live in. But if his works are prophetic, they are not prescriptively so. The value of his fiction lies to a great extent in his representative portraits of people.

Forster ardently believed in the right of every member of humanity to be as much himself as he can be within the bounds of community safety. As a supporter of a political system that grants each of us his uniqueness, he was willing to give democ-

racy two cheers at least: "Two cheers are quite enough: there is
no occasion to give three. Only Love the Beloved Republic deserves that." Yet that republic cannot function effectively in a
climate of prejudices and antagonisms. On the title page of one
of his two finest novels, *Howards End* (1910), Forster placed a
phrase representing the philosophy of one of his characters,
which is essentially his own philosophy: "Only connect."

Forster was born in 1879, the son of a London architect who
died when the boy was two years old. His education, his enjoyment of leisure time, as well as his ability to undertake his
earlier travels ("and travelling inclined me to write") were all
made possible by a legacy from his great-aunt, Marianne Thornton, who died when Forster was eight. Before attending the university, however, he had to undergo the torment of being a day
student at Tonbridge School, which seemed to him a concentration of injustice and misery. The wonder and freedom of Cambridge were a happy contrast, perhaps best summed up in Forster's novel, *The Longest Journey* (1907), and in his 1934
biography of Goldsworthy Lowes Dickinson.

During his first four years at Cambridge, 1897–1901, Forster
barely knew Dickinson, who was sixteen years older. Forster
had intended to study with him, but was "dished by Oscar
Browning," the fat and sharp-minded history teacher, who said,
"Yet must come to me." Forster's classics tutor was the forceful
Nathaniel Wedd, of whom he wrote in the 1934 Dickinson biography: "It is to him more than to Dickinson—indeed more to
him than to anyone—that I owe such awakening as has befallen
me. It is through him that I can best imagine the honesty and
fervor of fifty years back." There was conscious honesty and
concentrated fervor at Cambridge in Forster's time in the person
and philosophy of G. E. Moore, whose *Principia Ethica* became
highly popular at the university after its publication in 1903.

Moore, who stressed that the "good" was indefinable and who searched intently for the exact meaning of every statement, had an immense influence on undergraduates of the period, particularly in the circle in which Forster moved.

In 1901–2 Forster made his first visit to Italy and Greece and began writing short fiction and novels. The first novel to be published was *Where Angels Fear to Tread* (1905), followed by *The Longest Journey* (1907), *A Room with a View* (1908), *Howards End* (1910), and long after, *A Passage to India* (1924). His first volume of shorter work, *The Celestial Omnibus and Other Stories*, came out in 1911; *The Eternal Moment and Other Stories* appeared in 1928 (all the tales had been written before World War I). The nonfiction volumes began with Forster's guidebook to Alexandria in 1922. Before the war, Forster had become part of the Bloomsbury group, whose members included the daughters of Sir Leslie Stephen, Virginia (later Mrs. Woolf) and Vanessa (later Mrs. Bell), and their brothers, Adrian and Thoby, as well as J. M. Keynes, Lytton Strachey, Leonard Woolf, Clive Bell, Roger Fry, Duncan Grant, David Garnett, and several others prominent in London intellectual and artistic life.

In 1910 Forster returned to Cambridge for his M.A. He spent the winter of 1912–13 in India, accompanied part of the time by Dickinson. After war broke out, Forster volunteered for the Red Cross, which sent him to Alexandria, where he remained from 1915 to 1918. In 1922 he returned to India for six months as private secretary to the Maharajah of the State of Dewas Senior. In 1927 Forster became a fellow of his old college, King's. After World War II, he again traveled frequently—to South Africa, the United States, Italy, and Greece—but spent most of his time in residence at King's.

Although E. M. Forster may not have had an outwardly eventful life, this shy and gentle man lived intensely through adventures of the spirit: knowledge, personal relationships, a love of certain places, and the satisfaction of writing. Forster was not widely read even after *A Passage to India*, but his reputation has grown steadily, particularly since World War II. Although he had not brought out a novel for forty-six years, he had been, before his death in 1970, generally regarded as England's finest living novelist.

Before specific consideration of Forster's nonfiction works and his six novels, we may take his short stories as a good starting point for a discussion of his writing career. The outstanding characteristic of these stories should be noted at once: they are almost entirely given over to fantasy, mythology, magic, the supernatural. These elements are sometimes at the edge of Forster's novels, and in *A Passage to India* there is a suggestion that they have made a definite invasion; yet the novels for the most part are in the vein of everyday realism. They are pointed up by the comic and the ironic, but they remain largely within the area of the realistic (though rarely the naturalistic). This is to say that the novels proceed at the pace of probability; some of the episodes may seem melodramatic, some of the people may dip over into caricature, and some of the episodes may be tinged with mystery, yet in the main the books are about life as we confront it each morning, not always necessarily making in our minds a clear distinction between its real and apparent aspects, but accepting its surface manifestations within the scope of the probable and the predictable. Forster's short stories, on the other hand, are not like this. We may meet in any of them a group of plausible people, and they may say what we might expect them to say, but there is always the tense possibility that, without warning, a poltergeist will start tumbling the furniture about. No reader is quite safe in a Forster short story.

Still another aspect of his work in this medium should be

noted. The themes are essentially those of the novels. In other words, Forster in the short stories adopts the guise of fantasy to put across what he says realistically in his longer fiction. As one example, consider the fate of Mr. Bons in the story "The Celestial Omnibus." He is a man with pretensions, who, although he has no genuine love of poetry, keeps fancy editions of the poets. In one of Forster's novels, Mr. Bons would have been mocked at or would have suffered some spiritual defeat. But when Dante (yes, Dante) is driving Mr. Bons in the celestial omnibus, Bons is horribly punished for his literalness, dropped from a great height and smashed. Here, fantasy in a most unusual way combines with a naturalistic event. But fantasy is at the basis of the destruction, whereas it would not have been in one of the novels.

The first story that Forster wrote he placed at the beginning of *The Celestial Omnibus* and also of *The Collected Tales of E. M. Forster* (British edition, *Collected Short Stories*). In "The Story of a Panic," some English people picnicking in the Italian countryside are suddenly seized by terror, and flee. If the spirit of panic has entered into their systems, the spirit of Pan has taken over that of the fourteen-year-old Eustace, whose ecstasies cause his elders to lock him up in a small room at the hotel. A young Italian waiter, Gennaro, who is the only one capable of understanding what has happened, protests that Eustace will die if he is imprisoned. Gennaro, who has betrayed Eustace into captivity for ten lire, finally sets him free, and as Eustace rushes away toward the woodland uttering strange cries, Gennaro says, "Now, instead of dying, he will live!"—but Gennaro himself falls dead.

This is typical Forster fantasy, recurring in slightly different fashion in another of the stories in *The Celestial Omnibus*, "Other Kingdom." Here, Evelyn Beaumont has been brought to England from "uncivilized" Ireland to marry the handsome, stuffy, wealthy Harcourt Worters. But after experiencing the rigidity of his ideas, she makes an Ovidian flight and takes a dryad's refuge in a grove of trees. Another of Forster's stories contrasting the pettiness of the everyday world with another and better world, "The Other Side of the Hedge" is less successful, partly because its symbolism depends too much upon the methodical and too little upon the intuitive, and partly because the fable contains no true basis of dramatic conflict.

Several of the stories deal with the afterlife, at least with another world in close relationship to the present one. These include "The Celestial Omnibus," already mentioned, "The Point of It," "Mr. Andrews," and "Co-ordination." "The Celestial Omnibus" has something more to offer than the destruction of Mr. Bons (look at that name backwards and it becomes Snob): there is also a small boy with an eagerly imaginative mind who rides the omnibus and does not fall into (or fall in) the sin of literalness. Altogether, it is Forster's most charming story of the relation between the present world and eternity. "As for 'The Point of It,' " Forster says, "it was ill-liked when it came out by my Bloomsbury friends. 'What *is* the point of it?' they queried, nor did I know how to reply." But it seems to have several points. One of them is that Harold, who dies young, in glory (the text suggests the choice of Achilles), has the better of it, in contrast with his surviving friend Michael, who leads a long life devoted to humanity and the accumulation of honors. At death he finds himself in the soft hell of the humanists, separated from his wife, who is in the stony hell of the truth seekers; but there is a way out, the heaven of youth, if one can in an intense moment realize the point of it. "Mr. Andrews" is a brief, light allegory of an Englishman who finds that he and a Turk can enter paradise together and have everything they ask for, which is just a little too good, so they abandon heaven for the struggle of living again; they have, in the course of their meeting, achieved a new understanding and tolerance in that each has prayed that the other might be admitted to heaven. In "Co-ordination," the brevity again helps, and it sustains a light anecdote Forster knows better than to draw out: Beethoven and Napoleon cast, from the afterlife, an influence over a girls' school. The influence seems on the surface beneficent, but it is channeled through a series of confusions that make the final effect one of amusing irony.

In the vein of "The Story of a Panic," two other tales project mischief from the invisible world: "The Curate's Friend" and "The Story of the Siren." The title of "The Curate's Friend" seems at one level ironic, since the faun that appears to a Wiltshire curate, though not to those about him, breaks up the romance between the cleric and his fiancée; but the faun is in the longer view his friend, since the clergyman becomes, in his own eyes at least, a better man and a better clergyman. In "The Story of the Siren," a young boatman tells an English tourist the story of his brother Giuseppe, who had seen the Siren and had married Maria, who had also beheld the wonder. When Maria became pregnant, a priest murdered her: the child of this pagan-visioned Joseph and Mary must not be allowed to become the new non-Christian messiah. Giuseppe wandered over the world, his brother says, trying to find someone else who had seen the Siren, particularly a woman—for then a child could be created. But Giuseppe at last arrived at Liverpool ("Is the district probable?" his brother asks), where he became ill, and died coughing blood. The boatman says, "Silence and loneliness cannot last for ever. It may be a hundred or a thousand years, but the sea lasts longer, and she shall come out of it and sing." So ends the last-written and the finest of Forster's mythological stories, one that concentrates various themes of all the others, especially his preoccupation with the natural world (as represented by his vital Mediterranean figures), linked with the supernatural or mythological (here the Siren) against the false world of society (the priest and Giuseppe's conventional fellow Sicilians). The darkening grotto, the fanatical murder, and the wild sea in which the Siren lives all combine to give the story its particular force.

In "The Machine Stops," Forster made a somewhat similar statement in a quite different way: he showed how one element of the modern social complex—the machine—had triumphed over the natural life of man. Forster spoke of the story as "a re-action to one of the earlier heavens of H. G. Wells." But it is far more pessimistic than anything by Wells, and reflects none of his faith in science as it portrays a dehumanized world of the future. One of the earliest science-fiction stories, it was a forerunner of Aldous Huxley's *Brave New World* and, with the big-brother functioning of the machine, the tale also anticipated George Orwell's Nineteen Eighty-Four.

Forster in "The Road from Colonus" wrote in a fairly realistic vein, though the story has mysterious overtones, particularly in relation to an ironic coincidence. The elderly Mr. Lucas, on tour in Greece, finds a place at which he wants to stop, where in a dry landscape water gushes out of a hollow tree. But this Oedipus is not permitted to linger: his daughter enlists the aid of a young man in the touring party to carry her father gently away. Later, back in London, when the daughter is about to be married, apparently to the young man from the touring party, she discovers from an old newspaper that a huge tree had blown down at the place where her father had wanted to stop, and had killed all the people there. But Mr. Lucas hardly seems interested in the accident, for he is too deeply concerned over having to give up his house: he continually hears the gush of water, "and I cannot stand the noise of running water."

"The Eternal Moment," the best of Forster's short stories, begins with a situation that suggests Henry James, an author for whom Forster has expressed distaste. But the idea of the once-simple town (then in Italia Irredenta) which has become hideously commercialized because it was the setting of a popular novel is intrinsically Jamesian. Forster works it out, however, as James would not have: the story becomes another account of those failures of people to reach one another from their different worlds. Miss Raby, an aging spinster novelist, returns to Vorta (based on Cortina d'Ampezzo) to see what damage her book has really done. Colonel Leyland, a fairly sophisticated and tolerant member of his class, is the platonic traveling companion of this woman given to heedless plain speaking. She tells him that years before one of the porters at the hotel where she lodged had tried to make love to her on the mountainside, and that she had promptly rejected him.

At Vorta they find that new and grand hotels have pushed into the background the charming little place where she had stayed. And the once-handsome porter, Feo, has become the swaggering fat concierge of the most swaggering and fattest of the new hotels. The candid Miss Raby mentions to Feo the mountainside scene, which he finally remembers with shock and embarrassment, and he fears, unreasonably, that she plans to blackmail him. On learning that he is married and has three small sons, she offers to export one of them to England, to adopt and educate him. Feo, who has no feeling for the child beyond wondering how much Miss Raby will pay for taking him, withdraws by saying his wife might object: the proper world he now represents as the concierge at the Hôtel des Alpes, whose personnel have been watching and listening during this scene, can have no dealings with the plainspoken Englishwoman who cries out in the hotel lounge, "Don't think I'm in love with you now!" But she had been when she rejected him, and in a blazing revelation she sees that episode on the mountain as perhaps the greatest moment of her life, the eternal moment from which she has drawn all her subsequent inspirations. But she has now lost Colonel Leyland, who touches his forehead so that Feo will see the gesture; and Feo whispers, "Exactly, sir. Of course we understand." Whatever else has happened to her, however, Miss Raby has learned how to face old age. Leyland, who had seemed enlightened above his milieu, slips safely back into it. Henry James would have probably ended on a different note, full of those illuminating subtleties which made up for the lack of certain other elements in his work; Forster in that final scene in the lounge achieved a marvelous dramatic vigor.

After the two books of his short stories were put into a single volume in 1947, Forster published no more work along this line. But in 1972, two years after his death, there appeared *The Life to Come and Other Stories*, a volume of fourteen of his tales, only two of which had been published before. One of them, "Albergo Empedocle," had come out in a magazine in 1903. The other, "The Second Course," was an amusing part of a venture which he and the three other authors had contributed to the magazine *Wine and Food* in 1944, under the general title of "Three Courses and a Dessert"; Christopher Dilke contributed the first course, the beginning of a story set in the England of World War II; Forster continued the narrative and was followed by A. E. Coppard and James Laver. This amusing little side-effort must be mentioned, but it has none of the force of "Albergo Empedocle." The latter is one of Forster's better stories and somewhat typical of those he wrote in his youth, featuring British tourists in an ancient Mediterranean setting, in this case embodying an effective and destructive symbol, which leads to an appalling obsession.

Of the remaining dozen stories, four could probably have been published in the author's lifetime. After he became a well-known novelist he would have had little trouble in getting even the earliest among them (including one that was rejected) published in magazines. But in some cases he felt that the treatment wasn't completely right, as in the case of "The Rock," which is little more than an anecdote about a man who, after a brush with death, changes his life. "The Helping Hand" is also anecdotal, a genuinely amusing little piece about plagiarism, with a fine touch of irony at the end. "The Purple Envelope" is built around the complications which arise when a young man each morning finds words in the mist forming on his shaving mirror. The finest of these four stories, all of which were written in the early 1900s, is "Ansell," which, through the friendship between a young intellectual and a young gardener, anticipates the theme of male comradeship that flourishes in the remaining eight stories, apparently written between the early 1920s and the late 1950s. Forster didn't publish these because they dealt unmistakably—and unashamedly—with homosexuality.

He wrote them, he once noted, "not to express myself, but to excite myself," and he destroyed a number of them, apparently including "a jokey thing" which Christopher Isherwood remembered, concerning "a girl who thought that two young men were always fighting when in fact they were making love." But, according to a diary entry by Forster, quoted in Oliver Stallybrass's Introduction to *The Life to Come*, Forster said that one of his short stories, to be called "Adventure Week"—about some boys at a camp—had to be torn up and burnt because he felt about it the dissatisfaction of a craftsman.

But the eight stories of his later years—all except the title
story of the posthumous collection, which was apparently written after *A Passage to India*—don't usually represent him at his
strongest, perhaps because the same element in his nature that
would keep him from trying to publish them was a self-con-
sciousness that somewhat impeded them, however private they
were, or meant at the most to be seen only by a group of sympathetic friends. Yet for the most part they include components
which characterize his finest short stories, notably fantasy and
magic, in these later tales usually fitted neatly into the homosexual themes. Sometimes the combination of these strains becomes
too much, as in "The Classical Annex," the story of a museum
curator whose adolescent son merges into the pagan statuary, a
story not long enough to become tedious and one which is saved
somewhat by the irony of its final sentences, spoken by a local
councillor.

The latest of the stories, completed in 1957–58 but begun
long before, is "The Other Boat," in which a British officer and
a young Indian called Cocoanut, who had met as children on a
P. & O. steamship, encounter one another again on another boat
and engage in a love affair which proves disastrous, in the somewhat melodramatic way which Forster often adopted in his fiction; yet as in several such cases the obtrusive note is forgotten
against the vitality of the story. These last tales differ in many
respects, however much some of them may have in common; if
"The Other Boat" is realistic-psychological-dramatic, "Dr. Wool-
acott" is allegorical, with death and love combining, for a young
invalid, in the equally young figure of one of the attractive
youths of the lower classes to whom Forster's protagonists are so
often drawn. Another such young man appears in the more realistic "Arthur Snatchfold," in which an aging nobleman barely
escapes imprisonment. "The Obelisk" is realistic also, a neat,

mischievous little comedy about a young couple who in a few moments of separation undergo quite different kinds of love affairs in the area of a notable phallic symbol; a picture postcard of which at the end of the story abruptly provides the girl with a shock of recognition.

"What Does It Matter? A Morality," a story with a Ruritanian-Graustarkian setting, which the textual editor of the collection dates as "probably the 1930s," may have grown out of Forster's visit to Budapest, Bucharest, and Cracow in the spring of 1932; it is a rather superficial little comedy about a president-dictator and some sexual hijinks. Forster did a little better with "The Torque," involving some early-Christian Romans who become involved with Goths, and if the story itself isn't either too plausible, or genuinely comic, its atmosphere and "historical touches" suggest that Forster could probably have written a fine novel in the historical vein, though he felt that his one (unfinished) attempt to do so was a failure. Among the posthumous tales, the most satisfactorily balanced in terms of theme, action, and character is the title story, which is also the most vividly written. Even the violent ending of "The Life to Come," is acceptable because it thrusts out of an ironic situation that could have no other result: the rueful and persistent misunderstanding, by a dark-skinned chieftain, of an attractive missionary's use of the word love.

The story of Forster's stories, like that of his novels, is one of powerful simplicity. It was his manner almost as much as his matter that aroused the enthusiasm of young English writers of the 1930s: Christopher Isherwood, W. H. Auden, and other members of the group of new young radicals of the day. Cyril Connolly said admiringly in *Enemies of Promise* (1939) that Forster had broken away from the "mandarin" style of such writers as Walter Pater, Henry James, and Joseph Conrad: Forster tends to use everyday words and to avoid conjunctive and relative clauses. Although he has not been imitated, Connolly says, Forster was the stylistic forerunner of Virginia Woolf, Katherine Mansfield, Elizabeth Bowen, and David Garnett. One of these writers, Elizabeth Bowen, has pointed out (in *Collected Impressions*, 1950) that the prose of Forster's essays resembles that of his fiction: "Its rhythm is so inherent in its content that one cannot detect it without analysis. The least frigid of writing, it is the most impersonal; [Forster] is the enemy of all those lovable little tricks."

Alexandria: A History and a Guide (1922) came out of Forster's experiences in that city during World War I. It is one of those special-interest books which can be read with enjoyment for its own sake; that is, by those who know little or nothing about Alexandria and have no particular intention of going there. The history section that takes up nearly half the book is a well-informed and colorful survey of the city from its founding in 331 B.C. to the riots and bombardment of A.D. 1882, when the British moved in. Earlier, Egyptians, Greeks, Romans, Arabs, and the armies of Napoleon cross the pages of the book. Its guide section is thorough, with street maps and plans of important monuments and temples. Forster dealt with Alexandria again in *Pharos and Pharillon* (1923), a series of sketches named for two lighthouses of the city: "Under [the vast and heroic] Pharos I have grouped a few antique events; to modern events and to personal impressions I have given the name of Pharillon, the obscure successor of Pharos, which clung for a time to the low rock of Silsileh and then slid unobserved into the Mediterranean." *Pharos and Pharillon* is a continuation of the history-guidebook; most of its sketches reaffirm Forster's Hellenism and his dislike of Christianity. They are often done in the mischievous vein of

Anatole France, and at times they foreshadow a quite different kind of writer, the Lawrence Durrell of the *Alexandria Quartet.*

In 1927, three years after Forster's last novel (*A Passage to India*), he brought out his volume of expository criticism, *Aspects of the Novel*, originally delivered in that year as the Clark lectures at Trinity College, Cambridge. The book is best known for its distinction between the types of characters Forster calls "round" and "flat": "The test of a round character is that it is capable of surprising in a convincing way. If it never surprises, it is flat. If it does not convince, it is a flat pretending to be round." Forster elaborates on these ideas. Flat characters—humorous types, caricatures—are useful to the novelist, though they are not the great achievement that round characters are. The flat are best when comic, and more of them could have been profitably used, Forster thinks, in the great Russian novels. His own particular interests appear in the chapters on fantasy and prophecy, and in the one on "Pattern and Rhythm," in which he speaks of "the three large blocks of sound" that make up Beethoven's Fifth Symphony. Forster wonders whether there is any analogy to this type of rhythm in fiction. Although he says he knows of none, his own novels sometimes have this three-part pattern, and he has given the nod to at least one interpretation (Peter Burra's) of these books as "symphonic." Forster also has much to say in *Aspects* that is illuminating on the subject of plot and piquant on the subject of other novelists. Forster here wrote one of the first commentaries on Herman Melville's *Billy Budd* (in 1951 he was to prepare the libretto for Benjamin Britten's operatic version of *Billy Budd*). *Aspects of the Novel* is not only valuable for what it tells of Forster's ways and means of writing; but it is also an important study of the art of fiction.

Besides a number of short essays on the lives of authors, Forster produced two full-length biographies: *Goldsworthy Lowes Dickinson* (1934) and *Marianne Thornton* (1956). Both these books were in a way acts of piety, the first to commemorate a good friend, the second a benign relative. The Dickinson volume, which came out two years after its subject's death, will mainly catch the attention of those concerned with Forster or with the Cambridge of yesterday and the day before. Dickinson's life is in the outward sense unchallenging to a biographer, since it can be only an intellectual record. Dickinson had a fine intellect: *The Greek View of Life* (1896) is still a useful and readable book, and the same may be said of his subsequent imaginary letters and dialogues. It is even, Forster says, "possible that Dickinson invented the phrase 'League of Nations,' " and he certainly did significant work for that organization. But, since his biography must be an intellectual treatise, it suffers somewhat because its subject's mind was not of the first and highest order.

On the other hand, *Marianne Thornton, 1797–1887: A Domestic Biography*, is, despite its modest subtitle, a compelling story. It is exciting to learn that Forster knew this woman who was born in the eighteenth century. His great-aunt was a member of the Clapham Sect of evangelicals, and the family knew Thomas Babington Macaulay, Bishop Wilberforce, and other famous men of the Victorian era. Forster's history of this branch of his family, with the full-length portrait of his great-aunt "Monie," is an attractive addition to the history of Victorian manners.

Forster collected many of his miscellaneous writings—articles, along with pamphlets and other small books—in *Abinger Harvest* (1936) and *Two Cheers for Democracy* (1951). The first of these books takes its name from the Surrey village where Forster lived for a number of years until he moved permanently to Cambridge after World War II. The volume includes *The Pageant of*

Abinger, first performed in 1934 (music by Ralph Vaughan Williams), a series of episodes relating to the life of the town from the Middle Ages to modern times. In its Epilogue, the Woodman says, "Houses and bungalows, hotels, restaurants and flats, arterial roads, by-passes, petrol pumps and pylons—are these going to be England? Are these man's final triumph? Or is there another England, green and eternal, which will outlast them?"

The essays in *Abinger Harvest* are of various kinds, chiefly belletristic, with articles on Joseph Conrad, T. S. Eliot, Marcel Proust, and other authors, including Forster's great ideal, Jane Austen. Sometimes the chapters are personal, as the one devoted to a bit of family history: "Battersea Rise" tells something about the Thornton home, dealt with more expansively in *Marianne Thornton*. "Notes on the English Character" is just that, a series of notes neatly discussing well-known attributes and at one point providing an instructive comparison with Indian character. Nearly a third of the book comprises essays on the Orient, from Marco Polo to the situation of modern India. Lionel Trilling, usually an admirer of Forster's, finds some of the literary sketches coy, especially those dealing with Gibbon, Coleridge, and Keats; these pieces seem to have been influenced by Lytton Strachey's manner. But usually Forster is strictly himself in this book, never more so than in that Epilogue to *The Pageant of Abinger*:

If you want to ruin our Surrey fields and woodlands it is easy to do, very easy, and if you want to save them they can be saved. Look into your hearts and look into the past, and remember that all this beauty is a gift which you can never replace, which no money can buy, which no cleverness can refashion.

Here is the true Forster speaking. In some ways, although his manner is quite different, he resembles D. H. Lawrence, who

also, but more violently, disliked the encroachment of civilization, and who also in his fiction opposed Anglo-Saxon philis-
tines with vitalistic types reminiscent of such figures as the
young Italian, Gino, in Forster's first novel, *Where Angels Fear to
Tread*.

Forster's *Two Cheers for Democracy* is a miscellany similar to
Abinger Harvest, though its opening section, "The Second Darkness"—devoted to the author's pamphlets and broadcasts during
World War II—gives the book a somewhat different tone. These
pieces are dated now except as examples of the kind of intellectual leadership a writer can provide during a time of crisis:
Forster spoke out sanely against race theories, Nazism, and
various other manifestations of the period. The belletristic
essays that make up the rest of the book are some of Forster's
finest, often adapted from reviews or occasional journalism but
always sieved through a civilized and alert intelligence. The
1941 Rede lecture at Cambridge, in memory of Virginia Woolf,
is a helpful examination of her work but, even more important,
it is a knowledgeable presentation of her attitudes toward her
work.

The other literary essays indicàte the range of Forster's interests, from John Skelton to Gabriele D'Annunzio, while the
travel sketches ("America is rather like life. You can usually find
in it what you look for") are wittily perceptive, including "India
Again" (1946), describing Forster's third visit there, and some
informative English views, both London and Cambridge as well
as T. E. Lawrence's Clouds Hill cottage and "The Last of Abinger." But *Two Cheers for Democracy* is best known for the essay
"What I Believe," from a phrase of whose text the title was
taken. Forster says he does not believe in Belief, though in an
age of no faith and many militant creeds, one is compelled in
self-defense to formulate one's own creed. "My law-givers are

Erasmus and Montaigne, not Moses and St. Paul." He distrusts Great Men, who "produce a desert of uniformity around them, and often a pool of blood too." Forster continually keeps the emphasis on the individual and the personal: "If I had to choose between betraying my country and betraying my friend, I hope I should have the guts to betray my country."

It may seem a long leap back, from this point, to 1905 and Forster's first published novel, *Where Angels Fear to Tread*—and yet it is not really a very great leap because the novels and the stories, as well as even the later essays, are closely related, as a study of the novels will show. And they should properly be given the emphasis of last place, as the most important part of Forster's career.

Where Angels Fear to Tread begins on an irony, as the widowed Lilia Herriton is departing for Italy. "Love and understand the Italians," her brother-in-law, Philip Herriton, tells her at the end of the third paragraph of the story. She does not understand the Italians, but she soon falls in love with one of them. Caroline Abbott, her companion on what was to have been a long though temporary visit, telegraphs to the Herritons that the young man belongs to the nobility. This news is received skeptically; to the elder Mrs. Herriton it makes no difference whether the man is a duke or an organ-grinder. Philip goes out to Italy upon the command of his imperious mother: "If Lilia marries him she insults the memory of Charles, she insults Irma [her small daughter], she insults us." In an opening chapter of less than eighteen pages, Forster has, with deft strokes of social comedy, drawn the battle lines and provided at least rudimentary portraits of all the leading characters except Lilia's Italian, Gino Carella.

Philip, the stiff young barrister, has been to Italy before and has loved it. He is an ineffectual youth with two outstanding characteristics, a sense of beauty and a sense of humor. But the

sense of beauty is a kind of embittered *bovarisme,* the disease of
the provincial who dislikes his province but must live in it. And
the sense of humor has become an acrid cynicism. Arriving in
Italy, Philip finds out to his dismay that Lilia has already married; she is thirty-three, Gino twenty-one. But Philip has been
even more horrified to learn that Gino is the son of a dentist:
"False teeth and laughing gas and the tilting chair at a place
which knew the Etruscan League, and the Pax Romana, and
Alaric himself, and the Countess Matilda, and the Middle Ages,
all fighting and holiness, and the Renaissance, all fighting and
beauty!"

Philip returns home, accompanied by the rueful Caroline Abbott. The story then takes up Lilia's marriage, and her gradual
disillusionment with Italian life. Gino, a sexual anarchist ("I
always desired a blonde"), is soon being unfaithful. He keeps
Lilia as his wife, however, for his deepest need is to have a son.
Lilia dies giving birth to that son, dies in a single sentence with
the abruptness that so often marks the death of Forster characters. Before long, Irma begins to receive picture postcards supposedly from her "lital brother." Mrs. Herriton orders Philip to
Italy again, to "rescue" the baby, and with him she sends his
priggish sister Harriet.

In Italy they meet Miss Abbott, who also feels responsible for
the child; when Philip asks her whether she has come as traitor
or spy, she takes no offense at the offensive words and admits
she is there as a spy. She says that Mrs. Herriton, who cares
nothing about the baby (which indeed is not even related to
her), has behaved dishonorably; if her son and daughter really
want to get it, however, Caroline will help, and if they want to
fail, she will take the child. Later she withdraws altogether,
telling Philip that if the little boy stays in Italy, with his loving
father, he will be brought up badly, and that if he goes to En-

gland he will be brought up well, although nobody there loves him.

Gino in any event is not selling: he expects to marry a woman he does not love, but she has a little money and will be a mother to Lilia's baby. When Harriet grimly steals the child, she deepens the wrong by leading Philip to believe that she has bought him. Here, Philip the barrister proves to be poor at cross-examination, although the circumstances are admittedly against him, since he and Harriet are hurrying to the railway station in a carriage on a rain-swept night, and the baby is obviously ill. The carriage overturns, killing the child. Philip, with a broken elbow, goes to tell the news to Gino, who savagely twists Philip's fractured arm and begins to strangle him; he is saved only by the timely appearance of Caroline Abbott, who restores Gino to common sense and even a manifestation of friendship for Philip. When the housekeeper brings a jug of milk intended for the baby, Gino insists that Philip take it; and what Philip leaves, Gino ritually drinks.

On the way back to England, Philip starts to tell Caroline that he is in love with her—oddly enough, these two old friends still address each other as Mr. Herriton and Miss Abbott—but she forestalls him by confessing that she is in love with Gino, "crudely" though profoundly. She will keep him in her memory forever. At the end of the story, as their train is about to enter the Saint Gotthard Tunnel, Philip takes his last look at the campanile of Airolo, which in the first chapter he had told Lilia to watch for (it was the beginning of beauty, the promise of the future). But as Philip tries to catch a glimpse of the campanile just before the train plunges into the darkness of the tunnel, he sees "instead the fair myth of Endymion." Caroline Abbott remained a goddess to the last, for to her no love was degrading, since she stood beyond degradation. She lifted him to so great a height

that he could tell her that he was her worshiper, like Gino, who
also thought her a goddess. "But what was the use of telling her?
For all the wonderful things had happened."

Almost all of Forster's values are brought to play in this
novel, which foreshadows the rest of his work. Instead of the
fantasy of the short stories, however, *Where Angels Fear to Tread*
features accident and coincidence. Now and then the careful
progress of the plot suffers from an abrupt theatrical interrup-
tion. This is sometimes disturbing in a basically realistic story,
where the great points should be made through the psychological without too much assistance from the accidental. In "The
Story of a Panic," the reader's imagination readily accepts Pan's
possession of the soul of the boy Eustace, and the boy's subsequent ecstatic rush to the woodland. In Forster's first novel,
Gino's violence is plausible, and it gives him a certain fierce reality, but the arrival of Caroline Abbott just in time to rescue
Philip seems a little pat, coming as it does so soon after the accident in which Gino's baby has been killed. These are minor
objections, however, in the face of the story's achievements, its
remarkable maturity as a first novel. Philip's sudden realization
of his love for Caroline, and her spasmodic admission of her
feelings toward Gino, may seem to match the abruptness of
some of the outer effects, but actually these onsets of love are
substantially motivated, proceeding out of events. The characters are all well drawn, and Gino is Forster's most successful attempt at portraying the child of nature. Forster gives the travelogue element just the right amount of color, and he devises
certain episodes with notable skill. One of these is the performance of the provincial Italian opera company, at which Harriet
behaves with prissiness and Gino with uproarious geniality.
This is an important moment in the expansion of Philip's character: he is on Gino's side here rather than Harriet's.

As usual in Forster, the story contains a conflict between two worlds, as represented by the English town of Sawston (which Philip finally comes around to calling "that hole") and the Italian town of Monteriano (which in Forster's parody of Baedeker is described as "now of small importance, and seat of the district prison. The inhabitants are still noted for their agreeable manners"). But Forster, even as a young novelist of only twenty-six, shrewdly avoided oversimplification in his opposition of these two places, these two ways of life: he turned the full dry light of social comedy on Monteriano as well as on Sawston. Granted, Monteriano comes off better; but Forster never suggests that it is perfect or utopian.

Philip Herriton and Caroline Abbott are characters of the kind that Forster, years later (not speaking of his own work), would designate as round: they change, they are capable of surprising the reader. Caroline is young, in her early twenties, and it is doubtful that she will remain forever on the shelf because of Gino. For one thing, the episode in which she bathes his brown baby indicates her talent for motherhood. As for Philip, the experiences he has gone through with Caroline have restored his sense of beauty and presumably will restore his sense of humor. At the end of the book he has decided to leave Sawston, for London. He would probably choose Monteriano if he could, but he has to make his living in London. At least he is abandoning Sawston and the values represented by his mother and sister. He tells Caroline Abbott that he is nothing more than a spectator of life, but surely he will from now on be a better and wiser spectator and possibly, at necessary times, a participant.

In *The Longest Journey* (1907), the detestable Sawston appears again. It gives its name to the middle section of the novel, whose first part takes its title from enlightened Cambridge and its third from pagan Wiltshire. Rickie Elliot, the sensitive, clubfooted young man, has in childhood lost his unlikable father and his lovable mother in a few terse sentences (Rickie's own death will be described later with almost equal abruptness). Living in Sawston after the university, Rickie speaks to his wife Agnes of his time at Cambridge: "those are the magic years, and—with luck—you see up there what you couldn't see before and mayn't ever see again." Rickie's philosophical friend, Stewart Ansell, had not "seen" Agnes when she had visited Cambridge long before there was a possibility of marriage with Rickie. When she appeared at Cambridge, Ansell ignored her outstretched hand, and when Rickie later scolded him privately for his rudeness, Ansell said no one had been there. When Rickie reminded Ansell that he had "seen" a philosophic cow during a dialectical dispute, Ansell retorted that there are two kinds of phenomena: "*one,* those which have a real existence, such as the cow; *two,* those which are the subjective product of a diseased imagination, and which, to our destruction, we invest with the semblance of reality." But Rickie ignored this warning, and after Agnes's athletic hero, Gerald, an officer and a bully, was killed (in two sentences) at a Rugby match, Rickie struck precisely the right sympathetic note, and before long he and Agnes were married.

At Sawston, where Agnes's brother, Herbert Pembroke, finds him a teaching position, Rickie deteriorates. The school is a reflection of the Tonbridge where Forster was so unhappy as a boy. (Forster in 1920, in his *Abinger Harvest* essay "Notes on the English Character" wrote that the institution of public schools produced men with "undeveloped hearts.") At Sawston, Agnes gives birth to a little girl, who has Rickie's physical defect; but the child is exterminated in another of those one-sentence deaths ("After a short, painless illness, his daughter died"). Rickie, whose disillusionment with Agnes has grown, comes to see her as Ansell had: "Like the world she had created for him, she was unreal." Rickie has meanwhile acquired another relative. His aunt has told him that the hearty, crude young man she has brought up—Stephen Wonham—is Rickie's half brother.

Agnes persuades Rickie not to tell Stephen this. Rickie dislikes him because he thinks his own father was also Stephen's, but eventually he feels Stephen must be told: "The lie we acted has ruined our lives," he says to Agnes. But he still makes no move toward Stephen. Then Ansell, who has for the second and implacably final time failed to get his Cambridge fellowship—it is one of Forster's little jokes to have the tutors say that Ansell had read too much Hegel—bursts into Sawston School. Rickie, Agnes, Herbert, the masters, and the boys are all in the dining hall when Ansell makes a great trumpeting revelation, not only that Rickie has a bastard brother whom he will not acknowledge, but also that this half brother is the son of Rickie's mother. It is an effectively dramatic scene, the voice of Cambridge, with all the righteousness of the twisted Gregors Werle in Ibsen's *The Wild Duck*, shouting out the uncomfortable truth to hypocritical Sawston. Amid the tumult, Rickie faints, as he had when he first heard about Stephen's relationship to him—presumably on the hated paternal side.

Now Rickie feels differently about his mother's other son; he leaves Agnes and goes to live in Wiltshire with Stephen, who greets him sullenly. He and Rickie are not attuned—Rickie is particularly repelled by Stephen's heavy drinking—but they remain together. One night, however, when he learns that Stephen is drunk after promising "to behave decently," Rickie feels that for the second time in his life he has gone bankrupt: "Pretended again that people were real. May God have mercy on me!" Finding Stephen lying in a stupor across a railway track,

he just has time to push him out of the way before a train
comes. But he cannot save himself. And in a final chapter set
several years in the future, Stephen is married and a father, living on the soil as a farmer. In a scene of ironic comedy, he
haggles with Herbert Pembroke, now a clergyman, over Rickie's
literary remains. For Rickie had written some stories, which he
could not sell during his lifetime but which have become popular after his death. They are little fantasies, one of them about a
girl changing into a tree.

In *The Longest Journey*, the portraits of Rickie, Ansell, Agnes,
and others are expertly achieved: they come up from the page as
believable. Stephen Wonham alone seems difficult to accept as
actual. Rather extravagantly called Siegfried in the first draft of
the story, Stephen is a far less successful attempt at a child of
nature than Gino Carella in the previous novel. Forster was able
to catch all the exotic phases of Gino and make them credible,
while Gino's quick outburst of cruelty added to his vitality.
With Stephen, Forster—who did so well with a variety of
people—is not quite able to convey the quality of the English
boor: he seems to fall between idealizing him and portraying
him realistically, and never quite brings these two phases
together into a living characterization. Otherwise the book is
finely wrought, with people once again representing places and
ideas and yet for the most part behaving as individual human
beings rather than as types. Cambridge will not mix with Sawston, nor Cambridge and Sawston with Wiltshire; and Rickie,
torn by the three of them, pays a heavy price. His life is so miserable that his death comes almost as a relief to the reader.

Although the book presents a number of its important events
as headlines rather than as developed dramatic episodes, it contains some excitingly good scenes, such as Ansell's giving out
the truth in the school dining hall. There are bits of social com-

edy and shrewd observation learned from Jane Austen and
Samuel Butler who, with Proust, Forster said, "have helped me
most over my writing." Because the first part of Proust's novel
wasn't published until 1913, he can't be counted as an influence
before *Maurice* (possibly) and *A Passage to India;* Forster said that
Butler "did more than the other two to help me look at life the
way I do. What is that way? It is the undogmatic way." Forster
further said that from Jane Austen he "learned the possibilities
of domestic humour." It should perhaps be pointed out that
these writers are only partial influences on Forster, and not ob-
stacles to his originality. One of the phases of technique, for example, which he shares with Proust (and mentions in *Aspects of
the Novel*) is the leitmotiv, which Forster in speaking of Proust's
handling of the "Venteuil" sonata designates as a component of
rhythm. In his early period, Forster was already making use of
such devices. Consider the Hermes statue in *The Longest Journey,*
a figure associated with both Gerald and Stephen. And the one
picture in Stephen's room is, perhaps a bit too poetically, of
Demeter, goddess of grain.

But there is a more complicated example of rhythm in this
sense: the pictures in Rickie's Cambridge room in the first chapter. These are more than static symbols; they keep turning up as
themselves or in variations, and have therefore a kinetic function. One of them is George Frederick Watts's "Sir Percival,"
another is "a cheap brown madonna," still another is what some
visitors assume is Venice but the informed know to be Stockholm; and there is a picture of Rickie's mother, "looking rather
sweet." What the "Sir Percival" stands for we learn at the end of
the sixteenth chapter, when Rickie, hurt by a magazine editor's
rejection of his stories, is planning to marry Agnes and teach at
Sawston: "Rickie trusted that to him also benefits might accrue;
that his wound might heal as he laboured, and his eyes recap-

ture the Holy Grail." As for his "cheap" religious painting,
Rickie discovers that the superior Pembrokes have "madonnas of
acknowledged merit"; this is not emphasized, only mentioned,
but it points up some differences. Rickie does not know of his
mother's escapade in Stockholm with the man who became Stephen's father, but this is undoubtedly the source of the picture
of that city, near which Mrs. Elliot's Wiltshire-farmer lover
drowned. In the last scene the picture is in Stephen's possession,
and Herbert Pembroke accuses him of causing it "to be filched
from the walls of my house." The photograph of the mother had
turned up somewhat earlier, when Rickie held it out to Stephen
as a bond between them, and Stephen, who wanted to be loved
for himself, not out of relationship, tore the picture to pieces.
The use to which these objects are put indicates Forster's
method of expanding a story, deepening it, getting beyond the
usual effects of plot and character by means of what he was later
to define as rhythm.

His third novel to be published, *A Room with a View* (1908),
was begun before the other two: "The Italian half of the novel
was almost the first piece of fiction I attempted. I laid it aside to
write and publish two other novels, and then returned to it and
added the English half." It is lighter than the other two books,
and Forster has called it his "nicest" novel.

It begins in a Florentine *pensione* he calls the Bertolini, which
was actually the Simi, on the Lungarno alle Grazie (as Forster
said in a letter, "It no longer exists, though the building itself
has not been destroyed. It faces San Miniato. A pensione on the
other [San Miniato] side of the river is sometimes—and
wrongly—pointed out as its origin"). The story begins with confusion at the Bertolini: a young English girl, Lucy Honeychurch, and her elderly cousin-companion, Charlotte Bartlett,
are unhappy when they arrive and find that they will not have

the rooms which had been promised them overlooking the Arno. "I have a view, I have a view," a heavily built old man in the dining room cries out, insisting that they change rooms with him and his son George. Miss Bartlett tries to freeze out old Mr. Emerson, but without success, so the two sets of people make the transfer. The Emersons will from now on play an important part in Lucy's life: when she sees a murder committed in the Piazza della Signoria, the arms she falls back into are those of George Emerson; and on an excursion to Fiesole, when she stumbles down a little hillside onto a terrace full of violets, George is standing there and promptly embraces and kisses her. Before Lucy has a chance to react, a voice calls her name three times: "The silence of life had been broken by Miss Bartlett, who stood brown against the view."

Back in England at her home, Windy Corner, Lucy becomes engaged to Cecil Vyse. He is medieval and "like a Gothic statue" (Forster disliked the Middle Ages). But George Emerson and his father appear as householders in the Honeychurches' town in Surrey, and George takes another occasion to kiss Lucy, this time in the garden of her home. She rebuffs him, but that evening she breaks her engagement with Cecil, who could conceive only a feudal relationship, "that of protector and protected. He had no glimpse of the comradeship after which the girl's soul yearned." Later, old Mr. Emerson, who is childishly outspoken, pleads with Lucy on behalf of his son—and successfully. The story ends at the Bertolini, where George and Lucy have a room with a view. Happiness spreads before them, and even Miss Bartlett, whom Lucy speaks of as "dreadful frozen Charlotte," turns out not to be so bad after all, for George tells his bride that it was Charlotte who made possible the important interview between Lucy and the elder Emerson which resulted in the marriage: "from the very first moment we met, she hoped, far down in her mind, that we should be like this. . . ."

It is a crowded little comedy, but less complex and involved than the other two books. Some of the names of the people virtually suggest Restoration plays: not only Lucy Honeychurch, but the Reverend Mr. Eager and the lady novelist, Eleanor Lavish. Mr. Emerson, the loud humanist, may be mischievously named in parody of the ideals of self-reliance, friendship, compensation, and English traits. Yet, for all its sharpness as a comedy, *A Room with a View* has a thin quality. As social comedy, it lacks a rape-of-the-lock satiric sting, nor is it a vital picture of pride and prejudice melting before love. There is one unlikable clergyman, Mr. Eager, and a half-way unlikable one, Mr. Beebe, and in Victorian fashion there are little interpolated sermons and editorials by the author, as in his two earlier novels. Here, no atmospheres clash, as in the other books, though the influence of Tuscany seems more beneficent than that of Surrey.

A number of characters in the book fail to establish concord, especially Lucy and Cecil. The latter is somewhat on the order of Philip Herriton in *Where Angels Fear to Tread*. In the important moments, however, people do manage to communicate: George with his impulsive kisses, and his somewhat grotesque father with the ability to find just the right words to say to Lucy as she is about to leave for Greece. But none of these characters have the energetic attractiveness of several in the earlier novels (Caroline Abbott, Gino Carella, even the weak but sympathetic Rickie Elliot), or of so many of them in the later books. George Emerson, for all his ardor and energy, is moody and rather commonplace, though he shows promise at the end with his discerning remarks about Charlotte Bartlett. Lucy is a likable, ordinary, attractive girl, but not one with the luminous quality of the sharp-witted Elizabeth Bennett of *Pride and Prejudice*.

Perhaps the strongest social-comedy element in *A Room with a*

View is the opposition of the lower-middle-class Emersons with the upper-middle-class Cecil Vyse and his public-school background; but if Cecil is, in Lucy's eyes, limited to the medieval and the feudal, George Emerson has some of the eager vitality of the Renaissance, though without its classical learning or abundant creativity—yet he is right for Lucy, that admirer of Italy and the Renaissance, so the story as it works out is Forster's happiest, most optimistic novel.

Forster had a bit of fun imagining the future of these characters when, in 1958, to celebrate the fiftieth birthday of *A Room with a View*, he wrote an "Anniversary Postscript," for *The Observer*. George and Lucy, Forster imagines, would have settled in Highgate. ("Lucy . . . must now be in her late sixties, George in his early seventies— a ripe age though not as ripe as my own. They are still a personable couple, and fond of each other and of their children and grandchildren.") George, who had worked his way into a well-paid government clerkship, would have become a conscientious objector in World War I. Lucy, who insisted on playing Beethoven ("Hun music!"), received a call from the police, apparently at the instigation of neighbors. (When old Mr. Emerson, who lived with his son and daughter-in-law, lectured the policeman, they warned him. He died soon afterward, "still looking out and confident that Love and Truth would see humanity through in the end.") At the outbreak of World War II, George at the age of fifty enlisted at once because, "being intelligent and passionate, he could distinguish between a Germany that was not much worse than England and a Germany that was devilish." After being taken prisoner in Africa, George was removed to southern Italy, and when the Italian government collapsed he visited Florence on his way north. Although the city had been somewhat damaged, the Bertolini area was untouched, but the Bertolini itself was gone,

changed, some of the façades shrunken or extended, so that George had

to report to Lucy that the View was still there and that the Room must be there too but could not be found. She was glad of the news, although at that moment she was homeless and possessionless. It was something to have retained a View, and secure in it and in their love as long as they have one another to love, George and Lucy await the Third World War—the one that would end war and everything else too.

Forster ends his amusing little epilogue with a note on Cecil Vyse, who in 1914 "was seconded to Information or whatever the withholding of information was then entitled." At a party Forster attended in the outskirts of Alexandria during the war, the hostess was reluctant to have Beethoven played, but a young officer spoke up and said that someone who knew about such things had assured him that Beethoven was really a Belgian. The young officer was almost certainly Cecil, for "that mixture of mischief and culture is unmistakable. Our hostess was reassured, the ban was lifted, and the Moonlight Sonata shimmered into the desert."

In 1910, two years after publication of *A Room with a View*, *Howards End* appeared. It was a new Forster; he had arrived at his major phase as a novelist.

Howards End, one of the most famous of symbolic houses in English literature, was an actual place that a family of Howards once owned. Forster lived in this Hertfordshire house from the time he was four until he was fourteen. He says in *Marianne Thornton* that "the garden, the overhanging wych-elm, the sloping meadow, the great view to the west, the adjacent farm through the high tangled hedge of wild roses were all utilized by me in *Howards End*, and the interior is in the novel too." Forster had hoped to live and die there: "It certainly was a lovable little house, and still is, though it now stands just outside a twentieth-century hub and almost within sound of a twentieth-century hum."

In the novel, the first Mrs. Wilcox grew up there; she is of the yeoman stock Forster so much admires, and like Mrs. Moore in *A Passage to India*, she is a grand elderly woman whose influence lingers after her death. Before dying, she writes a note saying that she wants Howards End left to her younger friend Margaret Schlegel, but her family regards this bequest as an aberration and finds excuses to ignore it ("not legally binding"). The husband, Henry Wilcox, and his brutal and violent elder son Charles, are of the world of business and practicality, and although they have no proper feeling for Howards End, they cling to it.

Margaret Schlegel and her sister Helen represent a way of life opposite to that of the male Wilcoxes, with one of whom, Paul, Helen is briefly and embarrassingly involved at the beginning of the story. The late father of the Schlegel girls had left Germany because of his disgust with the materialist outlook, the militarist character, and the imperialist ambitions of the newly federated nation. The girls represent what was later to be called "the other Germany": the cultural side, particularly the musical. It is at a performance of Beethoven's Fifth Symphony that they meet Leonard Bast, a physically and spiritually undernourished young London clerk who is a walking testimonial to the fact that even the famous liberal reform movements of the nineteenth century had not, by the twentieth, done much toward alleviating the conditions one of Benjamin Disraeli's characters spoke of in 1845 in the novel *Sybil, or the Two Nations*. The "two nations" were the rich and the poor, between whom there is no intercourse and no sympathy; who are as ignorant of each other's habits, thoughts and feelings, as if they were dwellers in different zones, or inhabitants of different planets; who are formed by a different breeding, are fed by a different food, are ordered by different manners and are not governed by the same laws.

Forster, in describing Leonard Bast, says he did not belong to "the very poor," but "he knew that he was poor, and would admit it: he would have died sooner than admit any inferiority to the rich." So he reads Ruskin and attends concerts at Queen's Hall.

The Schlegel girls take him up seriously, and upon learning from Henry Wilcox that the insurance company which employs Leonard Bast might fail, they persuade him to leave it. At a lower salary, he goes to work in a bank, which soon lets him go in an employment reduction. Meanwhile, Henry Wilcox has proposed to Margaret and been accepted. At the wedding of Wilcox's daughter Evie, at his country house in Shropshire, Helen Schlegel suddenly appears with Leonard Bast and his wife Jacky, a blowsy slattern a dozen years older than he is. The Basts have been reduced to desperation because of the business advice, channeled through the Schlegels, that Henry Wilcox does not even remember giving. Helen has come down like an avenging angel to put matters right. Margaret shunts them all off to the village inn, but Jacky stays behind and gets drunk on the wedding wine. She encounters Henry, whom she addresses as Hen, and Margaret discovers that, years before, Jacky had been his mistress. Margaret decides not to let this stand between herself and Henry, and subsequently marries him.

Later, when Helen, back from a trip to the Continent, will communicate with Margaret only through letters, Henry and Margaret lure her to Howards End by telling her that the Schlegels' possessions are there and that she must unpack her books. Surprising Helen at the house, Margaret sees that she is pregnant. Helen wants to stay with the familiar furniture that night at Howards End—Margaret and Henry are located nearby at Charles's, but she wants Margaret to join her for that night, after which Helen will go to Munich for the birth of her child. Henry refuses: "Helen commands my sympathy . . . But I cannot treat her as if nothing had happened." Margaret goes to stay with her anyhow, and plans to leave her husband forever. That night she hears from Helen of her one joyless night with Leonard Bast, in Shropshire, at the time of Evie's wedding. Leonard, who does not know of the impending child, feels guilty because he has been Helen's lover and goes to Howards End to look for Margaret and confess that he is sorry. Leonard, like Stephen Wonham, becomes increasingly unreal: perhaps because of class differences in Victorian and Edwardian England, Forster could not have known such men well, as he apparently knew Italians and Indians in their own countries. Leonard in any event has been more than anything else an emblematic figure: when first introduced, he has an umbrella that is "all gone along the seams." But on his fatal visit to Howards End the symbols multiply. As he enters the house in the early morning he meets Charles, who has learned of what has happened: Charles seizes from its hanging place on the wall an old sword that had belonged to the Schlegel girls' father, and beats Leonard with it. Leonard falls, killed not by the sword but by a weak heart. As he crumples to the floor he catches hold of a bookcase, which is upset, showering books over him. It is a sword wielded by one of the Wilcoxes, the new conquerors of England, which has in effect killed Leonard, and it is the books of the Schlegels, representative of the culture he has aspired to, which symbolically bury him.

Although the autopsy shows that Leonard Bast was in the last stages of heart disease, Charles is tried and sentenced to three years' imprisonment for manslaughter. Margaret had told her husband that she planned to take Helen to Germany and stay there with her after the birth of the child, but when Henry turns to her pathetically after Charles is sentenced, Margaret goes with Henry to Howards End, to help him recover. At the end of the book he has called a family council there and told his children that he will leave them all his money, but that Howards End will go to Margaret, who learns for the first time, from something she overhears, that Mrs. Wilcox had wanted her to have the place. After her own death, it will become the property of her nephew—Leonard Bast's son—now a tiny child out in the adjoining fields with Helen, who on the last page of the novel bursts into the house rejoicing because there will be a great crop of hay.

Hay is one of the important symbols of *Howards End:* both the earlier Mrs. Wilcox and Margaret are associated with it. The former is introduced into the story with her hands full of hay, and Margaret several times twines grass in her own hands. In contrast to this, the male Wilcoxes are victims of hay fever. There are other suggestive images, such as the wych-elm mentioned in the earlier quotation by Forster describing the house that served as the original for Howards End: in an interview he said that this tree is symbolic, "the genius of the house," which itself stands for the enduring England (as Lionel Trilling was the first to point out). Today, this England is being cut down and cut up; Forster has been quoted earlier in a 1956 reference to "the twentieth-century hum" near the original Howards End, a reference he expanded three years later in a BBC broadcast ("Recollections of Nassenheide"), in which he said, "The tragedy of England is that she is too small to become a modern state and yet to retain her freshness. The freshness has to go." The loss of the freshness is accompanied by the loss of "the heritage which I used to see from my own doorstep in Hertfordshire when I was a child, and which has failed to outlast me." But even as early as 1910, the year of the novel, outspreading London threatened the peace of the countryside around Howards End: "Henry's kind had filched most of [the glebe]" that should have bordered the length of the Great North Road, on which the new monsters, the automobiles (Henry Wilcox's car is suggested as evil) are bringing to the fresh countryside the mechanization of the city. It is as if the recurrent goblins of Helen Schlegel's vision are taking over, the goblins she finds in the third movement of Beethoven's Fifth Symphony: "The music started with a goblin walking quietly over the universe, from end to end."

The "only connect" idea occurs when Margaret is pondering how she can point out to Henry Wilcox the salvation that is possible from within him and every man: "Only connect the prose and the passion, and both will be exalted, and human love will be seen at its height. Live in fragments no longer. Only connect, and the beast and the monk, robbed of the isolation that is life to either, will die." But she has not counted on Henry's obtuseness; she cannot get her ideas across to him. Throughout, the Schlegels and the Wilcoxes never really connect, though Margaret tries. Helen, early in the story, says that the Wilcoxes are "just a wall of newspapers and motor-cars and golf-clubs," and she is sure that behind that wall only emptiness and panic exist. Margaret tells her that "there is a great outer life" which she and Helen do not know, "in which telegrams and anger count." In it, personal relations do not govern, and love there "means marriage settlements, death, death duties." But "though obviously horrid," this outer life "often seems the real one—there's grit in it. It does breed character." Margaret tends throughout to defend the male Wilcoxes, and at one point she tells Helen that, without such men, "there would be no trains, no ships to carry us literary people about in, no fields even. Just savagery." The opposition between the Schlegel and Wilcox ways of life is somewhat thrown out of balance by Margaret's eagerness to connect. Forster skillfully has avoided an exactly balanced antithesis: rather he has presented a series of uncoordinated opposites.

As noted earlier, Henry's rigidity breaks whatever connection has been in the process of becoming established, and Margaret prepares to leave him. But she stays with him when she sees that he is shattered by the disgrace over Charles, and it is as a sick man that Henry lives at Howards End with her and Helen and the Bast child—a sick man, though not altogether a discontented one. Nevertheless, the true connection that Margaret had hoped for is not made. She has merely triumphed because of circumstances. She indulges in a rare moment of private gloating after Henry has announced that Howards End will be hers: "She, who had never expected to conquer anyone, had charged straight through these Wilcoxes and broken up their lives." This stresses breaking, not connecting—breaking followed by submission. But ultimately all will be well at Howards End, except for the encroachment of the symbolically evil city, and the child of Leonard Bast will inherit this earth. Leonard, ruined by the city, was two generations removed from the soil; his son, also the son of the cultivated Helen Schlegel, will settle into the life known by the family of the first Mrs. Wilcox, whose magic touch has made possible a hopeful future.

Forster's gifts of comedy and irony are again manifest, as well as the simple strength of his style, which in the present book ranges on the edge of the poetic, sometimes dangerously so. Some of the symbols of this novel have been referred to. Most of them are easily discernible, and yet they embody that intuitive quality of the symbolism of the modern school (which, after Baudelaire's pioneering sonnet "Correspondances," might be called correspondential symbolism). The element of the romantic in Forster's fiction, so often neglected in discussion of his work, appears forcibly in *Howards End*, not so much in relation to love as in relation to a romantic feeling for the earth, the places on it, and their influence. There is, above all, Howards End itself, the center of sanctification for both Mrs. Wilcoxes. It is a way of life upon the earth.

Before *Howards End*, Forster had begun a novel he never completed, *Arctic Summer:*

I had got my antithesis all right, the antithesis between the civilized man, who hopes for an Arctic summer in which there is time to get things done, and the heroic man. But I had not settled what is going to happen, and that is why the novel remains a fragment.

Late in 1910, after *Howards End* had come out, Forster made notes for a novel about a large and varied family; the setting was to be the English countryside and perhaps Paris. But he soon noted that he was too "tired" to write this. In 1911, the year he brought out *The Celestial Omnibus*, he tried his hand at what he has called "a bad unpublished play," *The Heart of Bosnia*. At another time, influenced by reading Anatole France, Forster attempted a novel about the Renaissance, but it remained unfinished. He wrote one more novel, however, the posthumous *Maurice* (1971), which he didn't publish in his lifetime because, like some of the previously mentioned short stories, it dealt with homosexuality.

The book cannot be discussed without a reference to Forster's explanation of its origin in 1913, a matter which he dealt with in his 1960 "Terminal Note" to the novel. He said that in 1913, when he had visited Edward Carpenter, a pioneer in the struggle to get homosexuality recognized and accepted, Carpenter's friend George Merrill "touched my backside—gently and just above the buttocks. I believe he touched most people's. The sensation was unusual and I still remember it. . . . It was as much psychological as physical. It seemed to go straight through the small of my back into my ideas, without involving my thoughts." When Forster returned to Harrogate, where he was then living, he at once began to write *Maurice:* "And the whole thing went through without a hitch." He completed the book in 1914.

The manuscript had a private circulation among Forster's friends, who approved of it in varying degrees. Lytton Strachey, an expert in such matters, who always greeted Carpenter's name "with a series of little squeaks," told Forster that the relationship between the Cantabrigian Maurice and the lower-class Alec "rested upon curiosity and lust and would only last six weeks." But Forster felt that "a happy ending was imperative. I shouldn't have bothered to write otherwise"; in 1960 he recorded his earlier determination that "two men should fall in love and remain in it for the ever and ever that fiction allows, and in this sense Maurice and Alec still roam the greenwood."

In the story, Maurice Hall doesn't realize that he is homosexual until he is at Cambridge. Forster noted that he tried to make him as different as possible from himself, "handsome, healthy, bodily attractive, mentally torpid, not a bad business man and rather a snob." He and Clive Durham fall in love, and Clive remains tormentingly apart. Later, after Clive has married and Maurice is visiting him and his wife, the young gamekeeper Alec Scudder climbs into Maurice's room one night, and their love affair begins. Maurice, who has been undergoing psychotherapy, abandons it. Sometime later, when Alec is to join his brother and sister-in-law to begin a new life in the Argentine, Maurice goes to Southampton to see Alec leave—amusingly enough, the ship is the *Normannia* from Forster's story "The Other Boat"—but Alec doesn't appear, and Maurice knows where to find him.

The book has some striking scenes, but a good deal of it seems flaccid in comparison with Forster at his best, as in *Howards End*, say, or *A Passage to India*, or in a story such as "The Eternal Moment." There is, particularly in the earlier parts, a lack of vividness, a deficiency of tension, which—despite Forster's courage in writing a novel he must have known would be published one day—may have come in part from an unconscious anxiety that inhibited his most notable gifts as a writer. Part of the apparent slackness may also derive from the general absence of concreteness of the kind which readers of a later time are accustomed to; yet Forster, as long ago as 1920, told Siegfried Sassoon in a letter, "Nothing is more obdurate to artistic treatment than the carnal, but it has to be got in, I'm sure: everything has to be got in." Yet most of *Maurice* is vague along the lines of the "carnal." Occasionally life manifests itself with a precise vitality, as at the end of the chapter in which Maurice, awakened in his bedroom at Clive's country house, receives an unexpected visitor:

But as he returned to his bed a little noise sounded, a noise so intimate that it might have arisen inside his own body. He seemed to crackle and burn and saw the ladder's top quivering against the moonlit air. The head and the shoulders of a man rose up, paused, a gun was laid against the window sill very carefully, and someone he scarcely knew moved towards him and knelt beside him and whispered, "Sir, was you calling out for me? . . . Sir, I know. . . . I know," and touched him.

The fourth and last part of the book, which follows, is far more animated, in its narrative and drama, than the earlier sections. Forster across the years kept working over the coda: according to his authorized biographer, P. N. Furbank, he revised it in 1919 and 1932 and, "fairly drastically, in 1959–60." The latest version is by far the best part of the book, containing not only the dramatic episode at Southampton, when the *Normannia* departs without Alec, the reunion of the lovers, and then the last dialogue, at once poignant and ironic, of Maurice and Clive, in which the latter will refer to Alec only as "Scudder" and in which Maurice will slip away during one of Clive's sentences inviting him to dinner the next week: "Dinner jacket's enough, as you know." Maurice left "no trace of his presence except a little pile of the petals of the evening primrose, which mourned from the ground like an expiring fire. To the end of his life Clive was not sure of the exact moment of departure, and with the approach of old age he grew uncertain whether the moment had yet occurred."

Maurice and *The Longest Journey* were, according to Forster's friend Oliver Stallybrass, the two "novels which meant most to" him, the latter perhaps because of his affinity with Rickie Elliott, who of all his characters is the one temperamentally closest to his author. Most critics, however, prefer either *Howards End* or *A Passage to India*, and in any dispute over their relative merits it might be noted that each of them is extremely excellent in its own way. *Howards End*, which is the only Forster novel apart from *The Longest Journey* whose action takes place entirely inside England, has an enriching complexity, but its theme can be understood without too much difficulty. *A Passage to India*, the only one of the novels set entirely outside England, has its own complexities and contains a mystery not too easy to resolve. As a novel, however, it is more satisfactory than any of the others, for a number of reasons. For one thing, it has more dramatization (and significant description that bears on the action) and fewer editorial comments than all the rest. More important, all its characters, English and Indian, are convincing: there are no imperfections in the portraiture such as there were in the instances of Stephen Wonham and Leonard Bast. And because the people of *A Passage to India* fuse so readily with theme and plot, the book is satisfactory in a way that no other Forster novel is: he had achieved a mastery of the medium.

Yet Forster had great difficulties with the story over a number of years. He began it in England after the 1912–13 visit to India, and then the war intervened. When he returned to that country in 1922, he took with him the chapters he had written, but discovered that he could not work on the book there: "What I had written wasn't India at all. It was sticking a photograph on a picture. However, I couldn't *write* it when I was in India. When I got away, I could get on with it." But he "still thought the book bad, and probably should not have completed it without the encouragement of Leonard Woolf."

A piquant introduction to the problems, as well as to the setting, of *A Passage to India* occurs in a book Forster brought out just twenty-nine years after the novel. *The Hill of Devi* (1953) is an account of his first two trips to India, in 1912–13 and 1922. It is made up largely of letters written to his mother and friends in England, chiefly concerning the Maharajah of Dewas Senior. He is "a bright and tiny young Indian" in the 1912–13 letters, and in those of 1922 a mature ruler with a sense of humor and a longing for affection. He could never be disturbed during his two-hour period of prayer: "I am so very sorry I am holy just now." Forster found on his first visit that "this amazing little state" could "have no parallel, except in a Gilbert and Sullivan opera." But during the six months of his second stay, which he could have made permanent but chose not to, Forster sank sympathetically into the place and its affairs.

The longest section of the book, "Gokul Ashtami," describes the festival of that name which Forster attended for nine days; it gave him the scenery of the Shri Krishna ceremonies in the last part of *A Passage to India*. He closes *The Hill of Devi* with an account of the last unhappy years of the Maharajah, whose son and heir fled from Dewas in 1927 because he thought his father was trying to poison him. This scandal intensified various political troubles the Maharajah was undergoing; in 1933 he left Dewas to live in Pondicherry, capital of French India, where he was a stranger. He prayed and fasted until his death in 1937.

Forster rounds off his notable portrait of this man by saying that it is impossible to think evenly of the dead, who slip out of sight and "go into silence. Yet we cannot help assigning some of them a tune." Usually, people do not leave a sound behind them, and cannot be evoked. But the Maharajah "has the rare quality of evoking himself, and I do not believe that he is here doing it for the last time."

Many interpretations of *A Passage to India* exist, but as in all Forster's novels the central theme is the inability of human beings to "connect." Here the two conflicting worlds are those of the colonial English and of the native Indian, both Mohammedan and Hindu. Forster in 1957 said that the India he had written of "no longer exists, either politically or socially . . . Assuredly the novel dates." But it distinctly does not, and one of the principal reasons for its continued existence is that in writing it Forster's "main purpose was not political, was not even sociological." He told a miraculously good story of a place and a time, and this should be enough. Criticisms of Forster's historical accuracy such as those made by Nirad C. Chaudhuri in "Passage to and from India" (*Encounter*, June, 1954) are merely literal and specious. For later events have demonstrated that the book is also timely not only for this moment of colonial troubles in different parts of the world and civil-rights uprisings in the United States, but emphatically appropriate on a larger scale because it is a picture of the human condition in our age. *A Passage to India* intensifies the message of *Howards End:* "Only connect."

This might well be the motto of Mrs. Moore, whose influence dominates the book somewhat in the manner of the first Mrs. Wilcox of *Howards End.* Both these elderly women—Mrs. Wilcox dies early in the story she appears in, Mrs. Moore at about the middle of the other novel—have a message that is stated only in action (Mrs. Wilcox's wish to give the house to Margaret Schlegel) or in a few cryptic but significant statements (Mrs. Moore's brief remarks about the innocence of an accused man, made "indifferently" to his accuser and later possibly repeated in her sleep and overheard). Both Mrs. Wilcox and Mrs. Moore are symbolic figures, among other things emblemizing the continuity of underlying truths: continuity, a sustained connection. Their intuitions as human beings are carried over into what they represent, for symbols at their most forceful are connotative rather than denotative and can best be apprehended through intuition. Each of these women is a form of the *magna dea* or *magna mater*, sharing this identity with such quite different women in modern literature as Mrs. Ramsay in Virginia Woolf's *To the Lighthouse* and Molly Bloom in James Joyce's *Ulysses*. Forster in his earlier books had tried with less success to project the intuitive, half-articulate, essentially nonintellectual character (and symbol) in males such as Gino Carella and Stephen Wonham. In his last two novels he succeeds marvelously with Mrs. Wilcox and Mrs. Moore, who even in death pervade the story: Margaret finally acquires Howards End in a way that promises a continuity Mrs. Wilcox could hardly have known, and Mrs. Moore has given Adela Quested the clarity of vision that helps her see truth. There is no easy solution in either case, certainly not in *A Passage to India*, in which the accused man who has been freed remains surly, but in each instance Forster has by indirection, by means of these grand elderly women, pointed a way toward some of the secrets of life, and toward true possibilities of connection.

A Passage to India is divided into three parts ("Mosque," "Caves," "Temple") which Forster says "represent the three seasons of the Cold Weather, the Hot Weather, and the Rains, which divide the Indian year." The central theme of the book concerns the attempts at friendship between the Englishman Cyril Fielding and the Mohammedan Indian Dr. Aziz. The central incidents, which have a drastic effect upon this friendship, are the occurrence at the Marabar caves and the subsequent trial of Dr. Aziz. Delighted to find some English people who are not snobbish, the eager Aziz has invited Fielding to visit the Marabar caves along with two newly arrived Englishwomen: Mrs. Moore, mother of the City Magistrate of Chandrapore, and the plain-looking Adela Quested, who considers marrying Mrs. Moore's son, Ronny Heaslop. Before consenting to a formal engagement, Adela has come out to see him in his new environment. Ronny only expresses the general attitude of the English colony when he disapproves of his mother's and Adela's association with Indians. And certainly the association does lead to catastrophe.

Adela staggers out of one of the caves, and after plunging downhill through cactus, is taken back to Chandrapore in a friend's car. In high hysteria, she says that Dr. Aziz had tried to assault her in the cave. He is arrested, and the antagonism between the English and the Indian sections of the community reaches a boiling point. Fielding, who was not a witness though he was nearby, is ostracized by the English for insisting that

Aziz could not have been guilty of the attempted assault. The sibylline Mrs. Moore, also not a witness, likewise believes in the innocence of Aziz, but leaves India before the trial. In dealing with these events, Forster shows the highest skill, brilliantly weaving the narrative through all the complications of the plot. To the admitted earlier influences of Samuel Butler and Jane Austen, Forster had added Proust: "I learned ways of looking at character from him. The modern subconscious way." Proust's writing also confirmed Forster in his use of the leitmotiv, taken from music. Here, such manifestations as the recurring wasp illustrate the technique: Mrs. Moore, seeing it as a creature of essential beauty, at least of prettiness, is close to Dr. Godbole, the Brahman mystic in the story who at the Shri Krishna festival in the last part of the book remembers a wasp he has seen and thinks of it in terms of union with God.

The trial itself is thematically and dramatically powerful, and pungent with humor. When Superintendent of Police McBryde opens the case for the prosecution, he cannot resist the temptation to harp on his favorite belief, "that the darker races are physically attracted by the fairer, but not vice versa," at which a disembodied voice asks, "Even when the lady is so uglier than the gentleman?" At once a native policeman seizes an Indian who had said nothing, and hustles him out of the courtroom. Later the name of Mrs. Moore is invoked: why had the prosecution got her out of the way so that she could not testify on behalf of Aziz? The native crowd begins to chant, "Esmiss Esmoor," horrifying Ronny, who does not want his mother transformed by parody into a Hindu goddess. No one there knows that Mrs. Moore has died on the ship taking her toward England. Some of her spirit may have infused itself into Miss Quested, who when called upon to testify, drily says that it was all a mistake, that Aziz did not follow her into the cave. Aziz is

freed amid uproar. Adela Quested, cut off from the English
colony and in possible danger of violence from the Indians, takes
refuge in the school Fielding directs. After she leaves India there
is a rumor that she and Fielding have been lovers there. Aziz accepts this preposterous story as fact: an intricately complicated
human being, he can be a sweet and gentle friend or a little
monster.

When Fielding and Aziz meet again two years later, Aziz
commits another mistake by thinking that the wife Fielding has
brought with him on an official visit to Mau (in Central India,
where Aziz has moved) is the former Adela Quested. But he
learns that Fielding's wife is Mrs. Moore's daughter, Stella.
Fielding and Aziz go for a last ride together, and Aziz is full of
hatred for the English and full of prophecy: when the next European war comes, and England is in trouble, "Aha! aha! Then
is our time." India will be free. Fielding, now "acquiring some
of [the] limitations" of Anglo-India, mocks him, but Aziz says
that every Englishman will be driven into the sea, and after that
he and Fielding can be friends. Fielding, leaning out of his
saddle to hold him affectionately, asks why they cannot be
friends now: they both want it. The closing passage of the book
says:

But the horses didn't want it—they swerved apart; the earth didn't
want it, sending up rocks through which riders must pass single file; the
temples, the tank, the jail, the palace, the birds, the carrion, the Guest
House, that came into view as they issued from the gap and saw Mau
beneath: they didn't want it, they said in their hundred voices, "No,
not yet," and the sky said, "No, not there."

The spirit of Mrs. Moore, that woman who was so beneficent
yet so imperfect, has not prevailed here, and the two worlds
remain apart. The causes are deeper than the experience at the
caves, yet ultimately it is that which has made Aziz what he is.

Selected Bibliographies

Arnold Bennett

NOTE. *We have listed here all Bennett's works of fiction, but given only a selection from his miscellaneous output. A complete bibliography can be consulted in J. G. Hepburn's book, listed below. The facts of publication for each volume are those of its publication in London.*

PRINCIPAL WORKS
Novels

A Man from the North. London, Lane, 1898.
Anna of the Five Towns. London, Chatto and Windus, 1902.
The Grand Babylon Hotel. London, Chatto and Windus, 1902.
The Gates of Wrath. London, Chatto and Windus, 1903.
Leonora. London, Chatto and Windus, 1903.
A Great Man: A Frolic. London, Chatto and Windus, 1904.
Teresa of Watling Street: A Fantasia on Modern Themes. London, Chatto and Windus, 1904.
Sacred and Profane Love: A Novel in Three Episodes. London, Chatto and Windus, 1905.
Hugo: A Fantasia on Modern Themes. London, Chatto and Windus, 1906.
Whom God Hath Joined. London, Nutt, 1906.
The Sinews of War. With E. Phillpotts. London, Laurie, 1906.
The Ghost. London, Chatto and Windus, 1907.
The City of Pleasure. London, Chatto and Windus, 1907.
Buried Alive. London, Chapman and Hall, 1908.
The Statue. With E. Phillpotts. London, Cassell, 1908.
The Old Wives' Tale. London, Chapman and Hall, 1908.

The Glimpse: An Adventure of the Soul. London, Chapman and Hall, 1909.
Helen with the High Hand: An Idyllic Diversion. London, Chapman and Hall, 1910.
Clayhanger. London, Methuen, 1910.
The Card. London, Methuen, 1911.
Hilda Lessways. London, Methuen, 1911.
The Regent: A Five Towns Story of Adventures in London. London, Methuen, 1913.
The Great Adventure. London, Methuen, 1913.
The Price of Love. London, Methuen, 1914.
These Twain. London, Methuen, 1916.
The Lions's Share. London, Cassell, 1916.
The Pretty Lady. London, Cassell, 1918.
The Roll Call. London, Hutchinson, 1918.
Lilian. London, Cassell, 1922.
Mr. Prohack. London, Methuen, 1922.
Riceyman Steps. London, Cassell, 1923.
Lord Raingo. London, Cassell, 1926.
The Strange Vanguard. London, Cassell, 1928.
Accident. London, Cassell, 1929.
Imperial Palace. London, Cassell, 1930.
Venus Rising from the Sea. London, Cassell, 1931.
Dream of Destiny. London, Cassell, 1932.

Short Stories

The Loot of the Cities. London, Rivers, 1905.
Tales of the Five Towns. London, Chatto and Windus, 1905.
The Grim Smile of the Five Towns. London, Chapman and Hall, 1907.
The Matador of the Five Towns. London, Methuen, 1912.
Elsie and the Child. London, Cassell, 1924.
The Woman Who Stole Everything. London, Cassell, 1927.
The Night Visitor. London, Cassell, 1931.

Essays

Things That Have Interested Me: Series I. London, Chatto and Windus, 1921.
Things That Have Interested Me: Series II. London, Chatto and Windus, 1923.
Things That Have Interested Me: Series III. London, Chatto and Windus, 1926.
The Savour of Life: Essays in Gusto. London, Cassell, 1928.
The Religious Interregnum. London, Benn, 1929.

Letters

Bennett, Dorothy Cheston. Arnold Bennett, A Portrait Done at Home, together with 170 Letters from A. B. New York, Kendall and Sharp, 1935.

The Letters of Arnold Bennett to His Nephew. New York and London, Harper & Brothers, 1935.

The Letters of Arnold Bennett. Edited by James G. Hepburn. 3 vols. London, Oxford University Press, 1966, 1968, 1970.

Gide, André and Arnold Bennett. Correspondance André Gide–Arnold Bennett, vingt ans d'amité littéraire (1911–1931). Introduction and notes by L. F. Brugmans. Geneva, 1964.

Travel

Those United States. London, Secker, 1912.

Paris Nights. London, Hodder and Stoughton, 1913.

Over There: War Scenes on the Western Front. London, Methuen, 1915.

Mediterranean Scenes. London, Cassell, 1928.

Florentine Journal, 1st April–25th May, 1910. London, Chatto and Windus, 1967.

Criticism

Literary Taste: How to Form It. London, New Age, 1909.

The Author's Craft. London, Hodder and Stoughton, 1914.

Books and Persons. London, Chatto and Windus, 1917.

Hynes, Samuel, ed. The Author's Craft and other Critical Writings of Arnold Bennett. Lincoln, University of Nebraska Press, 1968.

Journals

Journal, 1929. London, Cassell, 1930.

The Journals of Arnold Bennett. Edited by Newman Flower. 3 vols. London, Cassell, 1932–33.

BIBLIOGRAPHY

Emery, Norman. Arnold Bennett (1867–1931): A Bibliography. Revised ed. Stoke-on-Trent, Stoke-on-Trent City Libraries, 1967.

Gordan, John D. Arnold Bennett: The Centenary of His Birth. Catalogue of an Exhibition in the Berg Collection, New York Public Library, 1968.

CRITICAL WORKS AND COMMENTARY

Allen, Walter. Arnold Bennett. London, Home and Van Thal, 1948.

Arnold Bennett. (Commemorative Brochure.) Stoke-on-Trent, College of Art, School of Printing and Graphic Design, 1967.

Arnold Bennett Centenary, 1867–1967. City of Stoke-on-Trent, Town Clerk's Department, 1967.

Barker, Dudley. Writer by Trade: A View of Arnold Bennett. London, Allen and Unwin, 1966.

Beardmore, George, and Jean Beardmore. Arnold Bennett in Love: Arnold Bennett and His Wife Marguerite Soulié, a Correspondence. London, David Bruce and Watson, 1972.

Bennett, Marguerite. My Arnold Bennett. London, Ivor Nicholson and Watson, 1931.

Hepburn, James G. The Art of Arnold Bennett. Bloomington, Indiana University Press, 1963.

Lafourcade, Georges. Arnold Bennett: A Study. London, Frederick Muller, 1939.

Lucas, John. Arnold Bennett. London, Methuen, 1974.

Marriott, Frederick. My Association with Arnold Bennett. Keele Occasional Publications Series No. 3. Keele, University College of North Staffordshire Library, 1967.

Pound, Reginald. Arnold Bennett. London, Heinemann, 1952. (This is still the standard biography.)

Roberts, Thomas R. Arnold Bennett's Five Towns Origins. City of Stoke-on-Trent, Libraries, Museums, and Information Committee, 1961.

Simons, J. B. Arnold Bennett and His Novels: A Critical Study. Oxford, Blackwell, 1936.

Swinnerton, Frank. The Georgian Literary Scene. London, Heinemann, 1935.

Tillier, Louis. Arnold Bennett et ses romans réalistes. Paris, Didier, 1967.

———. Studies in the Sources of Arnold Bennett's Novels. Paris, Didier, 1969.

Warillow, E. J. D. Arnold Bennett and Stoke-on-Trent. Hanley, Etruscan Publications, 1966.

Wright, Walter F. Arnold Bennett, Romantic Realist. Lincoln, University of Nebraska Press, 1971.

Evelyn Waugh

NOTE: *Only first English and American editions of Waugh's works are listed, except where later editions are of special interest. Most of Waugh's fiction is published in a Uniform Edition by Chapman & Hall, London, and many titles are available in paperback editions, published mainly by Penguin in England and by Dell in the United States.*

PRINCIPAL WORKS

Rossetti: His Life and Works. London, Duckworth, 1928; New York, Dodd, Mead, 1928.

Decline and Fall. London, Chapman and Hall, 1928; New York, Farrar and Rinehart, 1929.

Vile Bodies. London, Chapman and Hall, 1930; New York, Cape and Smith, 1930.

Labels: A Mediterranean Journal. London, Duckworth, 1930; New York, Cape and Smith, 1930 (under the title, A Bachelor Abroad: A Mediterranean Journal).

Remote People. London, Duckworth, 1931; New York, Farrar and Rinehart, 1932 (under the title, They Were Still Dancing).

Black Mischief. London, Chapman and Hall, 1932; New York, Farrar and Rinehart, 1932.

Ninety-Two Days. London, Duckworth, 1934; New York, Farrar and Rinehart, 1934.

A Handful of Dust. London, Chapman and Hall, 1934; New York, Farrar and Rinehart, 1934.

Edmund Campion. London, Sheed and Ward, 1935; Boston, Little, Brown, 1946.

Mr. Loveday's Little Outing, and Other Sad Stories. London, Chapman and Hall, 1936; Boston, Little, Brown, 1936.

Scoop. London, Chapman and Hall, 1938; Boston, Little, Brown, 1938.

Robbery under Law: The Mexican Object Lesson. London, Chapman and Hall, 1939; Boston, Little, Brown, 1939 (under the title, Mexico: An Object-Lesson).

Work Suspended. London, Chapman and Hall, 1942. (See Tactical Exercise, below.)

Put Out More Flags. London, Chapman and Hall, 1942; Boston, Little, Brown, 1942.

Brideshead Revisited. London, Chapman and Hall, 1945; Boston, Little, Brown, 1945. Revised ed., London, Chapman and Hall, 1960.

When the Going Was Good (selections from earlier travel books). London, Duckworth, 1946; Boston, Little, Brown, 1946.

Scott-King's Modern Europe. London, Chapman and Hall, 1947; Boston, Little, Brown, 1949.

The Loved One. London, Chapman and Hall, 1948; Boston, Little, Brown, 1948.

Helena. London, Chapman and Hall, 1950; Boston, Little, Brown, 1950.

Men at Arms. London, Chapman and Hall, 1952; Boston, Little, Brown, 1952.

Love among the Ruins. London, Chapman and Hall, 1953.

Tactical Exercise. Boston, Little, Brown, 1954. (Includes Work Suspended and Love among the Ruins.)
Officers and Gentlemen. London, Chapman and Hall, 1955; Boston, Little, Brown, 1955.
The Ordeal of Gilbert Pinfold. London, Chapman and Hall, 1957; Boston, Little, Brown, 1957.
"The Private Diaries of Evelyn Waugh." Edited by Michael Davie. *Observer Magazine*, March 25, April 1, 8, 15, 22, and 29, and May 6, 1973.
Ronald Knox. London, Chapman and Hall, 1959; Boston, Little, Brown, 1959.
Unconditional Surrender. London, Chapman and Hall, 1961; Boston, Little, Brown, 1962 (under the title, The End of the Battle).
A Little Learning. London, Chapman and Hall, 1964; Boston, Little, Brown, 1964.
Sword of Honour. (One-vol. ed.) London, Chapman and Hall, 1965.

CRITICAL WORKS AND COMMENTARY

Bergonzi, Bernard. "Evelyn Waugh's Gentlemen," *Critical Quarterly*, V (1963), 23–36.
Bradbury, Malcolm. Evelyn Waugh. Edinburgh and London, Oliver and Boyd, 1964.
Carens, James F. The Satiric Art of Evelyn Waugh. Seattle and London, University of Washington Press, 1966.
De Vitis, A. A. Roman Holiday: The Catholic Novels of Evelyn Waugh. New York, Bookman Associates, 1956.
Donaldson, Frances. Evelyn Waugh: Portrait of a Country Neighbour. London, Weidenfeld & Nicolson, 1967.
Dyson, A. E. "Evelyn Waugh and the Mysteriously Disappearing Hero," *Critical Quarterly*, II (1960), 72–79.
Greenblatt, Stephen Jay. Three Modern Satirists: Waugh, Huxley and Orwell. New Haven, Yale University Press, 1965.
Jebb, Julian. "Evelyn Waugh: An Interview," *Paris Review*, VIII (1963), 73–85.
Kermode, Frank. "Mr. Waugh's Cities," in Puzzles and Epiphanies, pp. 164–75. London, Routledge, 1962.
O'Donnell, Donat (Conor Cruise O'Brien). Maria Cross: Imaginative Patterns in a Group of Modern Catholic Writers. London, Chatto and Windus, 1953.
Pryce-Jones, David. Evelyn Waugh and his World. London, Weidenfeld and Nicolson, 1973.
Stopp, Frederick J. Evelyn Waugh: Portrait of an Artist. London, Chapman and Hall, 1958.
Waugh, Alec. My Brother Evelyn and Other Profiles. London, Cassell, 1968.
Wilson, Edmund. "Never Apologize, Never Explain: The Art of Evelyn

Waugh," and "Splendors and Miseries of Evelyn Waugh," in Classics and Commercials. New York, Farrar, Straus, 1950.

Ford Madox Ford

NOTE: *Most of Ford's works have long been out of print. Exceptions are* Parade's End, *comprising the four Christopher Tietjens novels, currently available in the United States in a two-volume edition by Signet (New American Library);* The Good Soldier, *published in Vintage Books (Random House); and* The Fifth Queen *(trilogy), issued by the Vanguard Press, in 1964. The same works, minus* Last Post *but with lesser pieces, were included in* The Bodley Head Ford Madox Ford *(four volumes), London, 1962–63, with an Introduction by Graham Greene.*

The standard bibliography, both primary and secondary, is David Dow Harvey's Ford Madox Ford, 1873–1939: A Bibliography of Works and Criticism *(Princeton, Princeton University Press, 1962). See also Charles G. Hoffmann,* Ford Madox Ford *(New York, Twayne, 1967).*

PRINCIPAL WORKS

The Brown Owl: A Fairy Story. London, Unwin, 1892 [for 1891]; New York, Stokes, 1891.

The Shifting of the Fire. London, Unwin, 1892; New York, Putnam, 1892.

Ford Madox Brown: A Record of His Life and Work. London, Longmans, Green, 1896; New York, Longmans, Green, 1896.

The Cinque Ports: A Historical and Descriptive Record. London, Blackwood, 1900.

The Inheritors: An Extravagant Story. With Joseph Conrad. New York, McClure, Phillips, 1901; London, Heinemann, 1901.

Romance: A Novel. With Joseph Conrad. London, Smith, Elder, 1903; New York, McClure, Phillips, 1904.

The Benefactor: A Tale of a Small Circle. London, Brown, Langham, 1905.

The Fifth Queen: And How She Came to Court. London, Rivers, 1906.

Privy Seal: His Last Venture. London, Rivers, 1907.

England and the English: An Interpretation. (Combining The Soul of London, 1905; The Heart of the Country: A Survey of a Modern Land, 1906; The Spirit of the People, 1907. These were separately published in London by Alston Rivers.) New York, McClure, Phillips, 1907.

An English Girl: A Romance. London, Methuen, 1907.
The Fifth Queen Crowned: A Romance. London, Nash, 1908.
Mr. Apollo: A Just Possible Story. London, Methuen, 1908.
The "Half Moon": A Romance of the Old World and the New. London, Nash, 1909; New York, Doubleday, Page, 1909.
A Call: The Tale of Two Passions. London, Chatto and Windus, 1910.
The Portrait. London, Methuen, 1910.
Ancient Lights and Certain New Reflections: Being the Memories of a Young Man. London, Chapman and Hall, 1911; New York, Harper and Brothers, 1911. (The Harper edition was entitled Memories and Impressions: A Study in Atmospheres.)
Ladies Whose Bright Eyes: A Romance. London, Constable, 1911; Philadelphia, Lippincott, 1935. (The Lippincott edition is extensively revised.)
The Panel: A Sheer Comedy. London, Constable, 1912; Indianapolis, Bobbs-Merrill, 1913. (The Bobbs-Merrill edition, a revised text, was entitled Ring for Nancy: A Sheer Comedy.)
Mr. Fleight. London, Latimer, 1913.
The Young Lovell: A Romance. London, Chatto and Windus, 1913.
Henry James: A Critical Study. London, Secker, 1913 [for 1914]; New York, A. and C. Boni, 1915.
The Good Soldier: A Tale of Passion. London, John Lane, 1915; New York, John Lane, 1915.
Thus to Revisit: Some Reminiscences. London, Chapman and Hall, 1921; New York, Dutton, 1921.
The Marsden Case: A Romance. London, Duckworth, 1923.
Women and Men. Paris, Three Mountains Press, 1923.
Some Do Not . . . : A Novel. London, Duckworth, 1924; New York, Thomas Seltzer, 1924.
The Nature of a Crime. With Joseph Conrad. London, Duckworth, 1924; New York, Doubleday, Page, 1924.
Joseph Conrad: A Personal Remembrance. London, Duckworth, 1924; Boston, Little, Brown, 1924.
No More Parades: A Novel. London, Duckworth, 1925; New York, A. and C. Boni, 1925.
A Man Could Stand Up—A Novel. London, Duckworth, 1926; New York, A. and C. Boni, 1926.
The Last Post. New York, Literary Guild of America, 1928; London, Duckworth, 1928. (The Duckworth edition was entitled Last Post.)
A Little Less Than Gods: A Romance. London, Duckworth, 1928; New York, Viking Press, 1928.

No Enemy: A Tale of Reconstruction. New York, Macaulay, 1929.
Reminiscences, 1894–1914: Return to Yesterday. London, Gollancz, 1931; New York, Liveright, 1932. (The Liveright edition was entitled Return to Yesterday.)
When the Wicked Man. New York, Liveright, 1931; London, Cape, 1932.
The Rash Act: A Novel. New York, Long and Smith, 1933; London, Cape, 1933.
It Was the Nightingale. Philadelphia, Lippincott, 1933; London, Heinemann, 1934.
Henry for Hugh: A Novel. Philadelphia, Lippincott, 1934.
Provence: From Minstrels to the Machine. Philadelphia, Lippincott, 1935; London, Allen and Unwin, 1938.
Collected Poems. New York, Oxford, 1936.
Vive le Roy: A Novel. Philadelphia, Lippincott, 1936; London, Allen and Unwin, 1937.
Great Trade Route. New York and Toronto, Oxford, 1937; London, Allen and Unwin, 1937.
Portraits from Life: Memories and Criticisms. Boston and New York, Houghton Mifflin, 1937; London, Allen and Unwin, 1938. (The Allen and Unwin edition was entitled Mightier Than the Sword: Memories and Criticisms.)
The March of Literature from Confucius' Day to Our Own. New York, Dial, 1938; London, Allen and Unwin, 1939. (The Allen and Unwin edition was entitled The March of Literature from Confucius to Modern Times.)
The Fifth Queen. (Combining The Fifth Queen: And How She Came to Court, 1906; Privy Seal: His Last Venture, 1907; The Fifth Queen Crowned: A Romance, 1908.) New York, Vanguard, 1964.
Letters. Edited by Richard M. Ludwig. Princeton, Princeton University Press, 1965.

CRITICAL WORKS AND COMMENTARY

Aldington, Richard. Life for Life's Sake: A Book of Reminiscences. New York, Viking, 1941.
Bowen, Stella. Drawn from Life. London, Collins, 1941.
Cassell, Richard A. Ford Madox Ford: A Study of His Novels. Baltimore, Johns Hopkins University Press, 1961.
Goldring, Douglas. The Last Pre-Raphaelite. London, Macdonald, 1948; New York, Dutton, 1949. (The Dutton edition was entitled Trained for Genius: The Life and Writings of Ford Madox Ford.)
———. South Lodge: Reminiscences of Violet Hunt, Ford Madox Ford and the English Review Circle. London, Constable, 1943.

Hunt, Violet. The Flurried Years. London, Hurst and Blackett, 1926; New York, Boni and Liveright, 1926. (The Boni and Liveright edition was entitled I Have This to Say.)

Leer, Norman. The Limited Hero in the Novels of Ford Madox Ford. East Lansing, Michigan State University Press, 1966.

Lid, Richard W. Ford Madox Ford: The Essence of His Art. Berkeley and Los Angeles, University of California Press, 1964.

MacShane, Frank. The Life and Work of Ford Madox Ford. New York, Horizon, 1965.

Meixner, John A. Ford Madox Ford's Novels: A Critical Study. Minneapolis, University of Minnesota Press, 1961.

Mizener, Arthur. The Saddest Story: A Biography of Ford Madox Ford. New York, World, 1971.

Poli, Bernard J. Ford Madox Ford and the *Transatlantic Review*. Syracuse, N.Y., Syracuse University Press, 1967.

Wiley, Paul L. Novelist of Three Worlds: Ford Madox Ford. Syracuse, N. Y., Syracuse University Press, 1962.

Joseph Conrad

WORKS

The Works of Joseph Conrad. Uniform Edition, London, J. M. Dent, 1923–28. Collected Edition, London, J. M. Dent, 1946–54. Memorial Edition, Garden City, N. Y., Doubleday, Page, 1925.

BIBLIOGRAPHIES

Ehrsam, Theodore G. A Bibliography of Joseph Conrad. Metuchen, N. J., The Scarecrow Press, 1969.

Lohf, Kenneth A., and Eugene P. Sheehy. Joseph Conrad at Mid-Century: Editions and Studies, 1895–1955. Minneapolis, University of Minnesota Press, 1957.

CRITICAL WORKS AND COMMENTARY

Allen, Jerry. The Sea Years of Joseph Conrad. New York, Doubleday, 1965.

Aubry, G. Jean. Joseph Conrad: Life and Letters. New York, Doubleday, Page, 1927.

Baines, Jocelyn. Joseph Conrad. New York, McGraw-Hill, 1960.

Boyle, Ted Eugene. Symbol and Meaning in the Fiction of Joseph Conrad. The Hague, Mouton, 1965.

Bradbrook, Muriel Clara. Joseph Conrad: Poland's English Genius. Cambridge, Cambridge University Press, 1941.

Fleishman, Avrom. Conrad's Politics: Community and Anarchy in the Fiction of Joseph Conrad. Baltimore, The Johns Hopkins Press, 1967.

Gordan, John Dozier. Joseph Conrad: The Making of a Novelist. Cambridge, Mass., Harvard University Press, 1940.

Graver, Lawrence. Conrad's Short Fiction. Berkeley and Los Angeles, University of California Press, 1969.

Guerard, Albert. Conrad the Novelist. Cambridge, Mass., Harvard University Press, 1958.

Gurko, Leo. Joseph Conrad: Giant in Exile. New York, Macmillan, 1962.

Haugh, Robert. Joseph Conrad: Discovery in Design. Norman, University of Oklahoma Press, 1957.

Hay, Eloise Knapp. The Political Novels of Joseph Conrad. Chicago, University of Chicago Press, 1963.

Hewitt, Douglas John. Conrad: A Reassessment. Cambridge, Bowes and Bowes, 1952.

Karl, Frederick. A Reader's Guide to Joseph Conrad. New York, Noonday, 1960.

Leavis, Frank Raymond. The Great Tradition. New York, G. W. Stewart, 1948.

Megroz, Rodolphe Luis. Joseph Conrad's Mind and Method. London, Faber and Faber, 1931.

Meyer, Bernard C. Joseph Conrad: A Psychoanalytic Biography. Princeton, Princeton University Press, 1967.

Morf, Gustav. The Polish Heritage of Joseph Conrad. New York, R. R. Smith, 1930.

Moser, Thomas. Joseph Conrad: Achievement and Decline. Cambridge, Mass., Harvard University Press, 1957.

Mudrick, Marvin, ed. Conrad: A Collection of Critical Essays. Englewood Cliffs, N. J., Prentice-Hall, 1966.

Najder, Zdzislaw. Conrad's Polish Background. London and New York, Oxford University Press, 1964.

Palmer, John A. Joseph Conrad's Fiction. Ithaca, Cornell University Press, 1968.

Rosenfield, Claire. Paradise of Snakes: An Archetypal Analysis of Conrad's Political Novels. Chicago and London, The University of Chicago Press, 1967.

Said, Edward W. Joseph Conrad and the Fiction of Autobiography. Cambridge, Mass., Harvard University Press, 1966.
Sherry, Norman. Conrad's Eastern World. London, Cambridge University Press, 1966.
———. Conrad's Western World. Cambridge, University of Cambridge Press, 1971.
———, ed. Conrad: The Critical Heritage. London and Boston, Routledge and Kegan Paul, 1973.
Visiak, Edward Harold. The Mirror of Conrad. London, W. Laurie, 1955.
Wiley, Paul L. Conrad's Measure of Man. Madison, University of Wisconsin Press, 1954.
Wright, Walter Francis. Romance and Tragedy in Joseph Conrad. Lincoln, University of Nebraska Press, 1949.

Virginia Woolf

NOTE: *The Hogarth Press, London, has kept up to date its Uniform Edition of Virginia Woolf's volumes.*

PRINCIPAL WORKS

The Voyage Out. London, Duckworth, 1915; New York, Doran, 1920, Harcourt, Brace, 1926.

Night and Day. London, Duckworth, 1919; New York, Doran, 1920.

Monday or Tuesday. Richmond, Hogarth, 1921; New York, Harcourt, Brace, 1921. (Six of the eight sketches are reprinted in A Haunted House and Other Short Stories.)

Jacob's Room. Richmond, Hogarth, 1922; New York, Harcourt, Brace, 1923.

Mr. Bennett and Mrs. Brown. Hogarth Essays. London, Hogarth, 1924. (Reprinted in The Captain's Death Bed and Other Essays.)

The Common Reader. London, Hogarth, 1925; New York, Harcourt, Brace, 1925.

Mrs. Dalloway. London, Hogarth, 1925; New York, Harcourt, Brace, 1925. With Introduction, New York, Modern Library, 1928.

To the Lighthouse. London, Hogarth, 1927; New York, Harcourt, Brace, 1927.

Orlando: A Biography. London, Hogarth, 1928; New York, Crosby Gaige, 1928, Harcourt, Brace, 1929.

A Room of One's Own. London, Hogarth, 1929; New York, Fountain Press, 1929, Harcourt, Brace, 1929.

The Waves. London, Hogarth, 1931; New York, Harcourt, Brace, 1931.

A Letter to a Young Poet. Hogarth Letters No. 8. London, Hogarth, 1932. (Reprinted in The Death of the Moth and Other Essays.)

The Common Reader: Second Series. London, Hogarth, 1932; New York, Harcourt, Brace, 1932. (The Harcourt edition was entitled The Second Common Reader.)

Flush: A Biography. London, Hogarth, 1933; New York, Harcourt, Brace, 1933.

The Years. London, Hogarth, 1937; New York, Harcourt, Brace, 1937.

Three Guineas. London, Hogarth, 1938; New York, Harcourt, Brace, 1938.

Roger-Fry: A Biography. London, Hogarth, 1940; New York, Harcourt, Brace, 1940

Between the Acts. London, Hogarth, 1941; New York, Harcourt, Brace, 1941.

The Death of the Moth and Other Essays. London, Hogarth, 1942; New York, Harcourt, Brace, 1942.

A Haunted House and Other Short Stories. London, Hogarth, 1943 [for 1944], New York, Harcourt, Brace, 1944.

The Moment and Other Essays. London, Hogarth, 1947; New York, Harcourt, Brace, 1947.

The Captain's Death Bed and Other Essays. London, Hogarth, 1950; New York, Harcourt, Brace, 1950.

A Writer's Diary. London, Hogarth, 1953; New York, Harcourt, Brace, 1954.

Virginia Woolf & Lytton Strachey: Letters. Edited by Leonard Woolf and James Strachey. London, Hogarth Press with Chatto and Windus, 1956; New York, Harcourt, Brace, 1956.

Granite and Rainbow: Essays. London, Hogarth, 1958; New York, Harcourt, Brace, 1958.

Contemporary Writers. Edited by Jean Guiguet. London, Hogarth, 1965.

Collected Essays. 4 vols. London, Hogarth, 1966–67; New York, Harcourt, Brace, 1967.

Mrs. Dalloway's Party: A Short Story Sequence. Edited by Stella McNichol. London, Hogarth, 1973.

CRITICAL WORKS AND COMMENTARY

Amoruso, Vito. Virginia Woolf. Bari, Adriatica, 1968.

Bazin, Nancy Topping. Virginia Woolf and the Androgynous Vision. New Brunswick, N. J., Rutgers University Press, 1973.

Bell, Quentin. Virginia Woolf: A Biography. London, Hogarth, 1972; New York, Harcourt, Brace, 1972.

Bennett, Joan. Virginia Woolf: Her Art as Novelist. Cambridge, Cambridge University Press, 1945; 2d. ed., enlarged, 1964.

Blackstone, Bernard. Virginia Woolf: A Commentary. London, Hogarth, 1949.

Brewster, Dorothy. Virginia Woolf's London. London, Allen and Unwin, 1959.

———. Virginia Woolf. London, Allen and Unwin, 1963.

Chambers, R. L. The Novels of Virginia Woolf. Edinburgh, Oliver and Boyd, 1947.

Chastaing, Maxime. La Philosophie de Virginia Woolf. Paris, Presses Universitaires de France, 1951.

Daiches, David. Virginia Woolf. Norfolk, Conn., New Directions, 1942.

Forster, E. M. Virginia Woolf, The Rede Lecture, 1941. Cambridge, Cambridge University Press, 1942.

Guiguet, Jean. Virginia Woolf et son oeuvre: l'art et la quête du réel. Paris, Didier, 1962. Translated by Jean Stewart as Virginia Woolf and Her Works. London, Hogarth, 1965.

Hafley, James. The Glass Roof: Virginia Woolf as Novelist. University of California English Studies, No. 9. Berkeley and Los Angeles, University of California, 1954.

Holtby, Winifred. Virginia Woolf. London, Wishart, 1932.

Johnstone, J. K. The Bloomsbury Group: A Study of E. M. Forster, Lytton Strachey, Virginia Woolf, and Their Circle. London, Secker and Warburg, 1954; New York, Noonday, 1954.

Kirkpatrick, B. J. A Bibliography of Virginia Woolf. London, Hart-Davis, 1957.

Leaska, Mitchell A. Virginia Woolf's Lighthouse: A Study in Critical Method. New York, Columbia University Press, 1970; London, Hogarth, 1970.

Love, Jean O. Worlds in Consciousness: Mythopoetic Thought in the Novels of Virginia Woolf. Berkeley and Los Angeles, University of California Press, 1970.

McLaurin, Allen. Virginia Woolf: The Echoes Enslaved. Cambridge, Cambridge University Press, 1972.

Marder, Herbert. Feminism and Art: A Study of Virginia Woolf. Chicago, University of Chicago Press, 1968.

Naremore, James. The World without a Self: Virginia Woolf and the Novel. New Haven, Yale University Press, 1973.

Moody, A. D. Virginia Woolf. Edinburgh, Oliver and Boyd, 1963.

Nathan, Monique. Virginia Woolf par elle-même. Paris, Seuil, 1956. Translated by Herma Briffault as Virginia Woolf. London, Evergreen Books, 1961; New York, Grove, 1961.

Pippett, Aileen. The Moth and the Star: A Biography of Virginia Woolf. Boston, Little, Brown, 1955.

Rantavaara, Irma. Virginia Woolf's The Waves. Helsinki, Societas Scientiarum Fennica, 1960.

Noble, Joan Russell, ed. Recollections of Virginia Woolf. New York, Morrow, 1972.

Richter, Harvena. Virginia Woolf: The Inward Voyage. Princeton, Princeton University Press, 1970.

Schaefer, Josephine O'Brien. The Three-fold Nature of Reality in the Novels of Virginia Woolf. London, Mouton, 1965.

Sprague, Claire, ed. Virginia Woolf: A Collection of Critical Essays. Englewood Cliffs, N. J., Prentice-Hall, 1971.

Thakur, N. C. The Symbolism of Virginia Woolf. London and New York, Oxford University Press, 1965.

Woolf, Leonard. Sowing: An Autobiography of the Years 1880–1904. London, Hogarth, 1960.

——. Beginning Again: An Autobiography of the Years 1911–1918. London, Hogarth, 1964.

——. Downhill All the Way: An Autobiography of the Years 1919–1939. London, Hogarth, 1967; New York, Harcourt, Brace, 1967.

——. The Journey, Not the Arrival Matters: An Autobiography of the Years 1939–1969. London, Hogarth, 1969; New York, Harcourt, Brace, 1970.

E. M. Forster

NOTE: * means reprinted in The Collected Tales; † means reprinted in Abinger Harvest; ‡ means reprinted in Two Cheers for Democracy; § means reprinted in Marianne Thornton.

PRINCIPAL WORKS

Where Angels Fear to Tread. Edinburgh and London, Blackwood, 1905; New York, Knopf, 1920.

The Longest Journey. Edinburgh and London, Blackwood, 1907; New York, Knopf, 1922.

A Room with a View. London, Arnold, 1908; New York, Knopf, 1923.

Howards End. London, Arnold, 1910; New York, Knopf, 1921.

* The Celestial Omnibus and Other Stories. London, Sidgwick and Jackson, 1911; New York, Knopf, 1923.

* The Story of the Siren. Richmond, Hogarth, 1920.

Notes on Egypt. London, The Labour Research Department [1921]. ("The Government of Egypt: Recommendations by a Committee of the International Section of the Labour Research Department, with Notes on Egypt, by E. M. Forster.")

Alexandria: A History and a Guide. Alexandria, Morris, 1922; New York, Doubleday, 1961.

Pharos and Pharillon. Richmond, and London, Hogarth, 1923; New York, Knopf, 1923.

A Passage to India. London, Arnold, 1924; New York, Harcourt, Brace, 1924.

† Anonymity: An Enquiry. London, Hogarth, 1925.

Aspects of the Novel. London, Arnold, 1927; New York, Harcourt, Brace, 1927.

† The Eternal Moment and Other Stories. London, Sidgwick and Jackson, 1928; New York, Harcourt, Brace, 1928.

† A Letter to Mandan Blanchard. London, Hogarth, 1931.

† The Pageant of Abinger. London, Athenaeum, 1934.

Goldsworthy Lowes Dickinson. London, Arnold, 1934.

Abinger Harvest. London, Arnold, 1936; New York, Harcourt, Brace, 1936.

Reading as Usual. Tottenham, Tottenham Public Library, 1939.

† What I Believe. London, Hogarth, 1939.

England's Pleasant Land: A Pageant Play. London, Hogarth, 1940.

Nordic Twilight. London, Macmillan, 1940.

‡ Virginia Woolf. Cambridge, Cambridge University Press, 1942.

‡ The Development of English Prose Between 1918 and 1939. Glasgow, Jackson, 1945.

The Collected Tales of E. M. Forster. New York, Knopf, 1947; London, Sidgwick and Jackson, 1947. (The latter edition was entitled Collected Short Stories.)

Two Cheers for Democracy. London, Arnold, 1951; New York, Harcourt, Brace, 1951.

Desmond McCarthy. Stanford Dingley, Mill House Press, 1952.

The Hill of Devi. London, Arnold, 1953; New York, Harcourt, Brace, 1953.

§ Battersea Rise. New York, Harcourt, Brace [1955].

Marianne Thornton: A Domestic Biography, 1797–1887. London, Arnold, 1956; New York, Harcourt, Brace, 1956.

Maurice. London, Arnold, 1971; New York, Norton, 1971.

Albergo Empedocle and Other Stories. Edited by George H. Thomson. New York, Liveright, 1971.

The Life to Come and Other Stories. London, Arnold, 1972; New York, Norton, 1973.

CRITICAL WORKS AND COMMENTARY

Ackerley, J. R. E. M. Forster: A Portrait. London, Ian McKelvie, 1970.

Beer, J. B. The Achievement of E. M. Forster. London, Chatto and Windus, 1962.

Borrello, Alfred. An E. M. Forster Dictionary. Metuchen, N. J., Scarecrow Press, 1971.

——. An E. M. Forster Glossary. Metuchen, N. J., Scarecrow Press, 1972.

Boulton, J. A. Notes on E. M. Forster: "A Passage to India." Bath, Somerset, Brodie, 1966.

Bradbury, Malcolm, ed. Forster: A Collection of Critical Essays. Englewood Cliffs, N. J., Prentice-Hall, 1966.

Brown, E. K. Rhythm in the Novel. Toronto, University of Toronto Press, 1950.

Brander, Laurence. E. M. Forster: A Critical Study. London, Hart-Davis, 1968; Lewisburg, Pa., Bucknell University Press, 1970.

Burra, Peter. "Introduction" to A Passage to India. London, J. M. Dent and Sons, 1942.

Colmer, John. E. M. Forster: A Passage to India. London, Arnold, 1967.

Crews, Frederick C. E. M. Forster: The Perils of Humanism. Princeton, N. J., Princeton University Press, 1962.

Gardner, Philip, ed. E. M. Forster: The Critical Heritage. London and Boston, Routledge and Kegan Paul, 1973.

Godfrey, Denis. E. M. Forster's Other Kingdom. London, Oliver and Boyd, 1968; New York, Barnes and Noble, 1968.

Grandsen, K. W. E. M. Forster. Edinburgh, Oliver and Boyd, 1962; New York, Grove Press, 1962.

Johnstone, J. K. The Bloomsbury Group: A Study of E. M. Forster, Lytton Strachey, Virginia Woolf, and Their Circle. New York, Noonday, 1954; London, Secker and Warburg, 1954.

Joseph, David I. The Art of Rearrangement: E. M. Forster's Abinger Harvest. New Haven, Yale University Press, 1964.

Kelvin, Norman. E. M. Forster. With a Preface by Harry T. Moore. Carbondale, Southern Illinois University Press, 1967.

Kirkpatrick, B. J. A Bibliography of E. M. Forster. London, Hart-Davis, 1965.

Levine, June Perry. Creation and Criticism: A Passage to India. Lincoln, University of Nebraska Press, 1971; London, Chatto and Windus, 1972.

Macaulay, Rose. The Writings of E. M. Forster. London, Hogarth, 1938; New York, Harcourt, Brace, 1938.

McConkey, James. The Novels of E. M. Forster. Ithaca, N. Y., Cornell University Press, 1957.

McDowell, Frederick P. W. E. M. Forster. New York, Twayne, 1969.

Mason, W. H. A Passage to India (E. M. Forster). New York, Barnes and
    Noble, 1965; Oxford, Blackwell, 1965.
Natwahr-Singh, K., ed. E. M. Forster: A Tribute, with Selections from his
    Writings on India. New York, Harcourt, Brace and World, 1964.
Oliver, H. J. The Art of E. M. Forster. Melbourne, Melbourne University
    Press, 1960; London and New York, Cambridge University Press, 1960.
Rose, Martial. E. M. Forster. London, Evans Bros., 1970.
Rutherford, Andrew, comp. Twentieth Century Interpretations of A Passage to
    India: A Collection of Critical Essays. Englewood Cliffs, N. J., Prentice-
    Hall, 1970.
Shahane, Vasant A., ed. Perspectives on E. M. Forster's A Passage to India: A
    Collection of Critical Essays. New York, Barnes and Noble, 1968.
Stallybrass, Oliver, ed. Aspects of E. M. Forster: Essays and Recollections
    Written for His Ninetieth Birthday, January 1, 1969. London, Arnold,
    1969; New York, Harcourt, Brace and World, 1969.
Thomson, George H. Fiction of E. M. Forster. Detroit, Wayne State University
    Press, 1967.
Tindall, William York, The Literary Symbol. New York, Columbia University
    Press, 1955.
Trilling, Lionel. E. M. Forster. Norfolk, Conn., New Directions, 1943; Lon-
    don, Hogarth, 1944.
Wakefield, G. P. Howards End (E. M. Forster). Oxford, Blackwell, 1968.
Warner, Rex. E. M. Forster. London, Longmans, Green, 1950.
Wilde, Alan. Art and Order: A Study of E. M. Forster. New York, New York
    University Press, 1964.

The Contributors

JOHN WAIN is the author of a number of novels, several collections of short stories and poetry, and an autobiography. He has written the following volumes of criticism: *Preliminary Essays, Essays on Literature and Ideas, The Living World of Shakespeare,* and *A House for the Truth.*

DAVID LODGE is Senior Lecturer in English at the University of Birmingham. He is the author of *Language of Fiction, The Novelist at the Crossroads, Graham Greene* (in the Columbia Essays on Modern Writers series), and several novels.

GROVER SMITH is Professor of English at Duke University. His publications include *T. S. Eliot's Poetry and Plays: A Study in Sources and Meaning; Josiah Royce's Seminar, 1913–1914, As Recorded in the Notebooks of Harry T. Costello; Letters of Aldous Huxley;* and *Archibald MacLeish.*

ROBERT S. RYF is Professor of English and Comparative Literature and Dean of the Faculty at Occidental College. He is the author of *A New Approach to Joyce* and, in the Columbia Essays on Modern Writers series, *Henry Green.*

CARL WOODRING is Professor of English at Columbia University. He is the author of *Wordsworth, Politics in the Poetry of*

Coleridge, Victorian Samplers, and *Politics in English Romantic Poetry.*

HARRY T. MOORE is a Research Professor at Southern Illinois University. He is the author of a number of books, including *The Life and Works of D. H. Lawrence,* and editor of *The World of Lawrence Durrell, Selected Letters of Rainer Maria Rilke,* and *Collected Letters of D. H. Lawrence,* among others. He is a Fellow of the Royal Society of Literature.

Index